This
Rum Tasting Journal
Belongs To

Thank you for your purchase!

This journal has been created especially for Rum Lovers, Connoisseurs & Aficionados.

Hope you enjoy using this journal for all your Rum Tasting Sessions.

If you like this, please share your feedback. Your Amazon rating and review will help us reach more people and will also help us improve

Thanks Again!

Copyright © 2021 Sam Patterson
All rights reserved. Contents of this book may not be reproduced, duplicated or transmitted without permission from the author or publisher.

Index

01 _____
02 _____
03 _____
04 _____
05 _____
06 _____
07 _____
08 _____
09 _____
10 _____
11 _____
12 _____
13 _____
14 _____
15 _____
16 _____
17 _____
18 _____
19 _____
20 _____
21 _____
22 _____
23 _____
24 _____
25 _____
26 _____
27 _____
28 _____
29 _____
30 _____
31 _____
32 _____
33 _____
34 _____
35 _____
36 _____
37 _____
38 _____
39 _____
40 _____
41 _____
42 _____
43 _____
44 _____
45 _____
46 _____
47 _____
48 _____
49 _____
50 _____

Index

51 _____   76 _____
52 _____   77 _____
53 _____   78 _____
54 _____   79 _____
55 _____   80 _____
56 _____   81 _____
57 _____   82 _____
58 _____   83 _____
59 _____   84 _____
60 _____   85 _____
61 _____   86 _____
62 _____   87 _____
63 _____   88 _____
64 _____   89 _____
65 _____   90 _____
66 _____   91 _____
67 _____   92 _____
68 _____   93 _____
69 _____   94 _____
70 _____   95 _____
71 _____   96 _____
72 _____   97 _____
73 _____   98 _____
74 _____   99 _____
75 _____   100 _____

NAME	Hawksbill		
DISTILLERY		TYPE	Spiced
ORIGIN		AGE	
PRICE		SAMPLED	29.1.22

COLOR METER

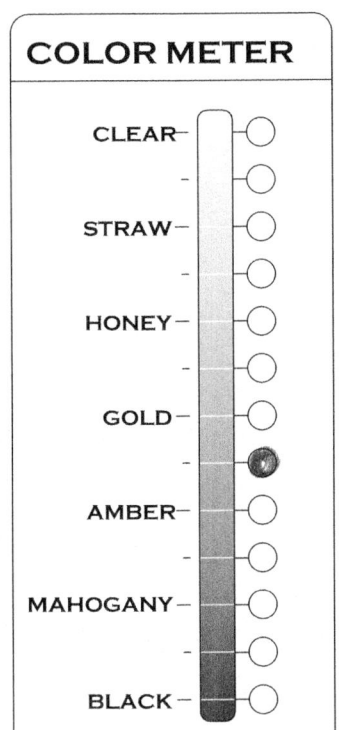

(Gold selected)

FLAVOR WHEEL

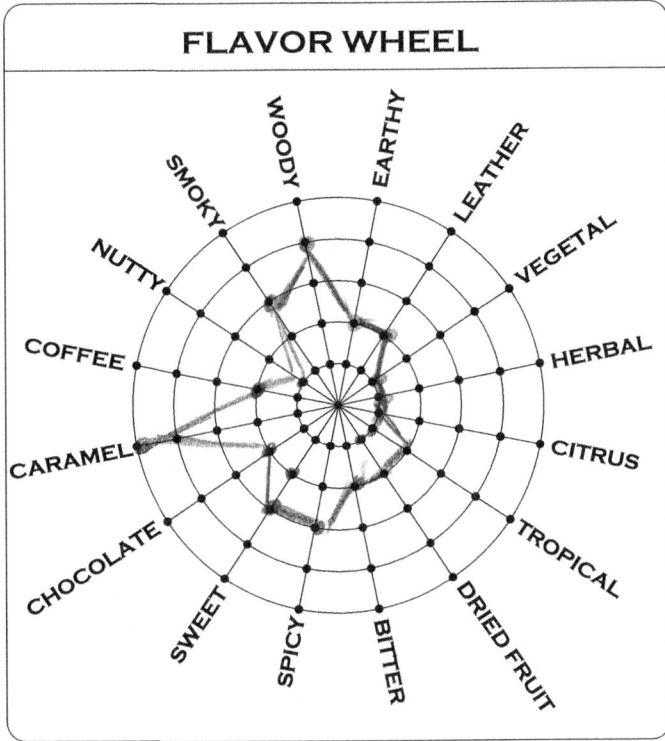

ADDITIONAL NOTES

FINAL RATING

- APPEARANCE ★★☆☆☆
- TASTE ★★★☆☆
- MOUTHFEEL ★★☆☆☆
- OVERALL ★★☆☆☆

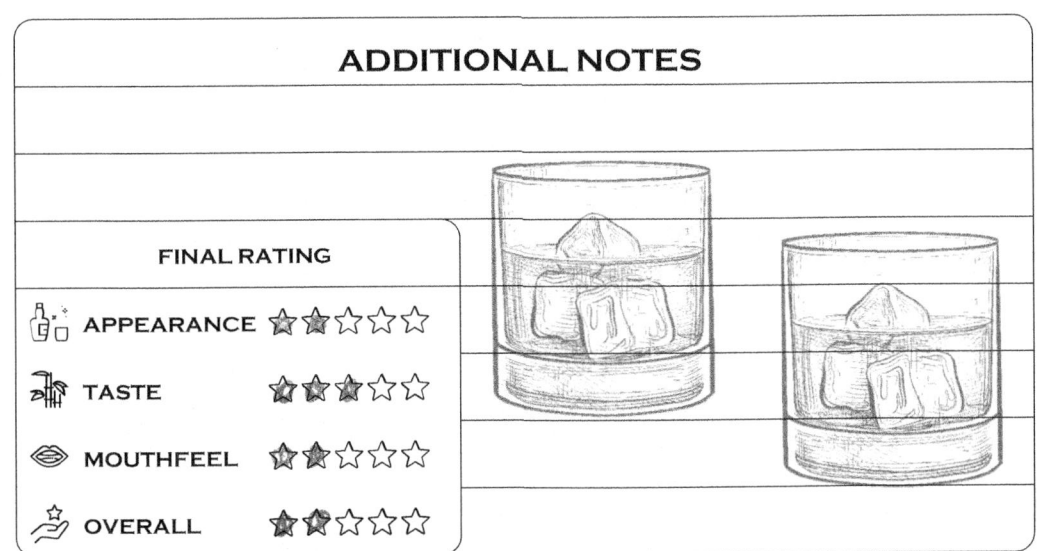

NAME	Rumbullion
DISTILLERY	
ORIGIN	
PRICE	
TYPE	Spiced
AGE	
SAMPLED	18.2.22

COLOR METER

Amber

FLAVOR WHEEL

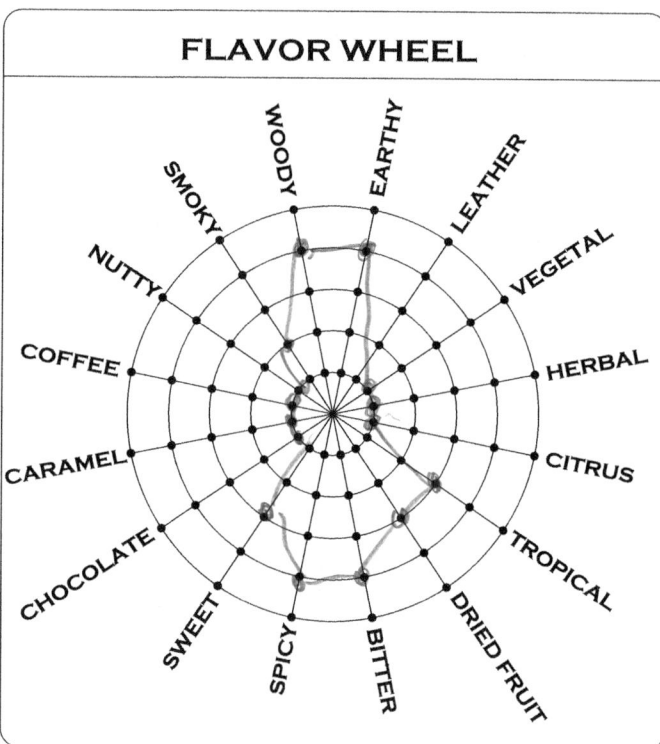

ADDITIONAL NOTES

Smell is fecking amazing!

FINAL RATING

- APPEARANCE ★★★☆☆
- TASTE ★★★★☆
- MOUTHFEEL ★★★☆☆
- OVERALL ★★★☆☆

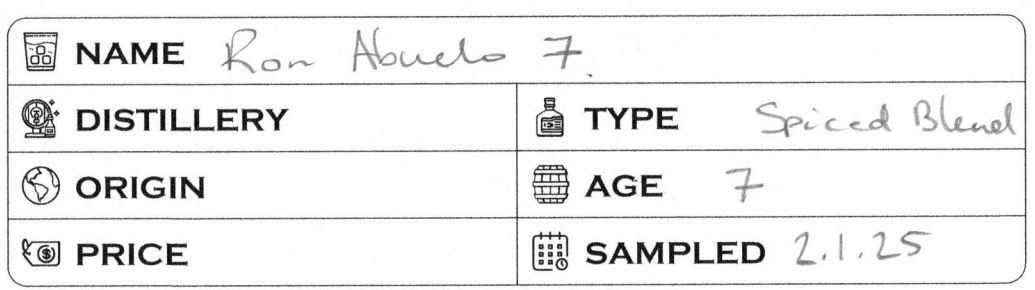

NAME	Ron Abuelo 7		
DISTILLERY		TYPE	Spiced Blend
ORIGIN		AGE	7
PRICE		SAMPLED	2.1.25

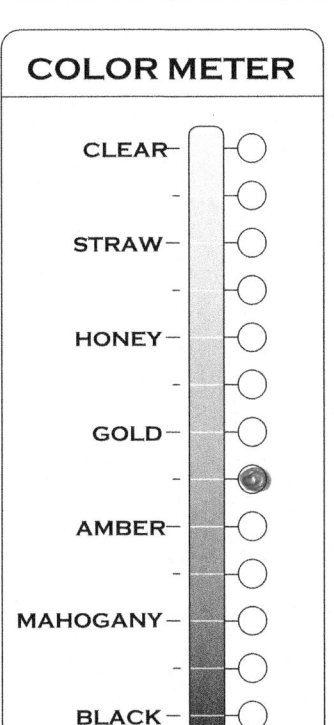

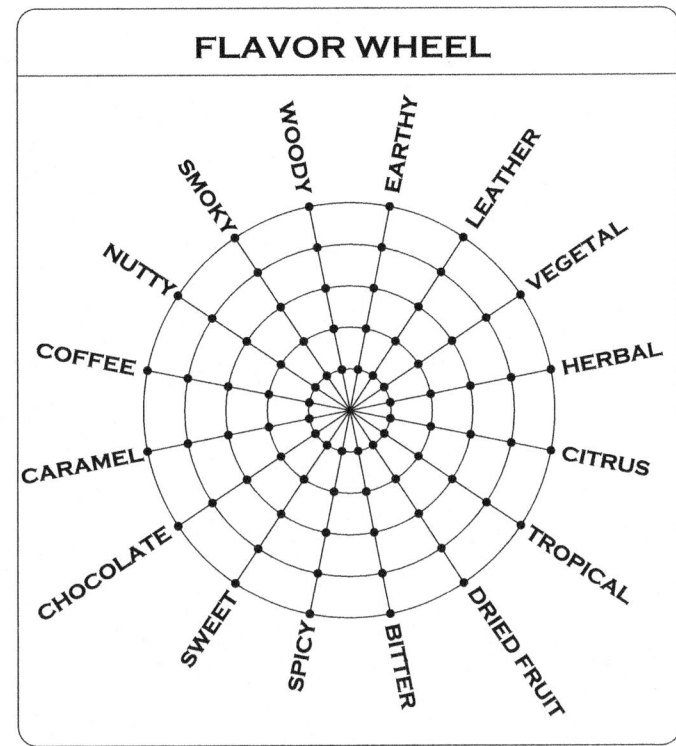

ADDITIONAL NOTES

FINAL RATING

- APPEARANCE ★★★☆☆
- TASTE ★★★★★
- MOUTHFEEL ★★★★☆
- OVERALL ★★★★☆

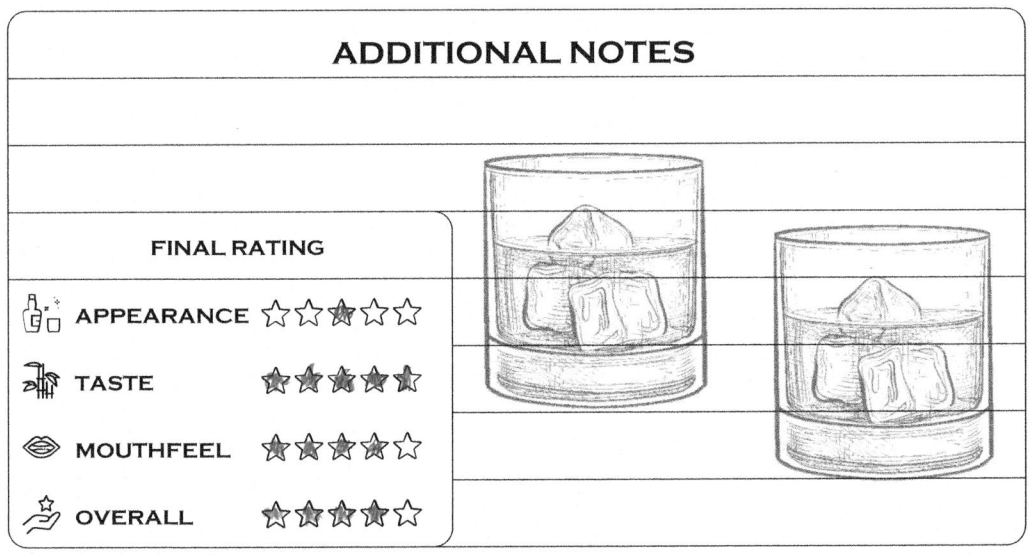

NAME	Meyers
DISTILLERY	
TYPE	Dark
ORIGIN	Jamaica
AGE	Blend
PRICE	£25
SAMPLED	11.1.25

COLOR METER
Mahogany / Black (near bottom)

FLAVOR WHEEL
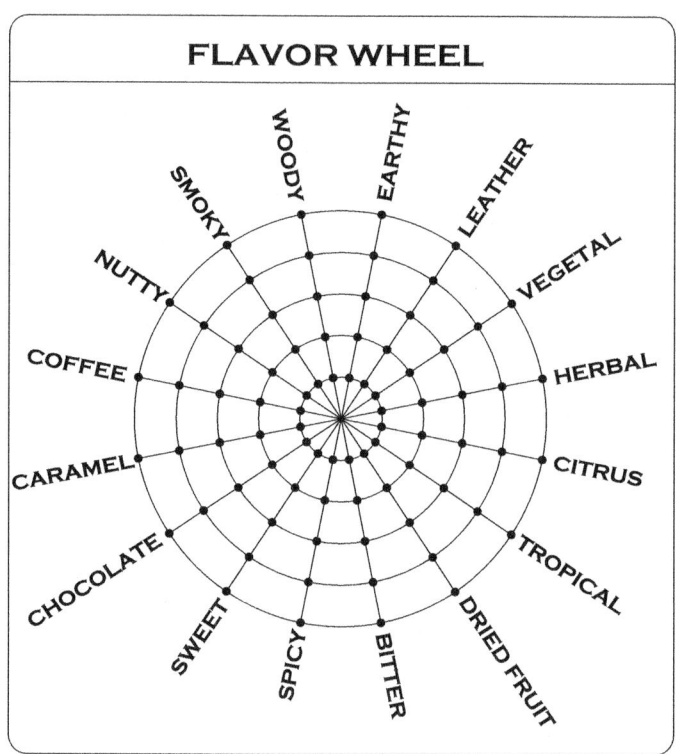

ADDITIONAL NOTES
Great mixer rum.

FINAL RATING
- APPEARANCE ★★★☆☆ (3/5)
- TASTE ★★★☆☆ (3/5)
- MOUTHFEEL ★★★★☆ (4/5)
- OVERALL ★★★★☆ (4/5)

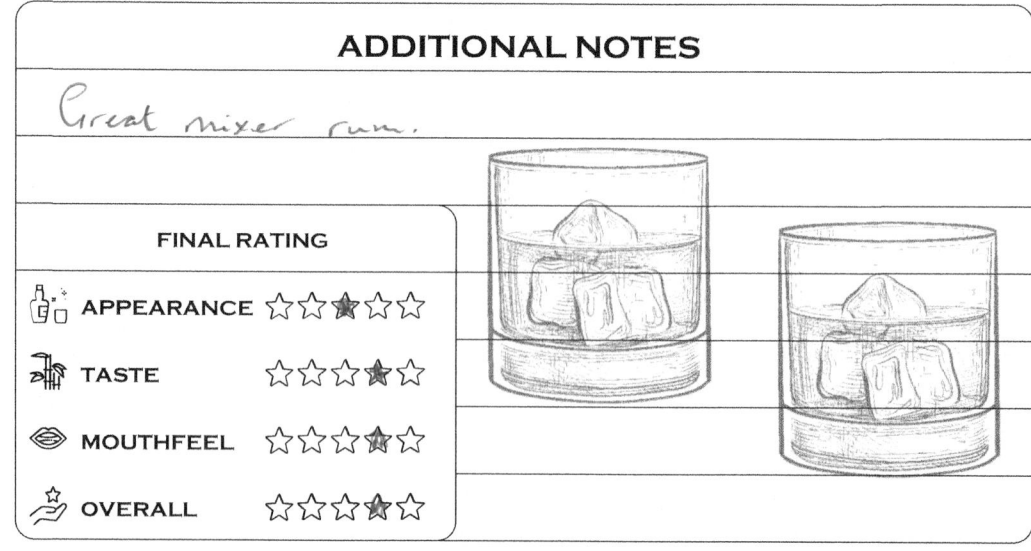

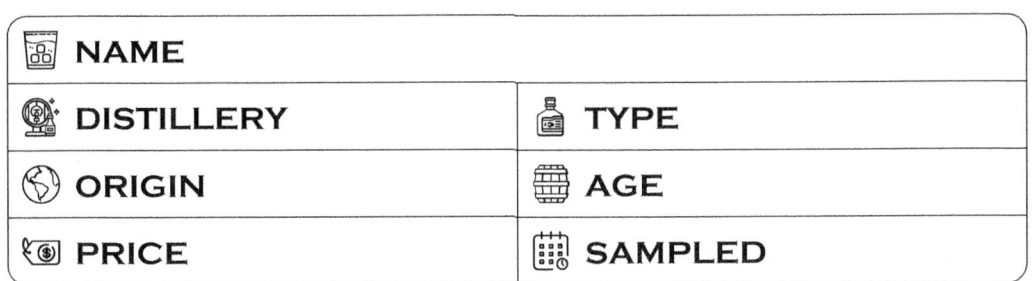

COLOR METER

- CLEAR
- STRAW
- HONEY
- GOLD
- AMBER
- MAHOGANY
- BLACK

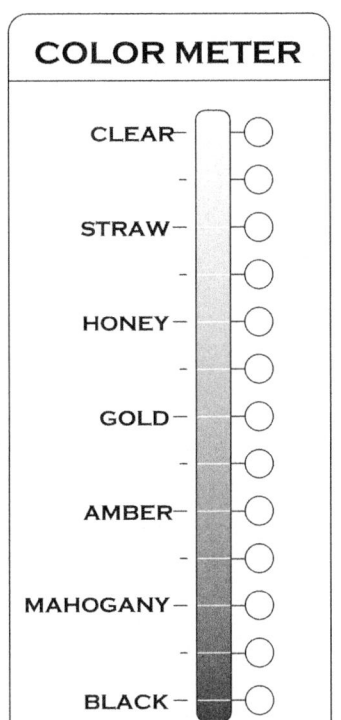

FLAVOR WHEEL

SMOKY, WOODY, EARTHY, LEATHER, VEGETAL, HERBAL, CITRUS, TROPICAL, DRIED FRUIT, BITTER, SPICY, SWEET, CHOCOLATE, CARAMEL, COFFEE, NUTTY

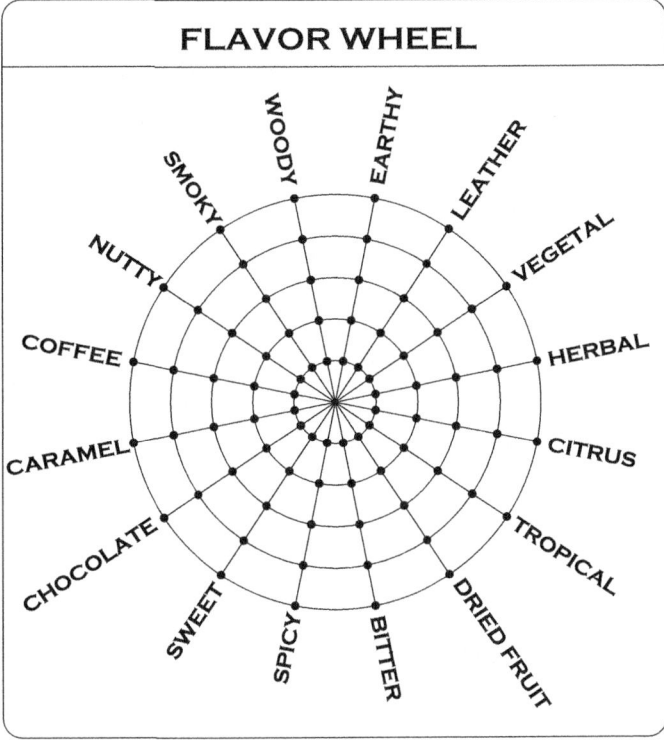

ADDITIONAL NOTES

FINAL RATING

- APPEARANCE ☆☆☆☆☆
- TASTE ☆☆☆☆☆
- MOUTHFEEL ☆☆☆☆☆
- OVERALL ☆☆☆☆☆

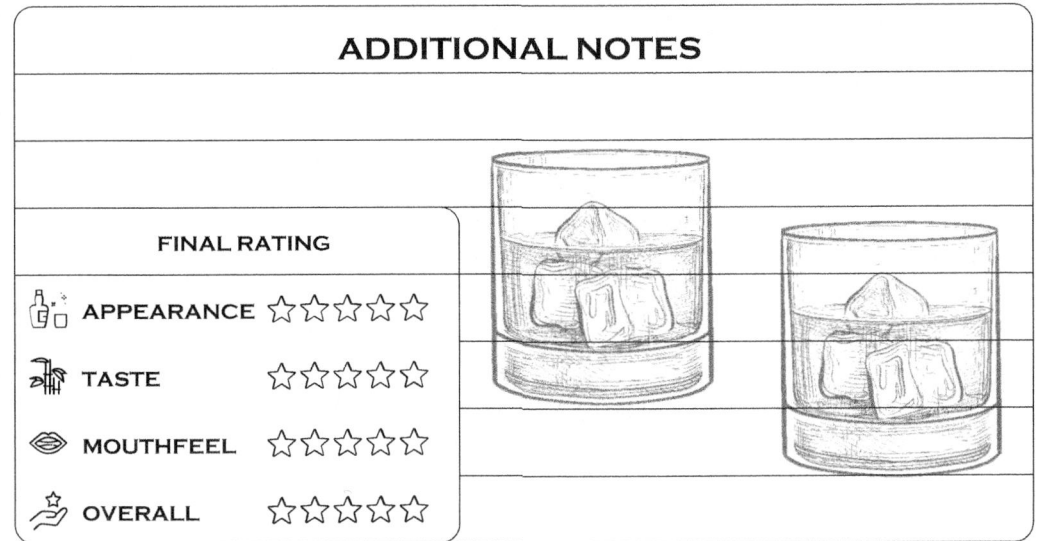

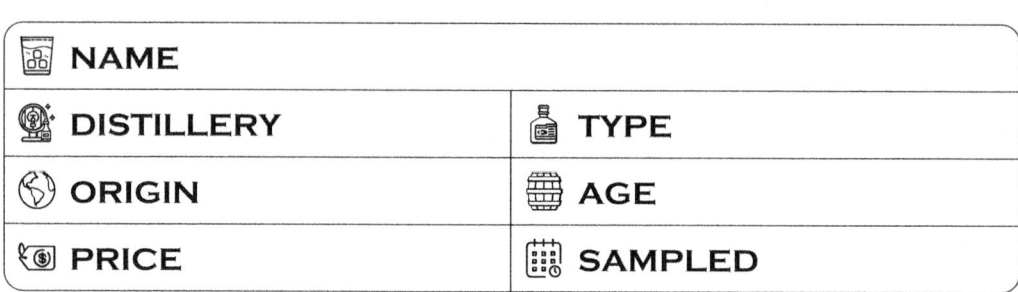

🥃 NAME	
🏭 DISTILLERY	🍾 TYPE
🌍 ORIGIN	🛢 AGE
💰 PRICE	📅 SAMPLED

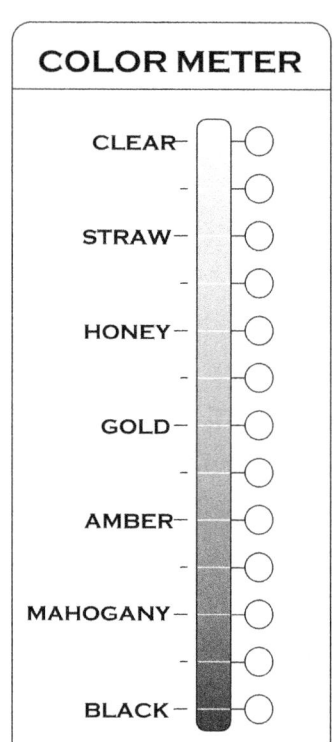

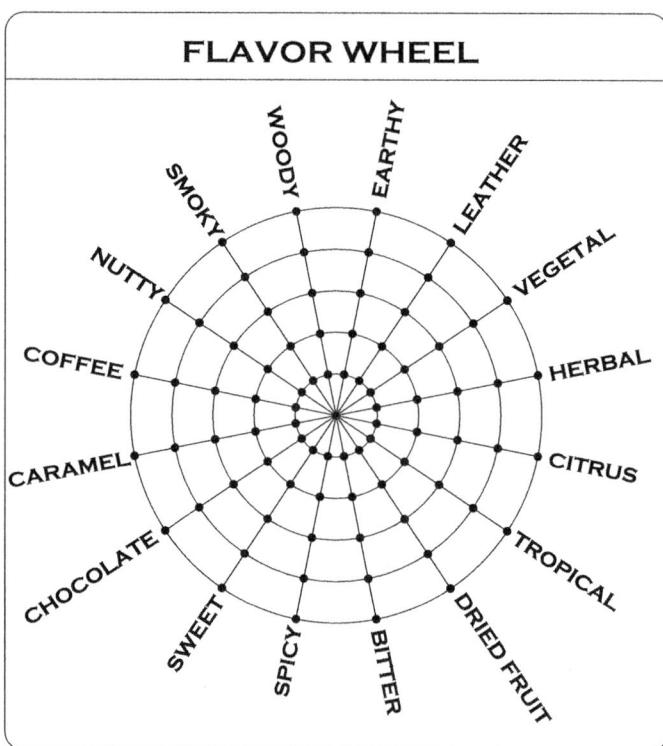

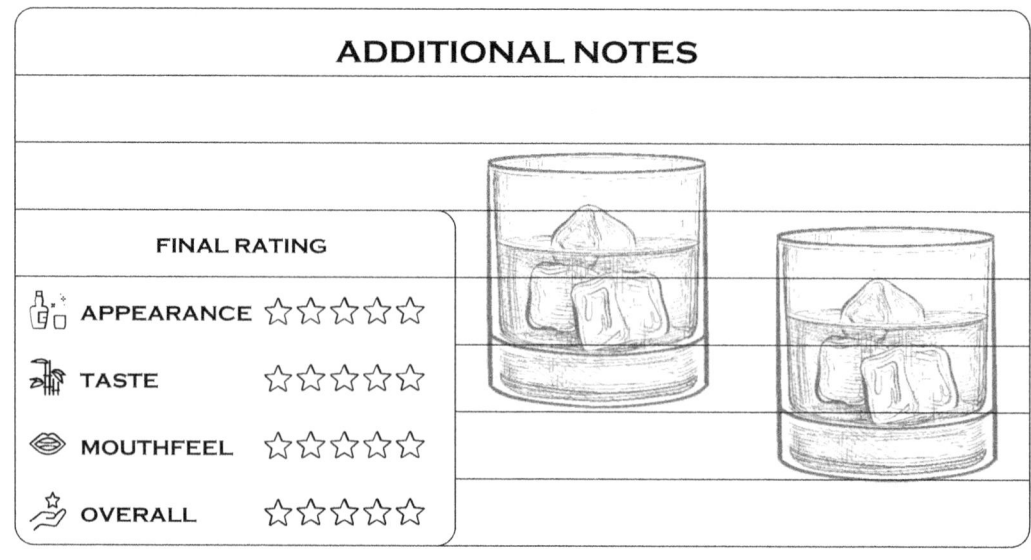

ADDITIONAL NOTES

FINAL RATING

- 🍶 APPEARANCE ☆☆☆☆☆
- 🌾 TASTE ☆☆☆☆☆
- 👄 MOUTHFEEL ☆☆☆☆☆
- 🖐 OVERALL ☆☆☆☆☆

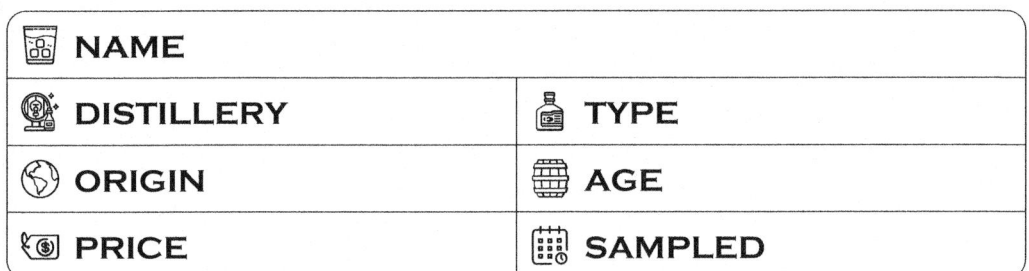

- NAME
- DISTILLERY
- ORIGIN
- PRICE
- TYPE
- AGE
- SAMPLED

COLOR METER

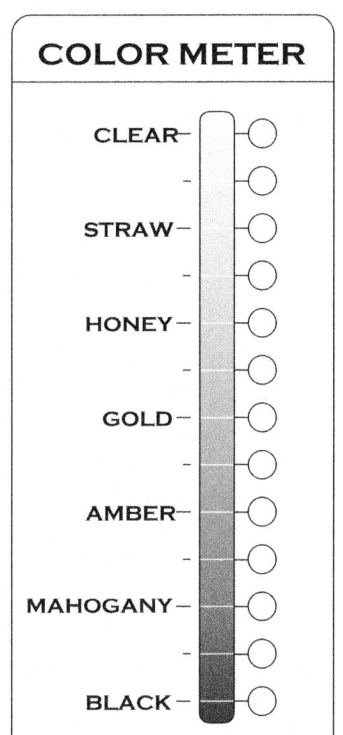

- CLEAR
- STRAW
- HONEY
- GOLD
- AMBER
- MAHOGANY
- BLACK

FLAVOR WHEEL

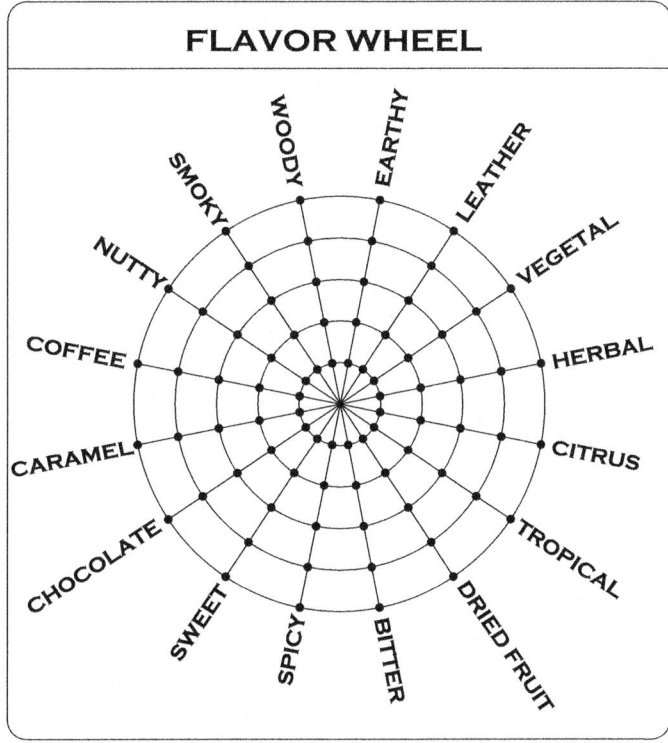

WOODY, EARTHY, LEATHER, VEGETAL, HERBAL, CITRUS, TROPICAL, DRIED FRUIT, BITTER, SPICY, SWEET, CHOCOLATE, CARAMEL, COFFEE, NUTTY, SMOKY

ADDITIONAL NOTES

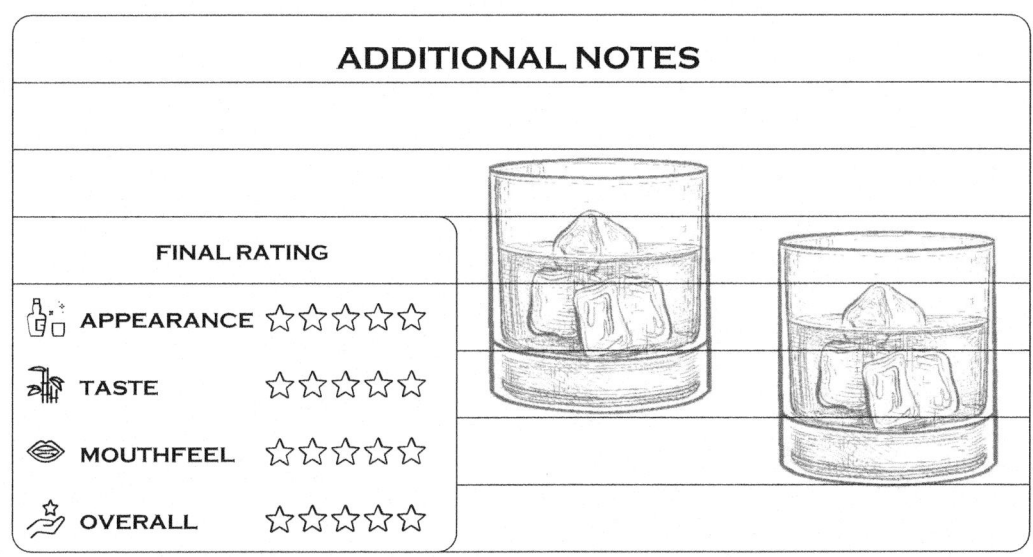

FINAL RATING

- APPEARANCE ☆☆☆☆☆
- TASTE ☆☆☆☆☆
- MOUTHFEEL ☆☆☆☆☆
- OVERALL ☆☆☆☆☆

NAME	
DISTILLERY	TYPE
ORIGIN	AGE
PRICE	SAMPLED

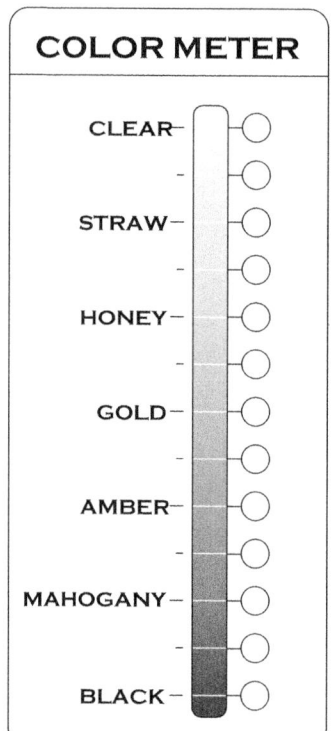

COLOR METER

- CLEAR
- STRAW
- HONEY
- GOLD
- AMBER
- MAHOGANY
- BLACK

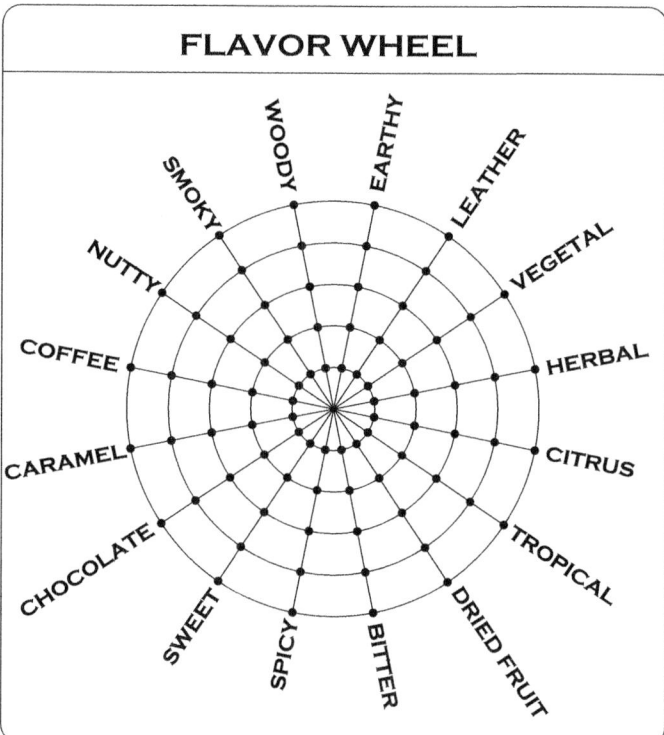

FLAVOR WHEEL

WOODY, EARTHY, LEATHER, VEGETAL, HERBAL, CITRUS, TROPICAL, DRIED FRUIT, BITTER, SPICY, SWEET, CHOCOLATE, COFFEE, CARAMEL, NUTTY, SMOKY

ADDITIONAL NOTES

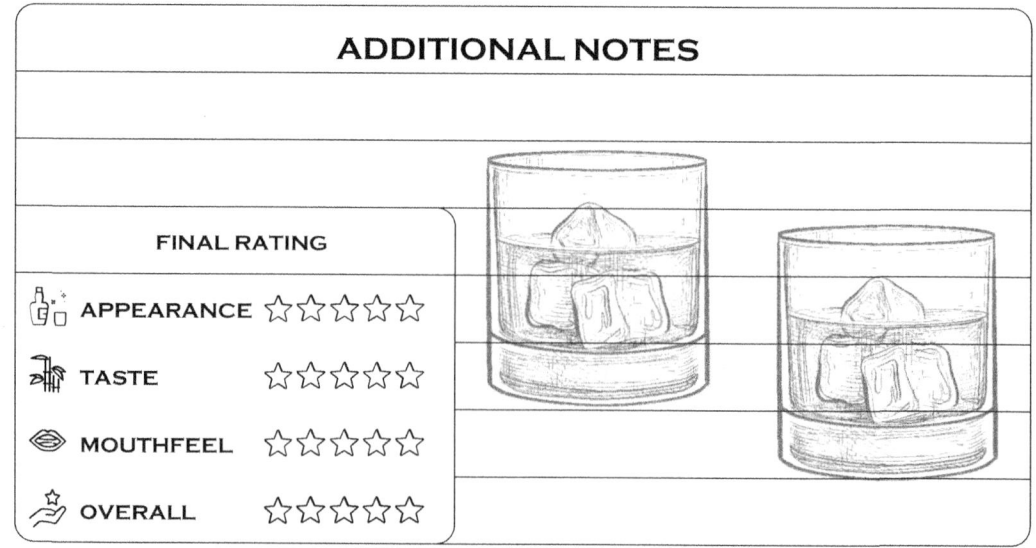

FINAL RATING

- APPEARANCE ☆☆☆☆☆
- TASTE ☆☆☆☆☆
- MOUTHFEEL ☆☆☆☆☆
- OVERALL ☆☆☆☆☆

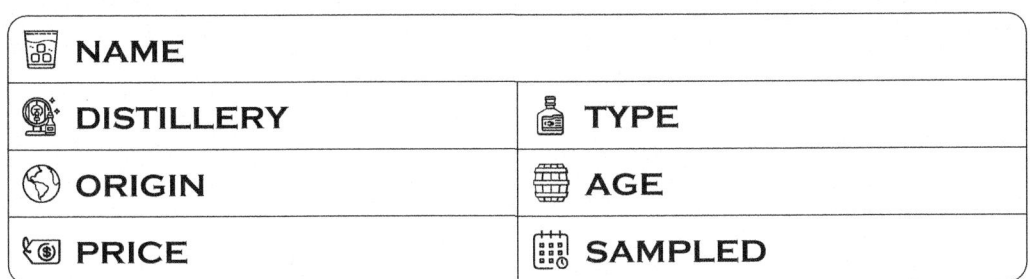

NAME	
DISTILLERY	TYPE
ORIGIN	AGE
PRICE	SAMPLED

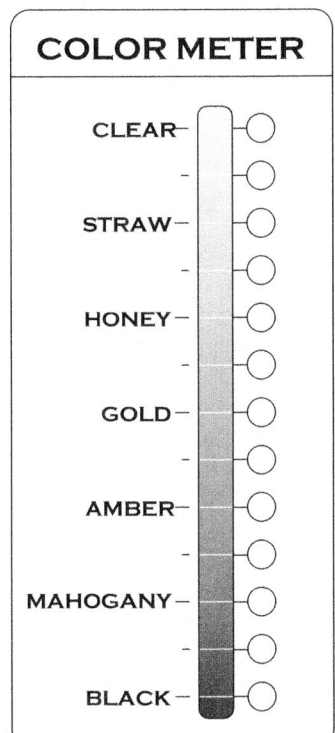

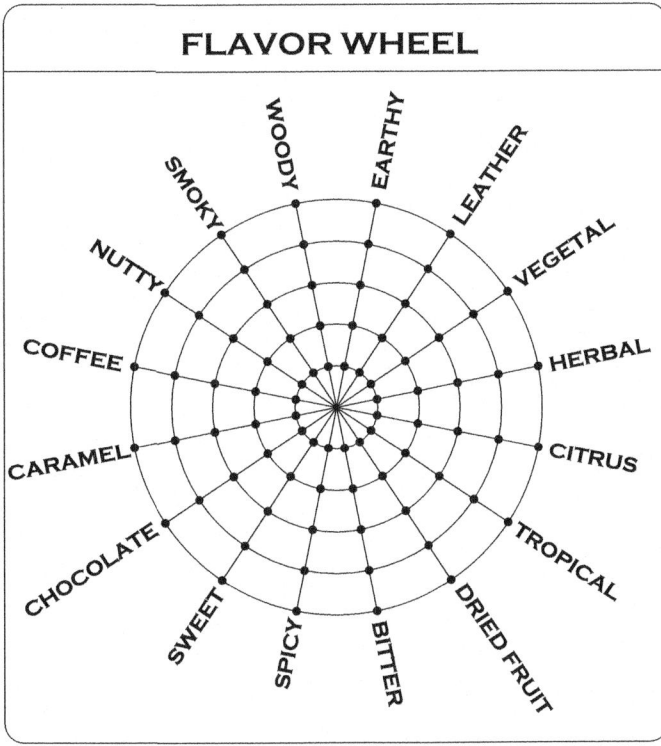

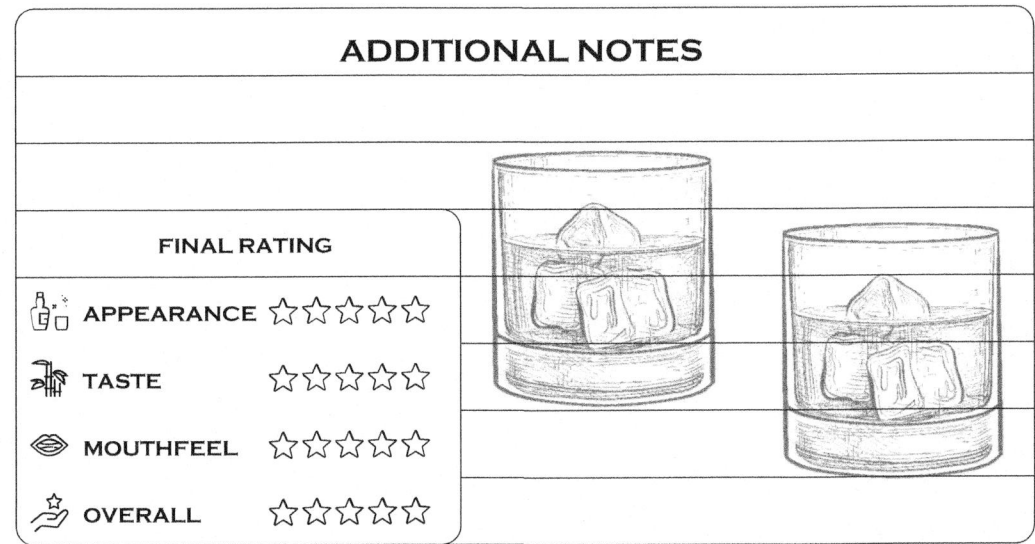

ADDITIONAL NOTES

FINAL RATING

- APPEARANCE ☆☆☆☆☆
- TASTE ☆☆☆☆☆
- MOUTHFEEL ☆☆☆☆☆
- OVERALL ☆☆☆☆☆

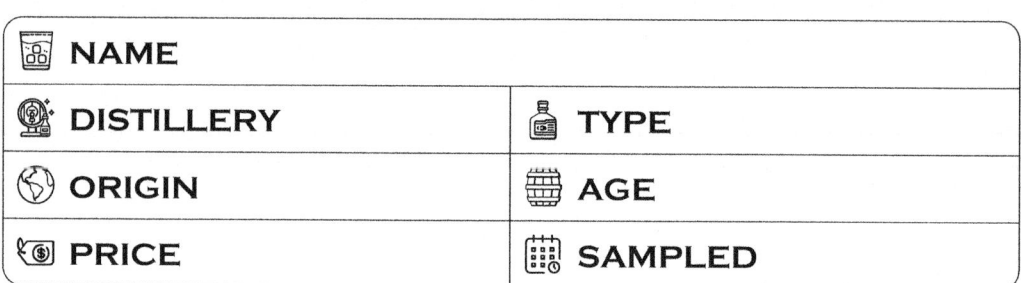

NAME

DISTILLERY

TYPE

ORIGIN

AGE

PRICE

SAMPLED

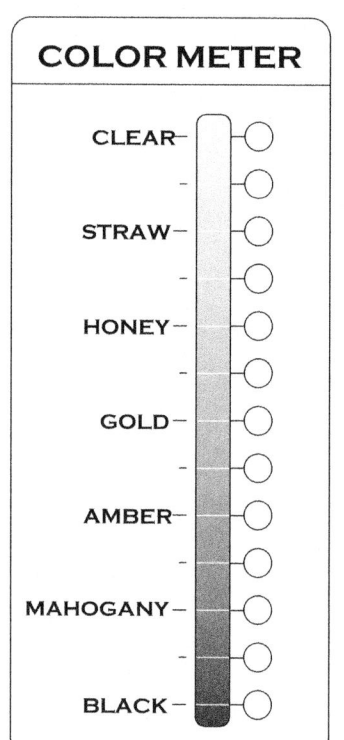

COLOR METER

- CLEAR
- STRAW
- HONEY
- GOLD
- AMBER
- MAHOGANY
- BLACK

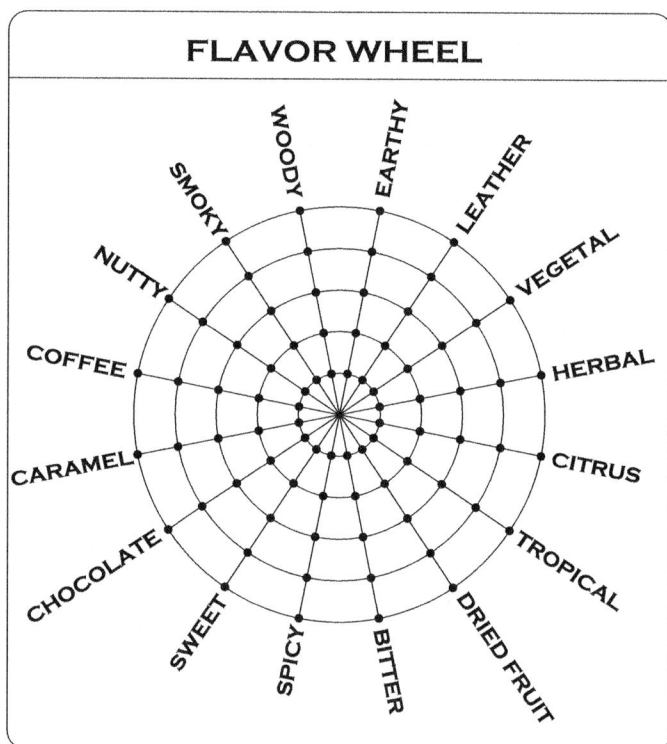

FLAVOR WHEEL

WOODY, EARTHY, LEATHER, VEGETAL, HERBAL, CITRUS, TROPICAL, DRIED FRUIT, BITTER, SPICY, SWEET, CHOCOLATE, CARAMEL, COFFEE, NUTTY, SMOKY

ADDITIONAL NOTES

FINAL RATING

- APPEARANCE ☆☆☆☆☆
- TASTE ☆☆☆☆☆
- MOUTHFEEL ☆☆☆☆☆
- OVERALL ☆☆☆☆☆

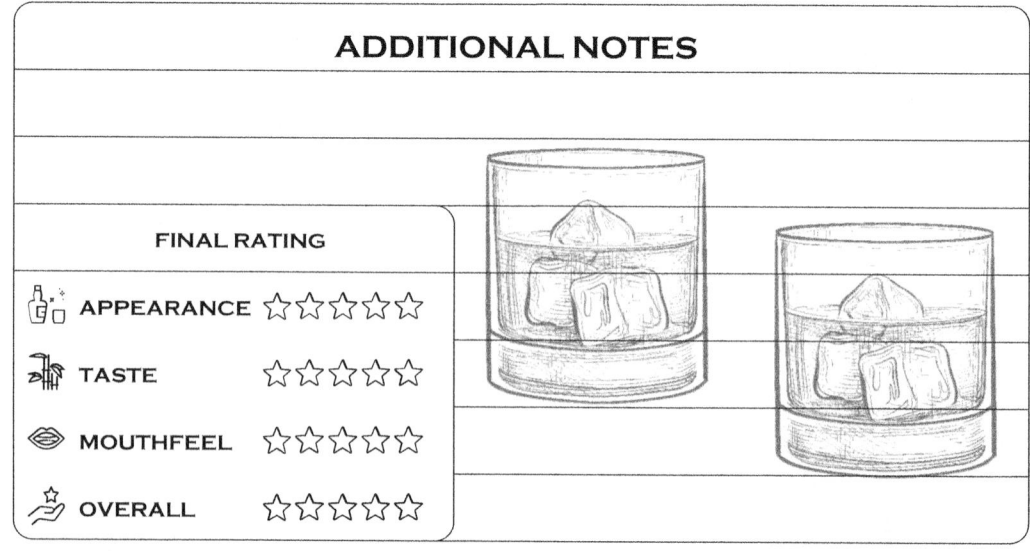

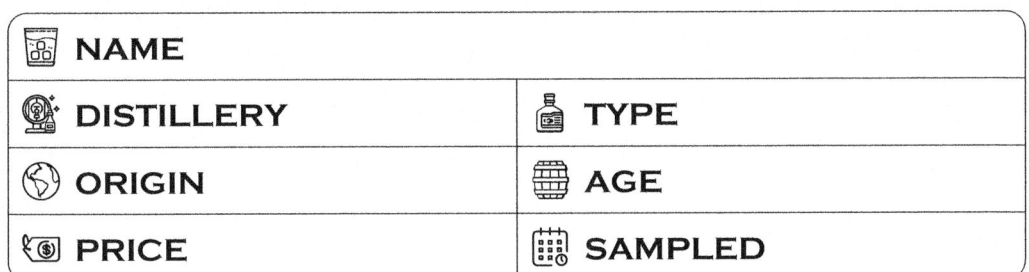

🥃 NAME		
🏭 DISTILLERY	🍾 TYPE	
🌍 ORIGIN	🛢 AGE	
💲 PRICE	📅 SAMPLED	

COLOR METER

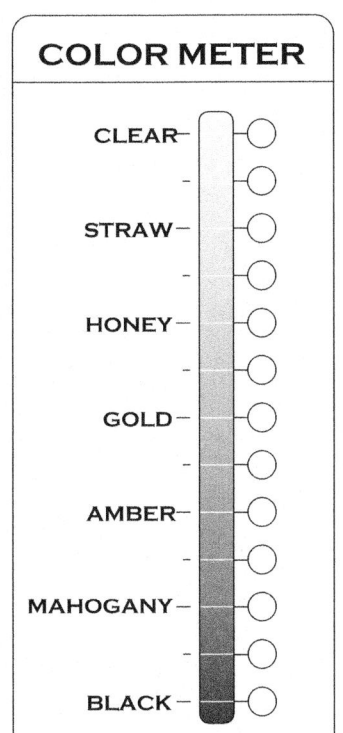

- CLEAR
- STRAW
- HONEY
- GOLD
- AMBER
- MAHOGANY
- BLACK

FLAVOR WHEEL

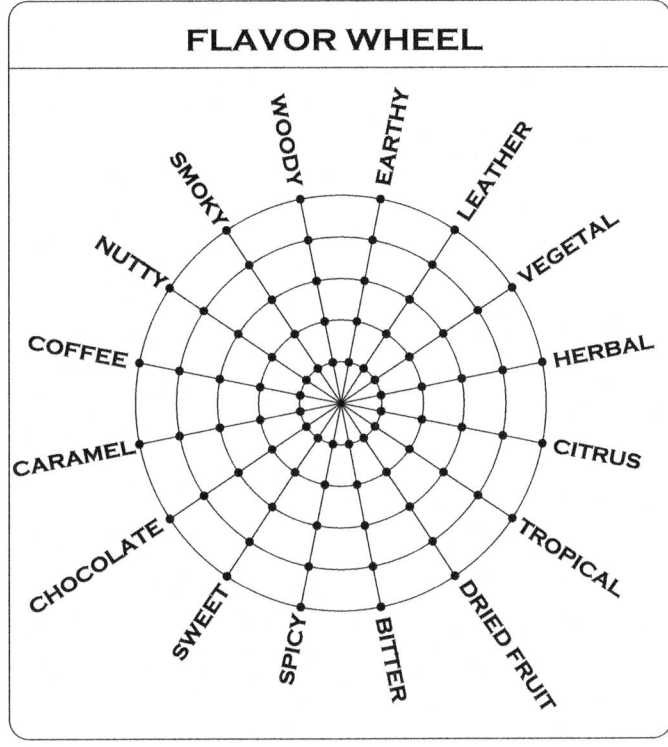

WOODY, EARTHY, LEATHER, VEGETAL, HERBAL, CITRUS, TROPICAL, DRIED FRUIT, BITTER, SPICY, SWEET, CHOCOLATE, CARAMEL, COFFEE, NUTTY, SMOKY

ADDITIONAL NOTES

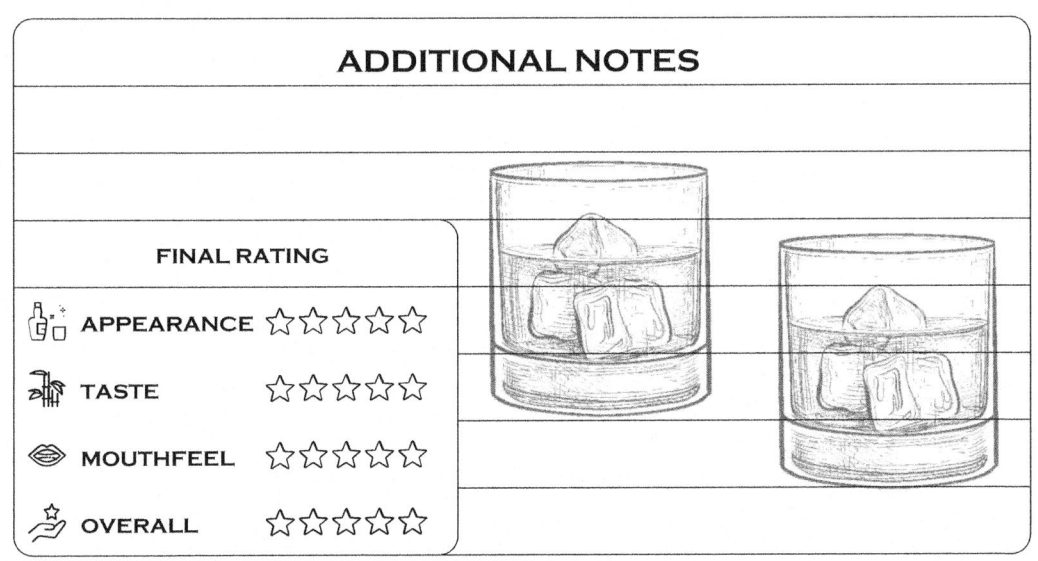

FINAL RATING

- 🍾 APPEARANCE ☆☆☆☆☆
- 👅 TASTE ☆☆☆☆☆
- 👄 MOUTHFEEL ☆☆☆☆☆
- 🖐 OVERALL ☆☆☆☆☆

🥃 NAME	
🛢️ DISTILLERY	🍾 TYPE
🌍 ORIGIN	🛢️ AGE
💰 PRICE	📅 SAMPLED

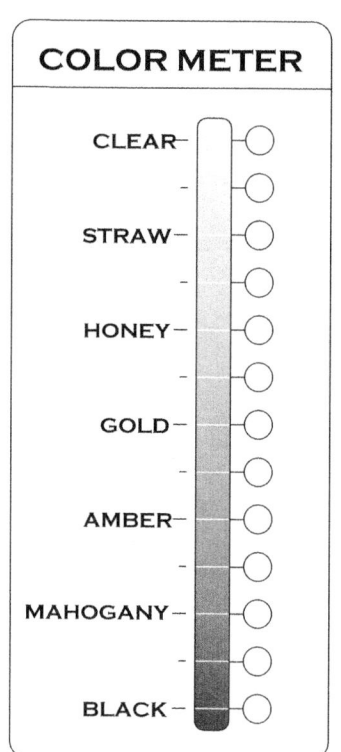

COLOR METER

- CLEAR
- STRAW
- HONEY
- GOLD
- AMBER
- MAHOGANY
- BLACK

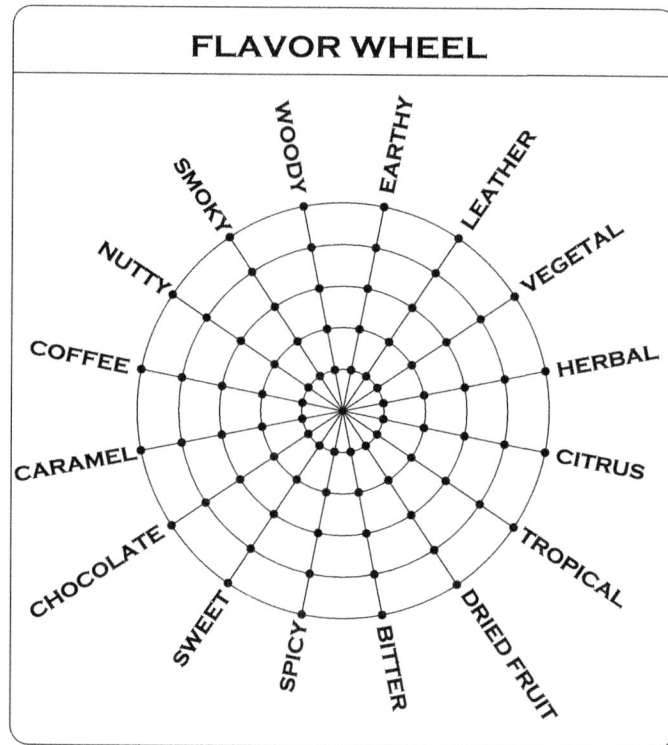

FLAVOR WHEEL

SMOKY, WOODY, EARTHY, LEATHER, NUTTY, VEGETAL, COFFEE, HERBAL, CARAMEL, CITRUS, CHOCOLATE, TROPICAL, SWEET, SPICY, BITTER, DRIED FRUIT

ADDITIONAL NOTES

FINAL RATING

- 🍾 APPEARANCE ☆☆☆☆☆
- 🥃 TASTE ☆☆☆☆☆
- 👄 MOUTHFEEL ☆☆☆☆☆
- 🤲 OVERALL ☆☆☆☆☆

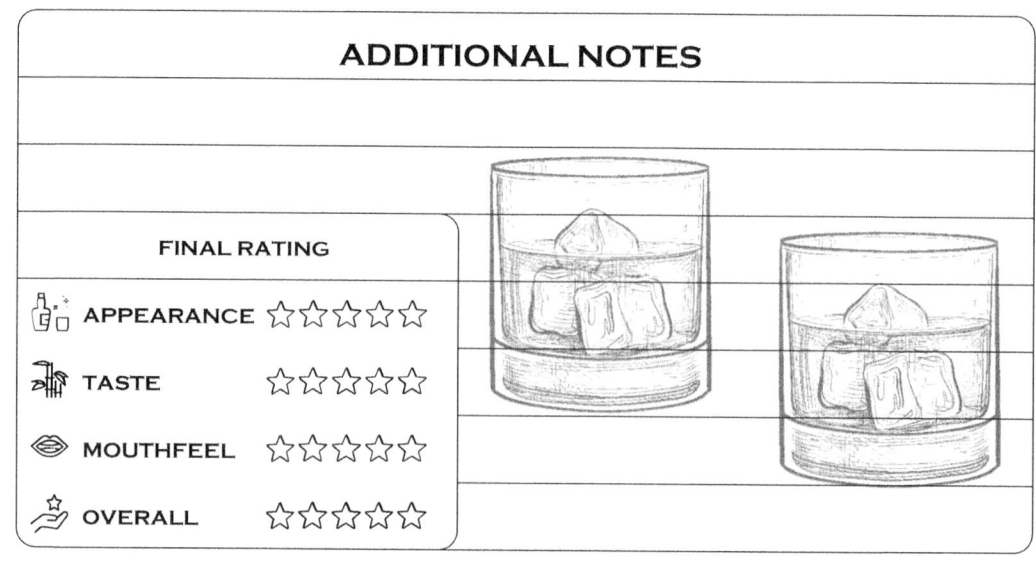

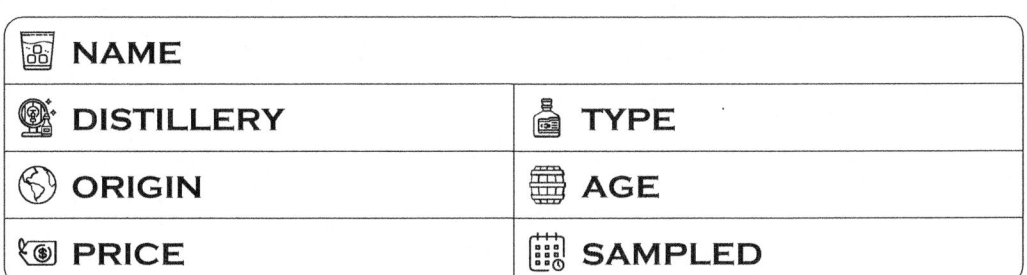

🥃 NAME	
🎡 DISTILLERY	🍾 TYPE
🌐 ORIGIN	🛢 AGE
💰 PRICE	📅 SAMPLED

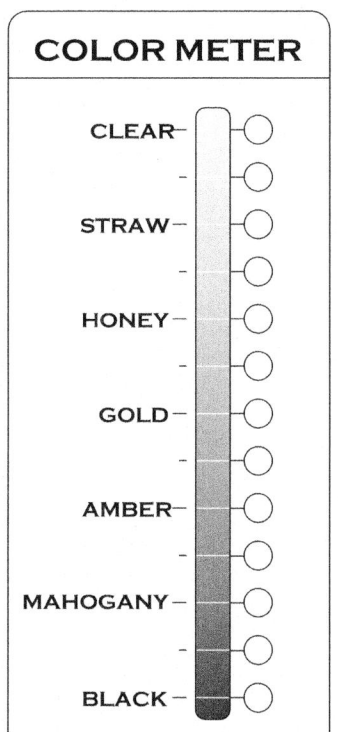

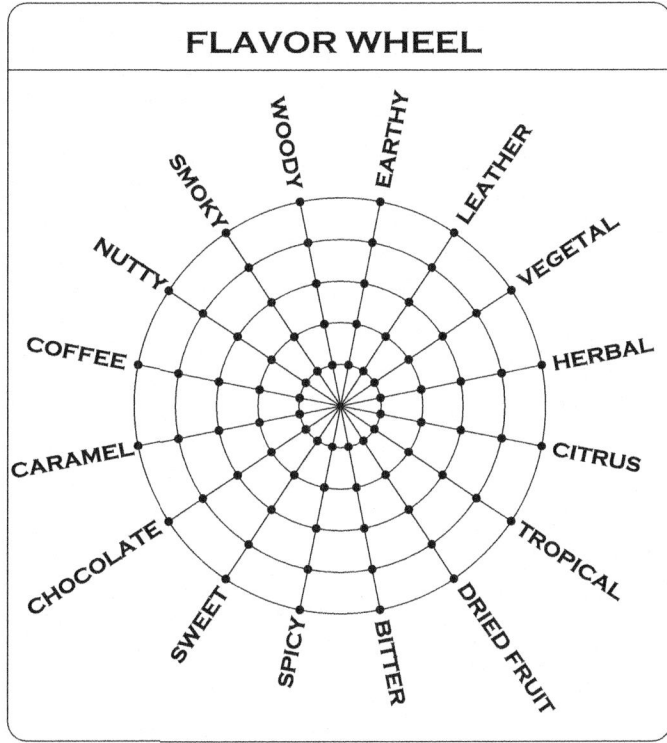

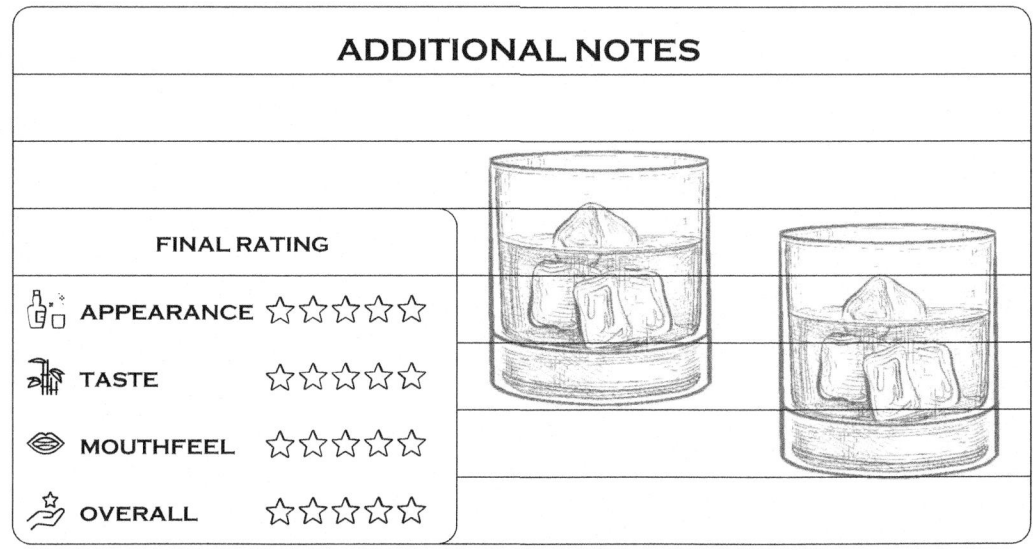

ADDITIONAL NOTES

FINAL RATING

- 🍾 APPEARANCE ☆☆☆☆☆
- 👅 TASTE ☆☆☆☆☆
- 👄 MOUTHFEEL ☆☆☆☆☆
- 🤲 OVERALL ☆☆☆☆☆

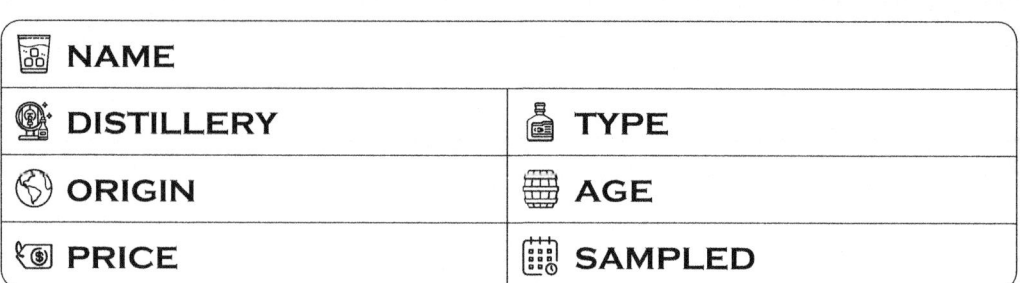

	NAME		
	DISTILLERY		TYPE
	ORIGIN		AGE
	PRICE		SAMPLED

COLOR METER

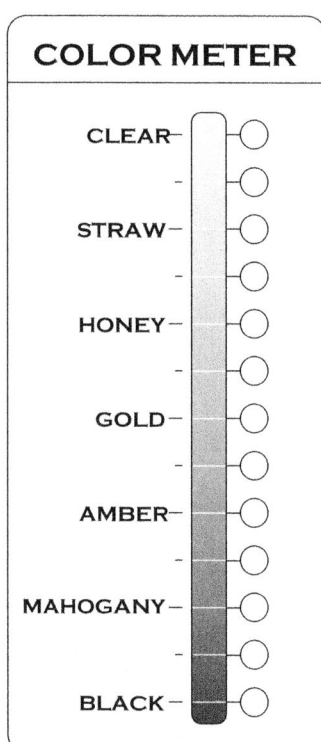

- CLEAR
- STRAW
- HONEY
- GOLD
- AMBER
- MAHOGANY
- BLACK

FLAVOR WHEEL

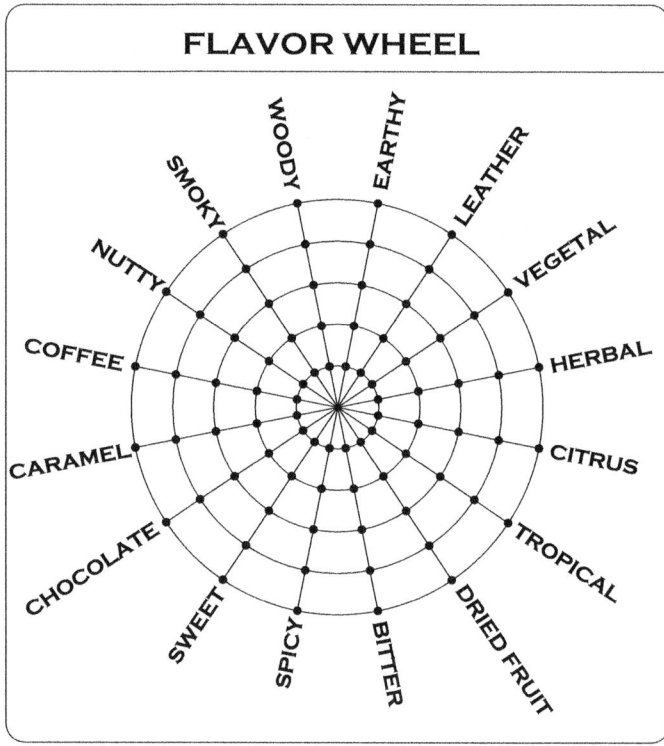

WOODY, EARTHY, LEATHER, VEGETAL, HERBAL, CITRUS, TROPICAL, DRIED FRUIT, BITTER, SPICY, SWEET, CHOCOLATE, CARAMEL, COFFEE, NUTTY, SMOKY

ADDITIONAL NOTES

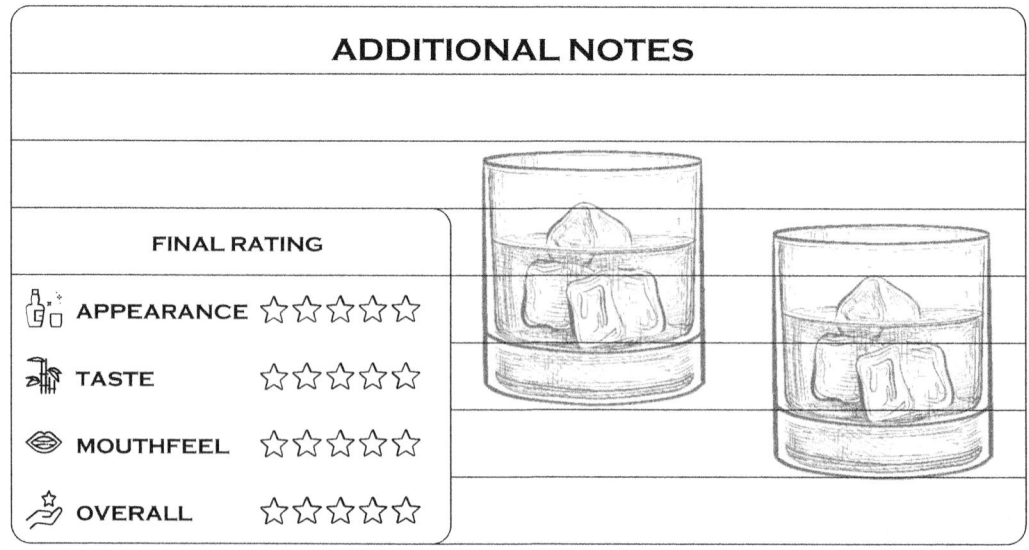

FINAL RATING

- APPEARANCE ☆☆☆☆☆
- TASTE ☆☆☆☆☆
- MOUTHFEEL ☆☆☆☆☆
- OVERALL ☆☆☆☆☆

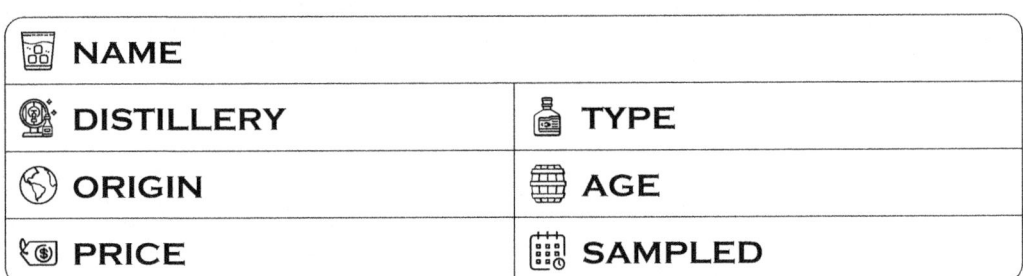

🥃 **NAME**	
🏭 **DISTILLERY**	🍾 **TYPE**
🌍 **ORIGIN**	🛢 **AGE**
💰 **PRICE**	📅 **SAMPLED**

COLOR METER

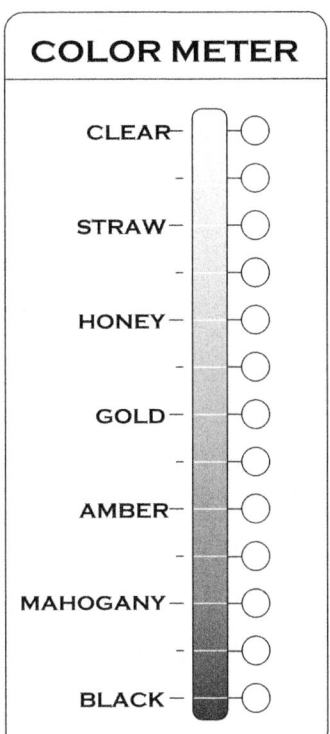

- CLEAR
- STRAW
- HONEY
- GOLD
- AMBER
- MAHOGANY
- BLACK

FLAVOR WHEEL

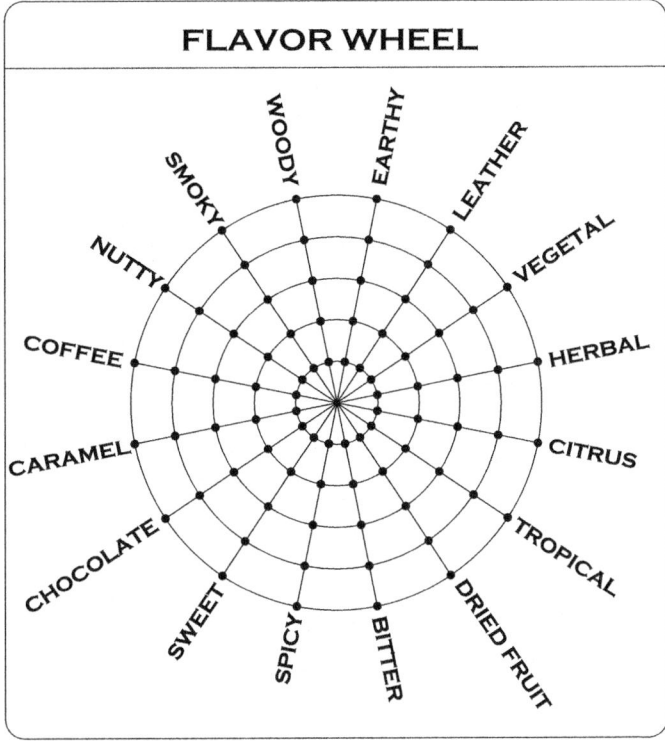

SMOKY, WOODY, EARTHY, LEATHER, VEGETAL, HERBAL, CITRUS, TROPICAL, DRIED FRUIT, BITTER, SPICY, SWEET, CHOCOLATE, CARAMEL, COFFEE, NUTTY

ADDITIONAL NOTES

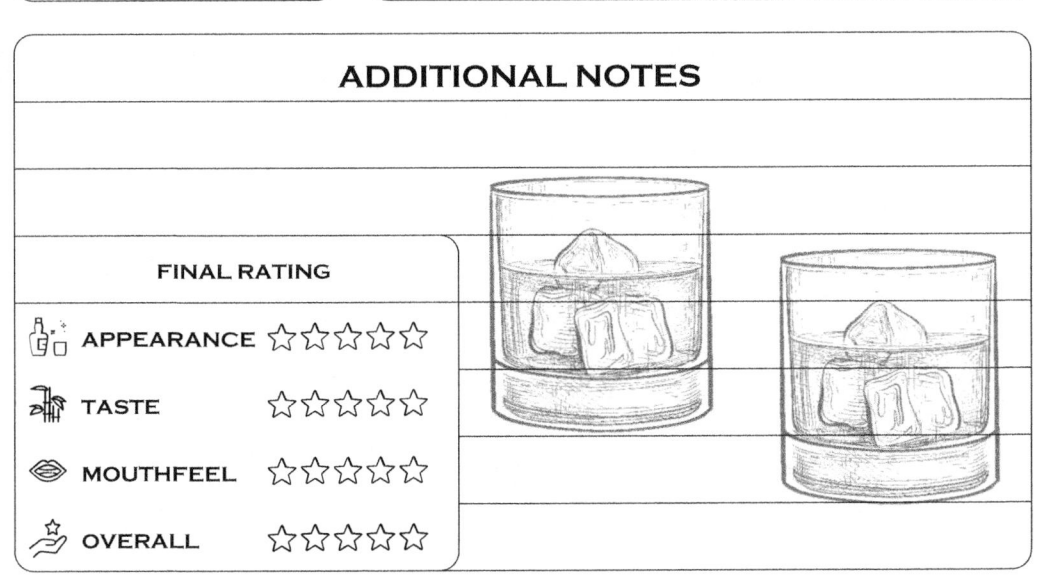

FINAL RATING

- 🍾 APPEARANCE ☆☆☆☆☆
- 👅 TASTE ☆☆☆☆☆
- 👄 MOUTHFEEL ☆☆☆☆☆
- 🙌 OVERALL ☆☆☆☆☆

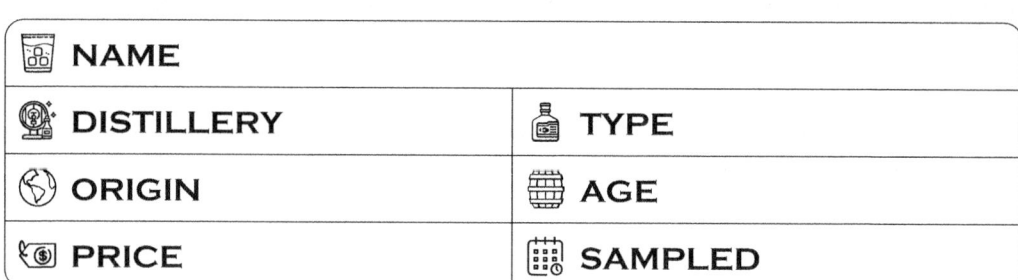

COLOR METER

- CLEAR
- STRAW
- HONEY
- GOLD
- AMBER
- MAHOGANY
- BLACK

FLAVOR WHEEL

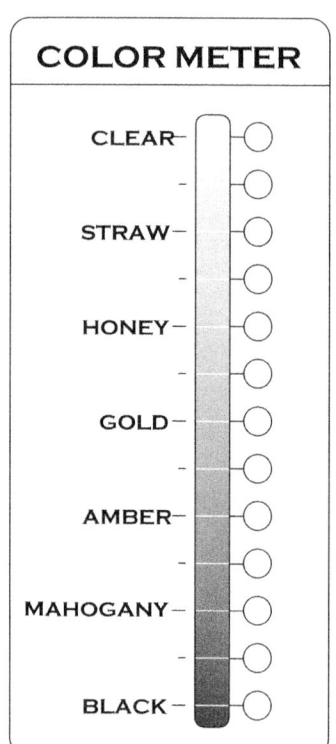
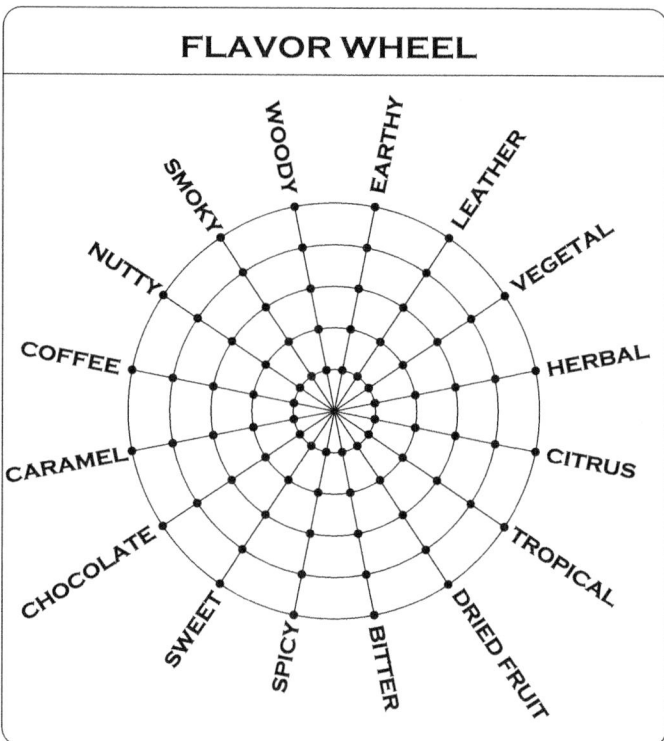

ADDITIONAL NOTES

FINAL RATING

- APPEARANCE ☆☆☆☆☆
- TASTE ☆☆☆☆☆
- MOUTHFEEL ☆☆☆☆☆
- OVERALL ☆☆☆☆☆

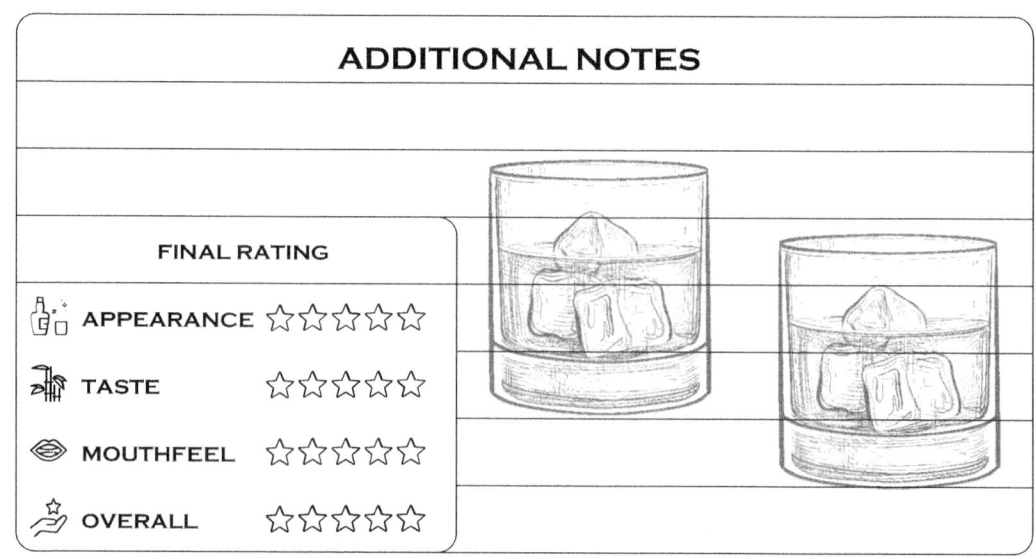

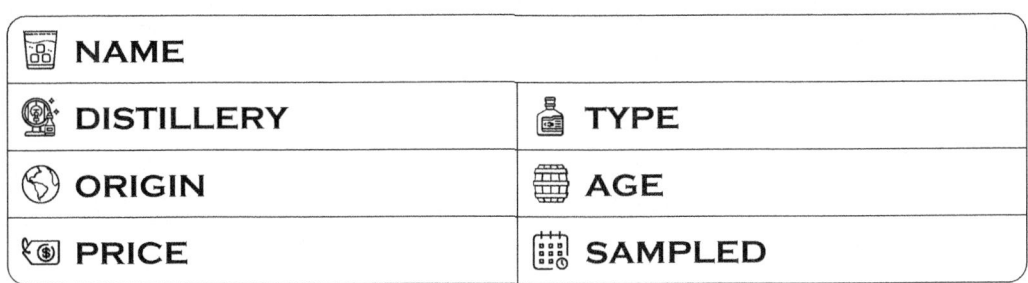

🥃 NAME	
🌐 DISTILLERY	🍾 TYPE
🌍 ORIGIN	🛢 AGE
💰 PRICE	📅 SAMPLED

COLOR METER

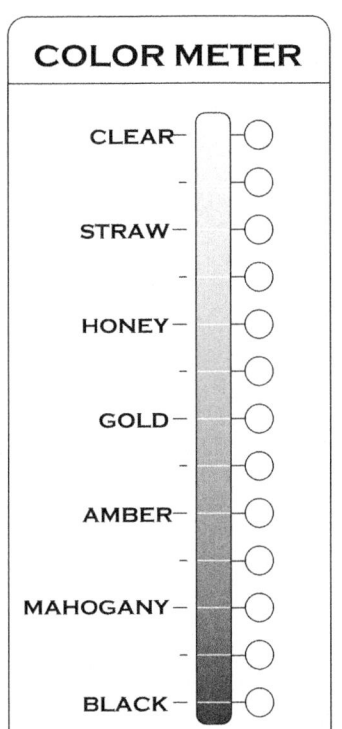

- CLEAR
- STRAW
- HONEY
- GOLD
- AMBER
- MAHOGANY
- BLACK

FLAVOR WHEEL

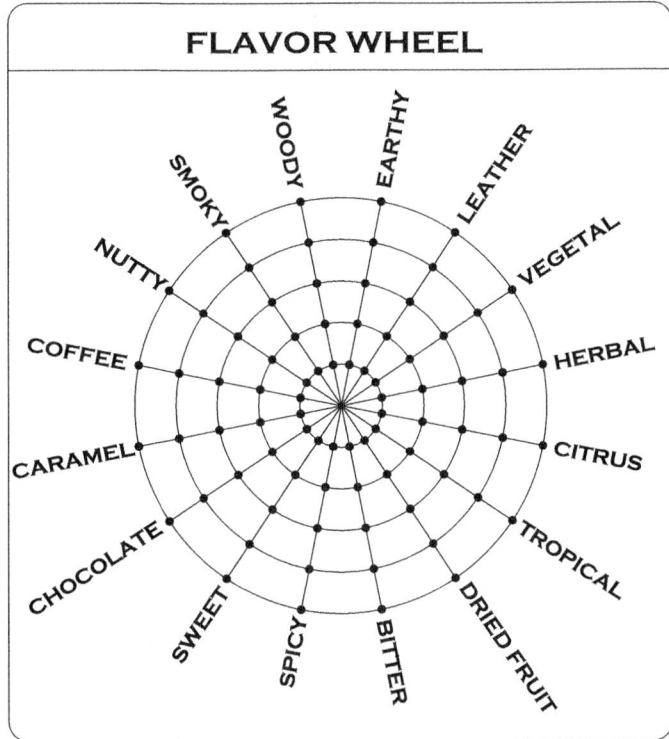

SMOKY, WOODY, EARTHY, LEATHER, VEGETAL, HERBAL, CITRUS, TROPICAL, DRIED FRUIT, BITTER, SPICY, SWEET, CHOCOLATE, CARAMEL, COFFEE, NUTTY

ADDITIONAL NOTES

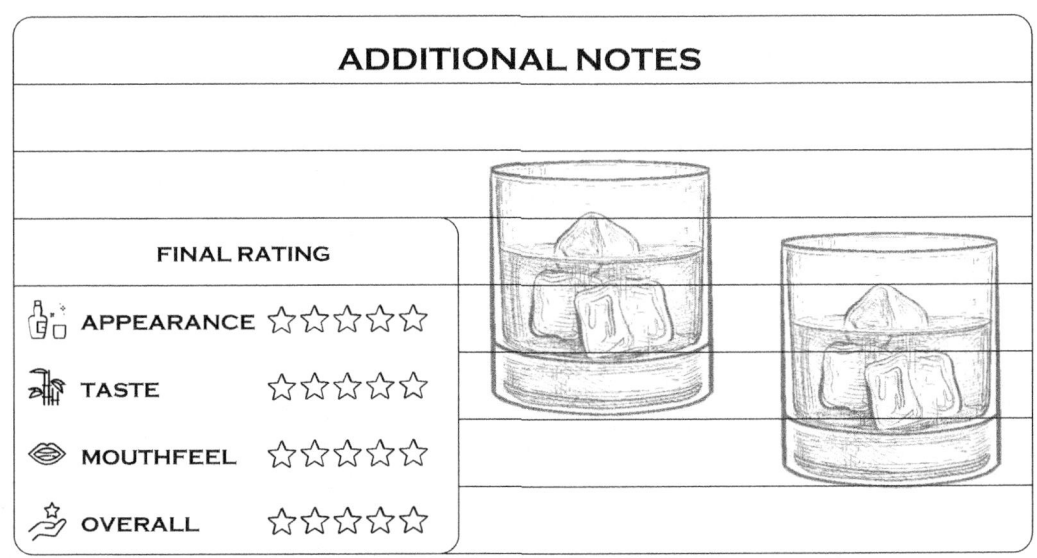

FINAL RATING

- 🍾 APPEARANCE ☆☆☆☆☆
- 👅 TASTE ☆☆☆☆☆
- 👄 MOUTHFEEL ☆☆☆☆☆
- 🏆 OVERALL ☆☆☆☆☆

🥃 NAME	
🛢️ DISTILLERY	🍾 TYPE
🌍 ORIGIN	🛢️ AGE
💲 PRICE	📅 SAMPLED

COLOR METER

- CLEAR
- STRAW
- HONEY
- GOLD
- AMBER
- MAHOGANY
- BLACK

FLAVOR WHEEL

WOODY, EARTHY, LEATHER, VEGETAL, HERBAL, CITRUS, TROPICAL, DRIED FRUIT, BITTER, SPICY, SWEET, CHOCOLATE, CARAMEL, COFFEE, NUTTY, SMOKY

ADDITIONAL NOTES

FINAL RATING

- 🍾 APPEARANCE ☆☆☆☆☆
- 🥃 TASTE ☆☆☆☆☆
- 👄 MOUTHFEEL ☆☆☆☆☆
- 🤚 OVERALL ☆☆☆☆☆

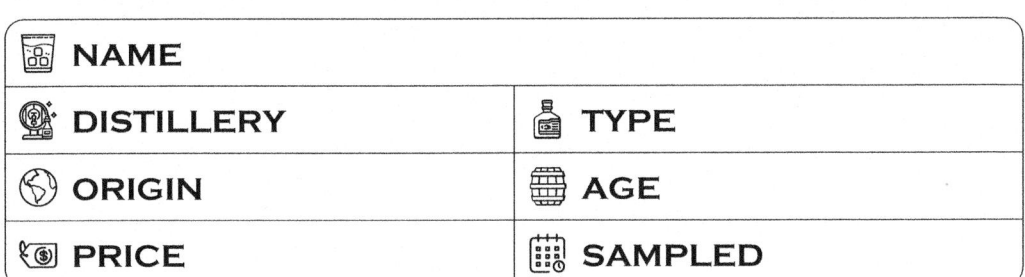

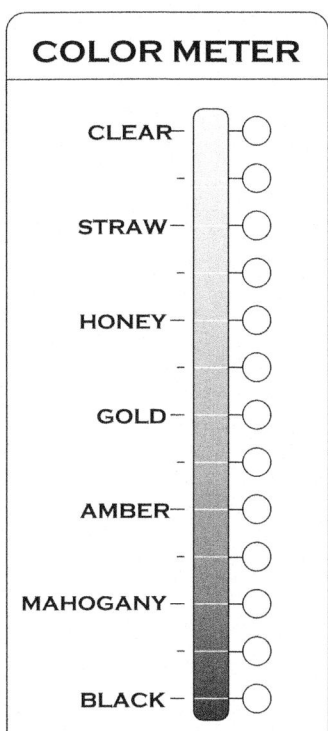

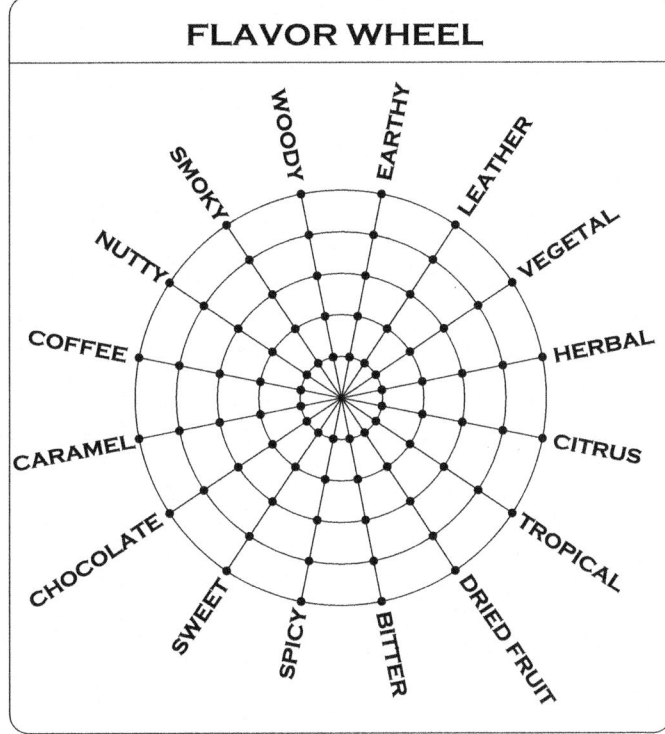

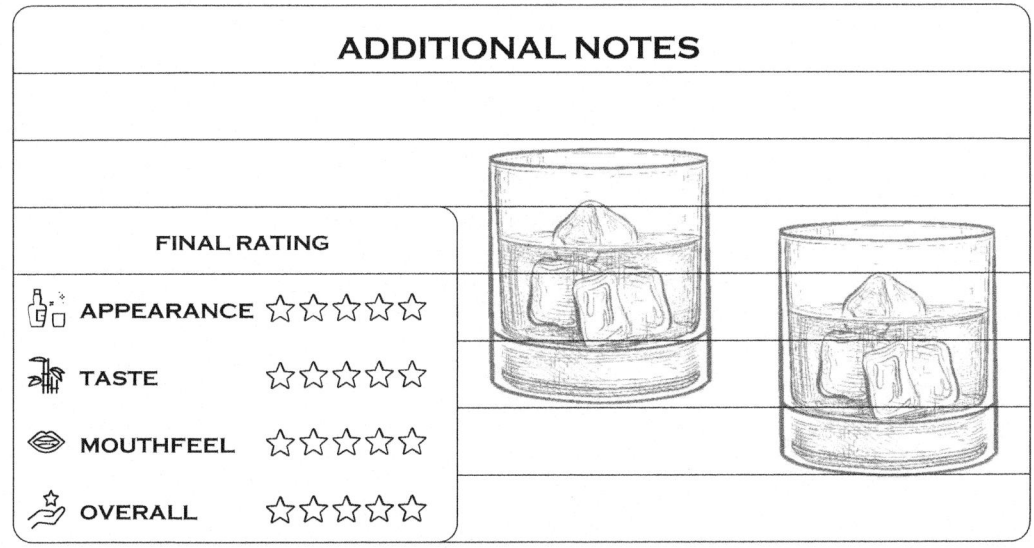

🥃 NAME	
🏭 DISTILLERY	🍾 TYPE
🌍 ORIGIN	🛢 AGE
💰 PRICE	📅 SAMPLED

COLOR METER

- CLEAR
- STRAW
- HONEY
- GOLD
- AMBER
- MAHOGANY
- BLACK

FLAVOR WHEEL

WOODY, EARTHY, LEATHER, VEGETAL, HERBAL, CITRUS, TROPICAL, DRIED FRUIT, BITTER, SPICY, SWEET, CHOCOLATE, CARAMEL, COFFEE, NUTTY, SMOKY

ADDITIONAL NOTES

FINAL RATING

- 🍾 APPEARANCE ☆☆☆☆☆
- 🌾 TASTE ☆☆☆☆☆
- 👄 MOUTHFEEL ☆☆☆☆☆
- 🙌 OVERALL ☆☆☆☆☆

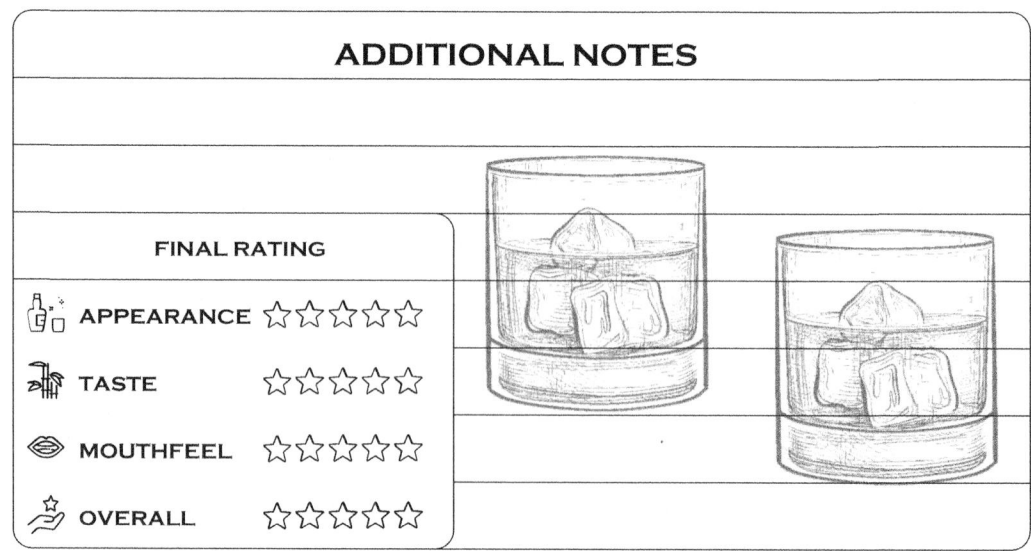

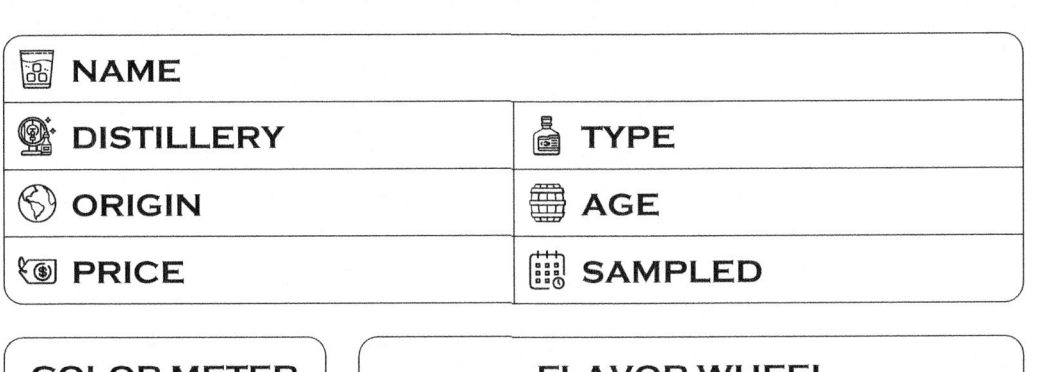

NAME	
DISTILLERY	TYPE
ORIGIN	AGE
PRICE	SAMPLED

COLOR METER

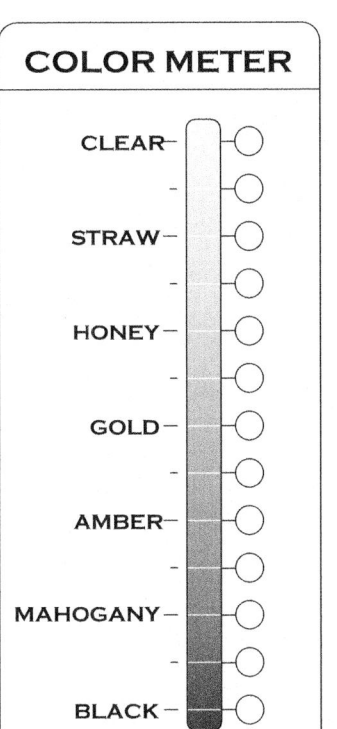

- CLEAR
- STRAW
- HONEY
- GOLD
- AMBER
- MAHOGANY
- BLACK

FLAVOR WHEEL

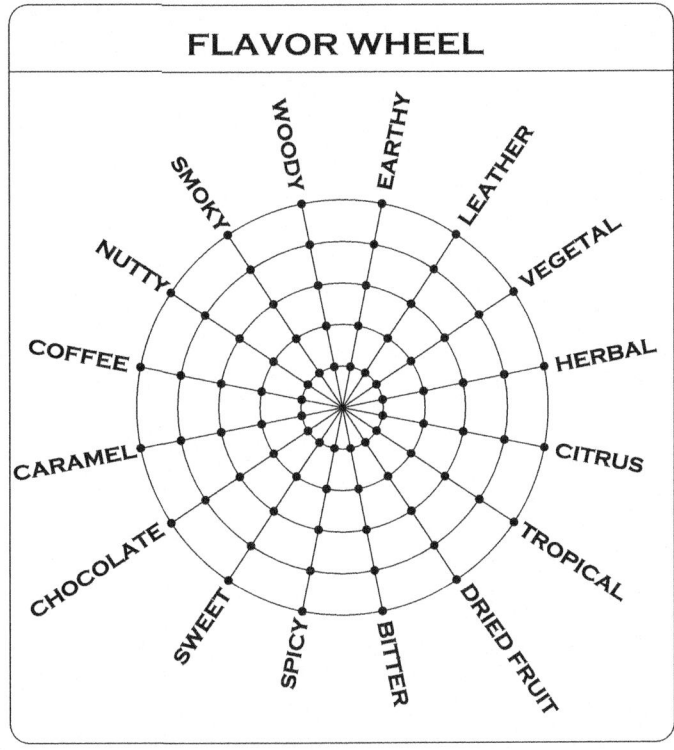

WOODY, EARTHY, LEATHER, VEGETAL, HERBAL, CITRUS, TROPICAL, DRIED FRUIT, BITTER, SPICY, SWEET, CHOCOLATE, CARAMEL, COFFEE, NUTTY, SMOKY

ADDITIONAL NOTES

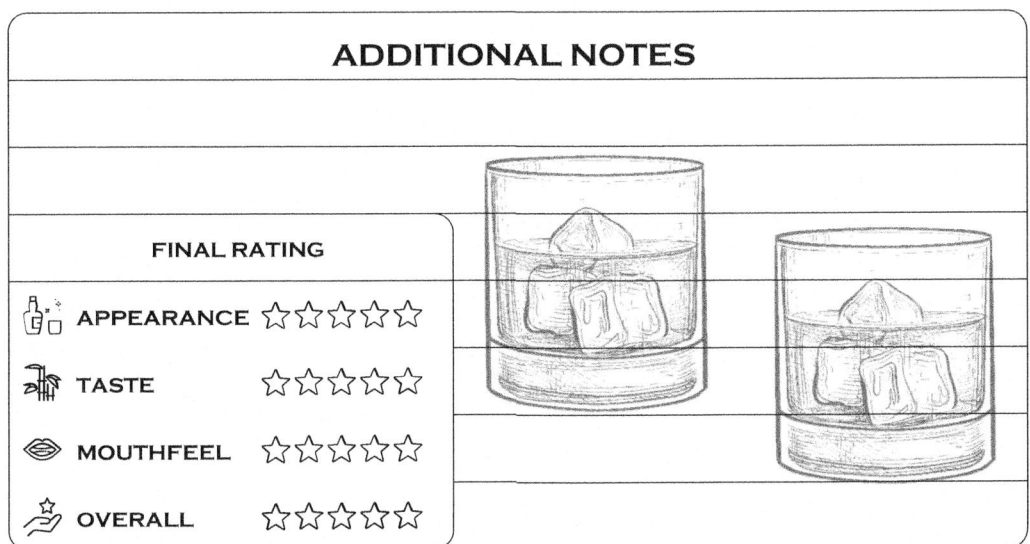

FINAL RATING

- APPEARANCE ☆☆☆☆☆
- TASTE ☆☆☆☆☆
- MOUTHFEEL ☆☆☆☆☆
- OVERALL ☆☆☆☆☆

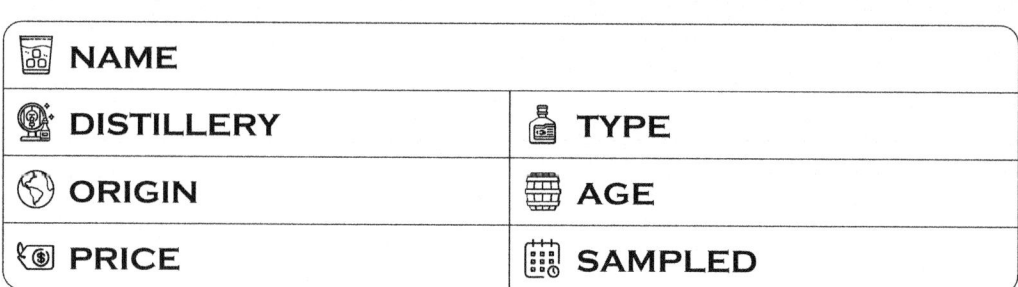

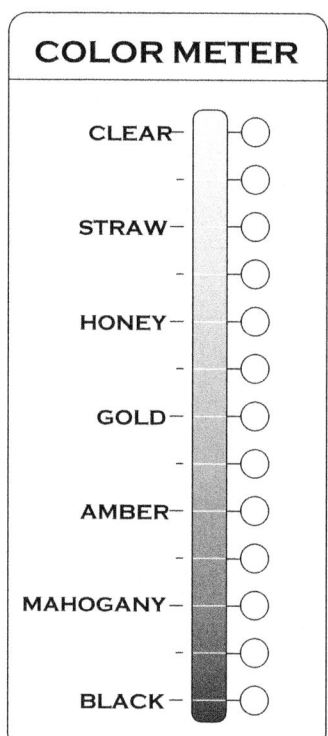

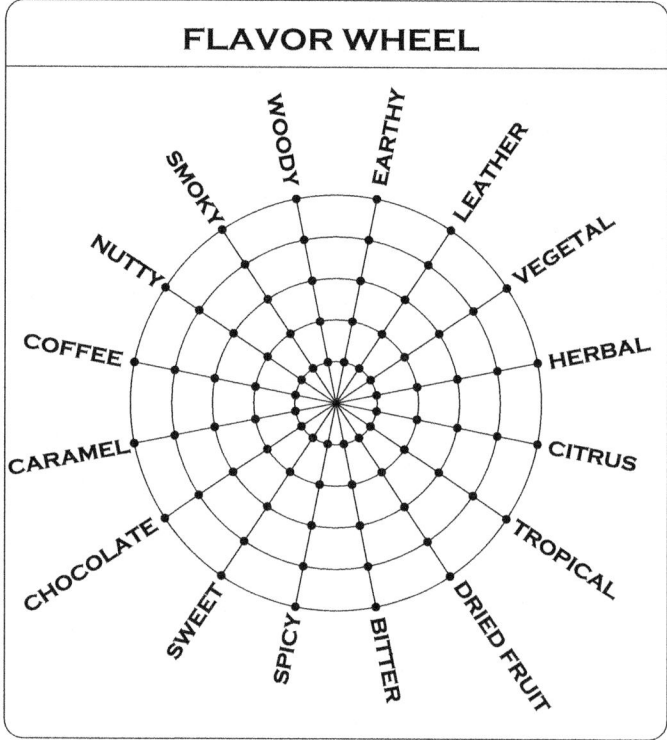

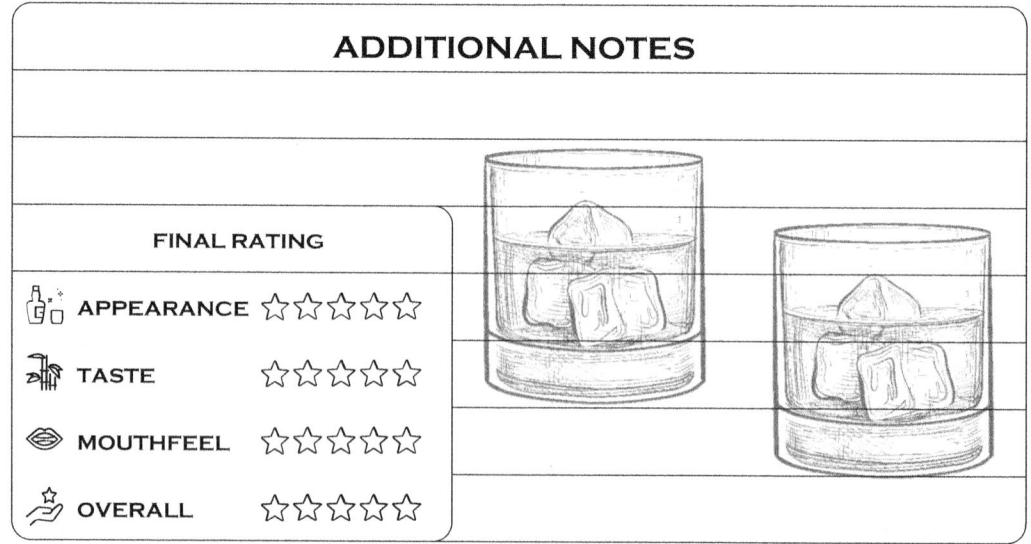

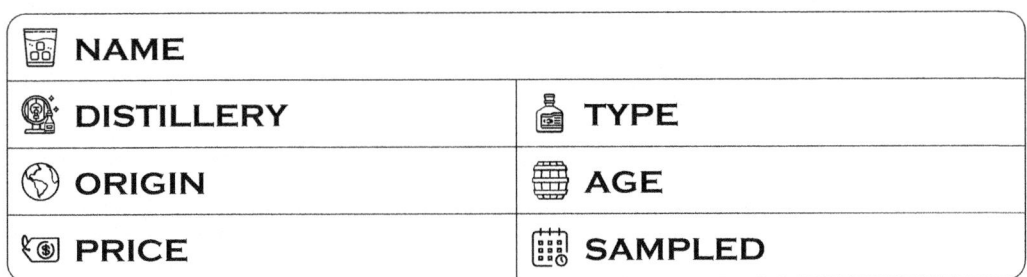

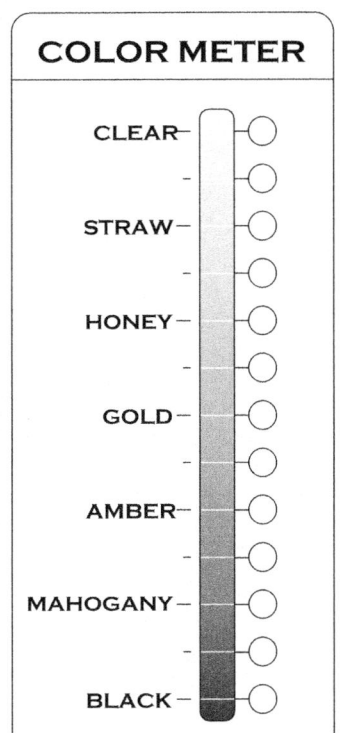

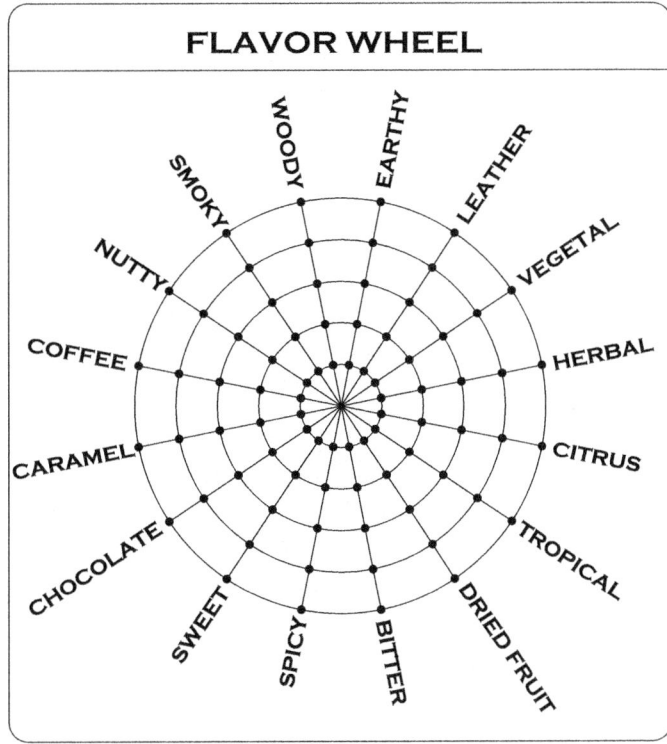

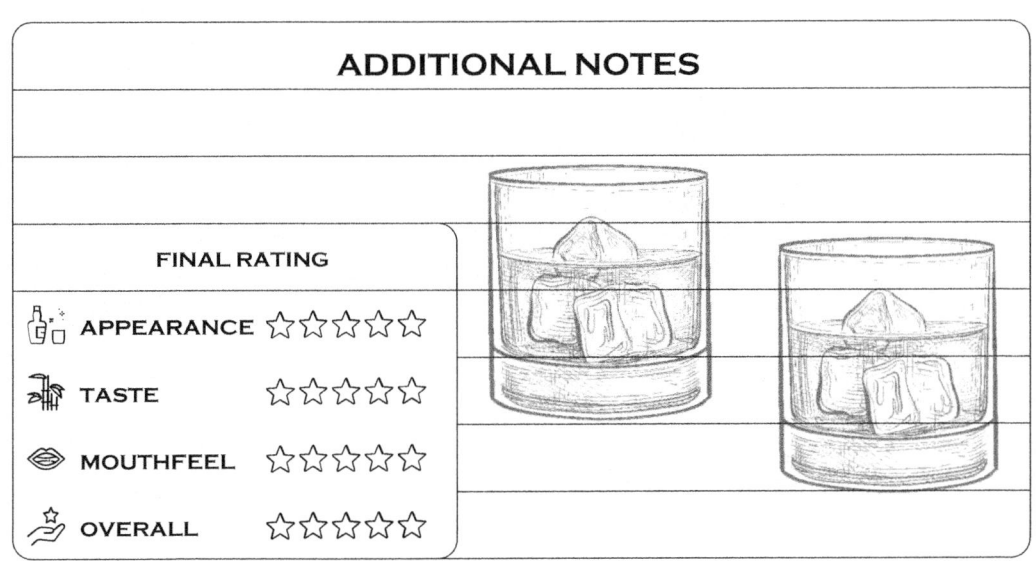

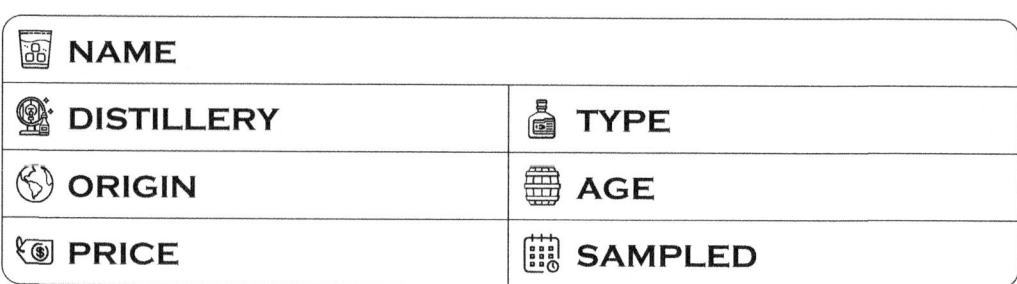

NAME	
DISTILLERY	TYPE
ORIGIN	AGE
PRICE	SAMPLED

COLOR METER

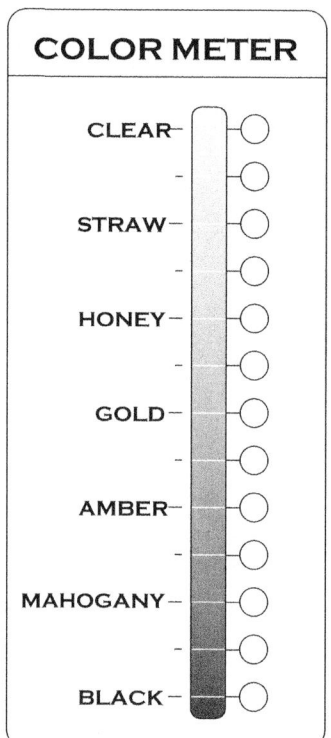

CLEAR
STRAW
HONEY
GOLD
AMBER
MAHOGANY
BLACK

FLAVOR WHEEL

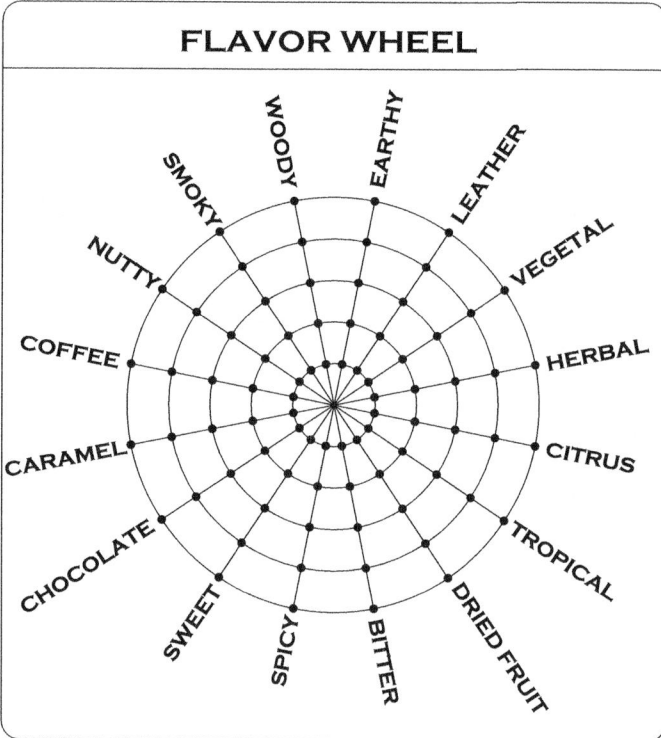

SMOKY, WOODY, EARTHY, LEATHER, NUTTY, VEGETAL, COFFEE, HERBAL, CARAMEL, CITRUS, CHOCOLATE, TROPICAL, SWEET, SPICY, BITTER, DRIED FRUIT

ADDITIONAL NOTES

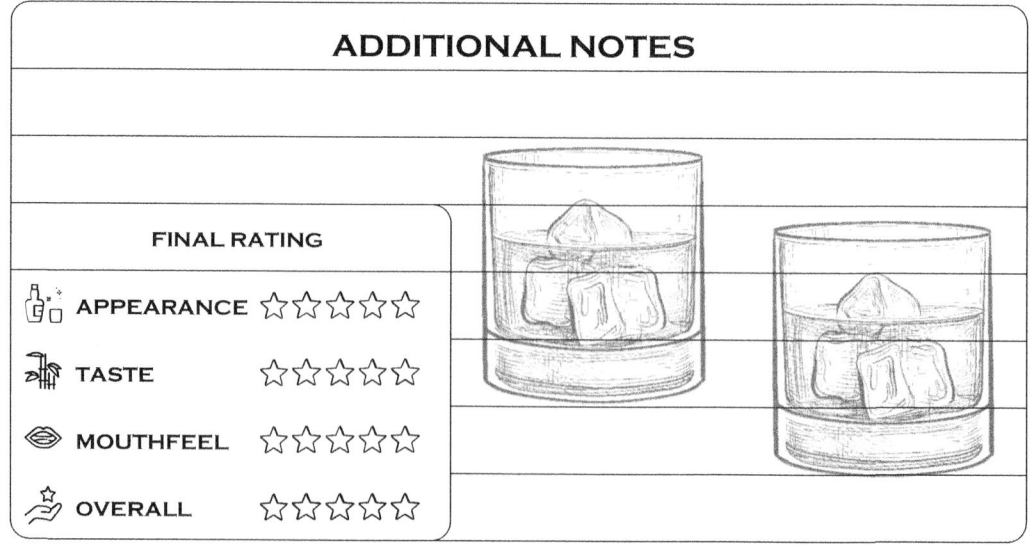

FINAL RATING

- APPEARANCE ☆☆☆☆☆
- TASTE ☆☆☆☆☆
- MOUTHFEEL ☆☆☆☆☆
- OVERALL ☆☆☆☆☆

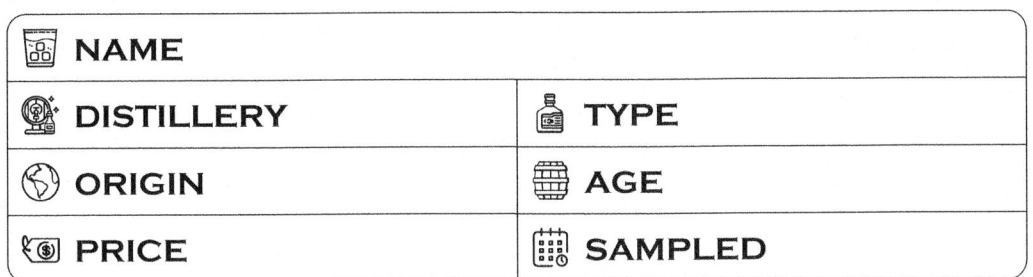

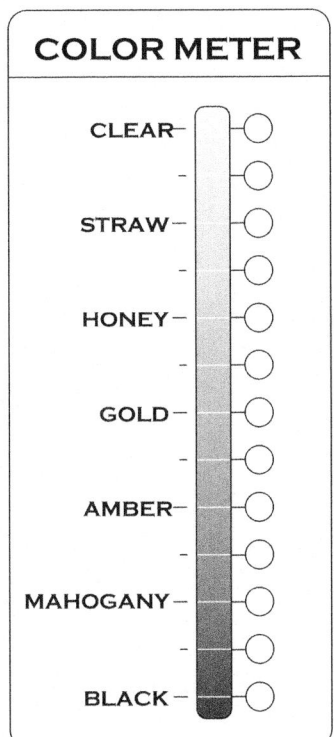

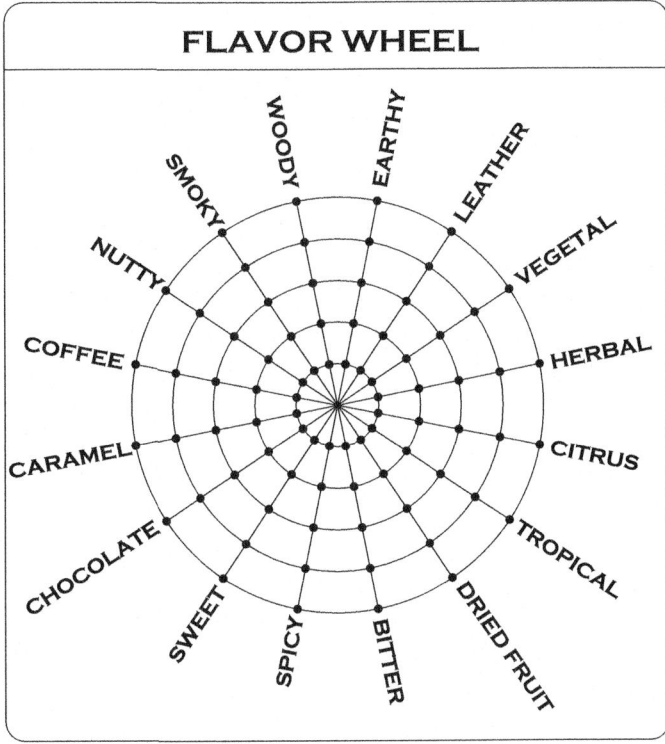

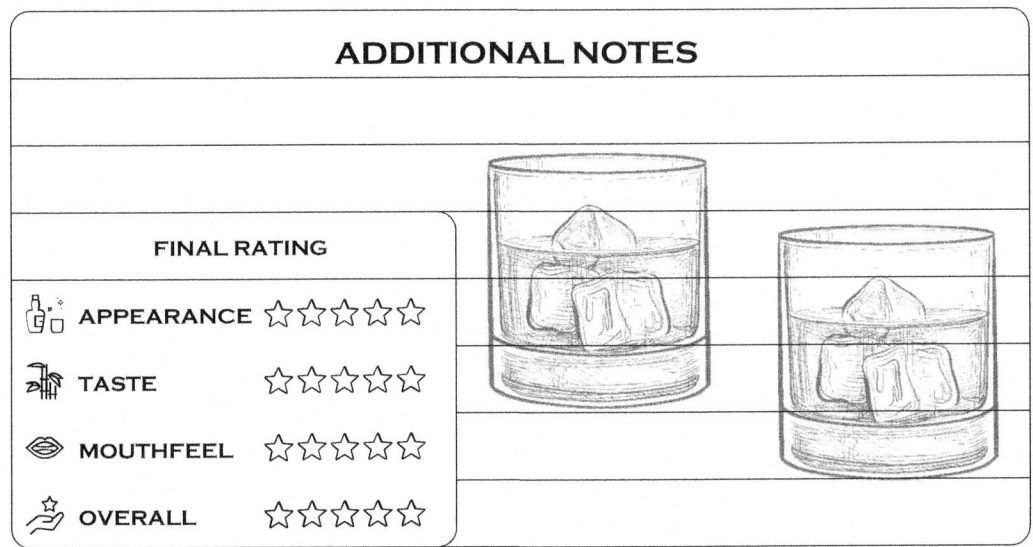

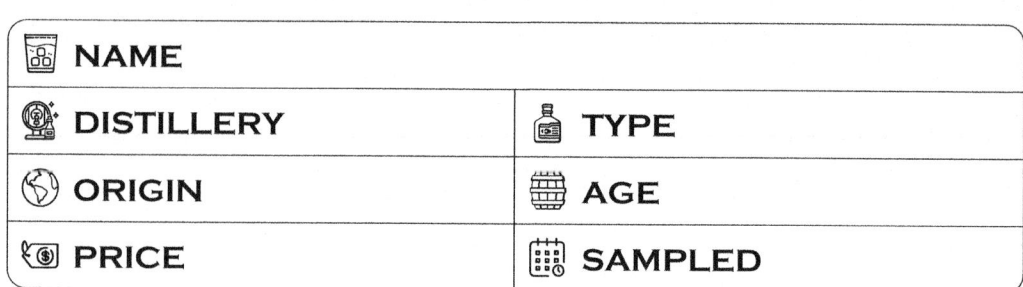

NAME	
DISTILLERY	TYPE
ORIGIN	AGE
PRICE	SAMPLED

COLOR METER

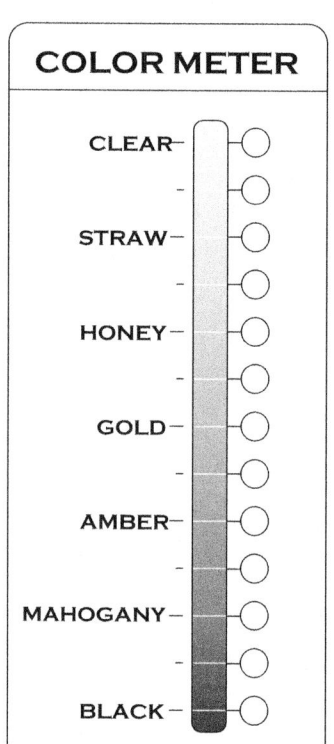

FLAVOR WHEEL

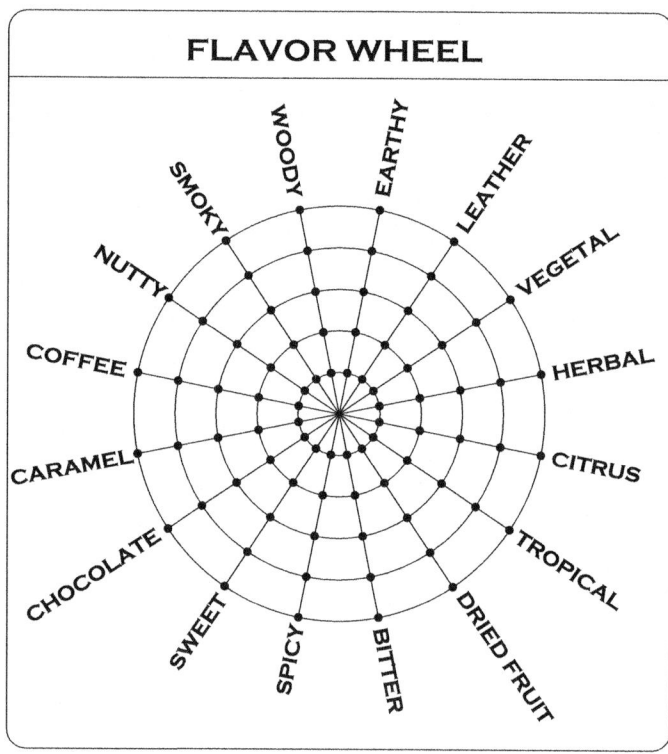

ADDITIONAL NOTES

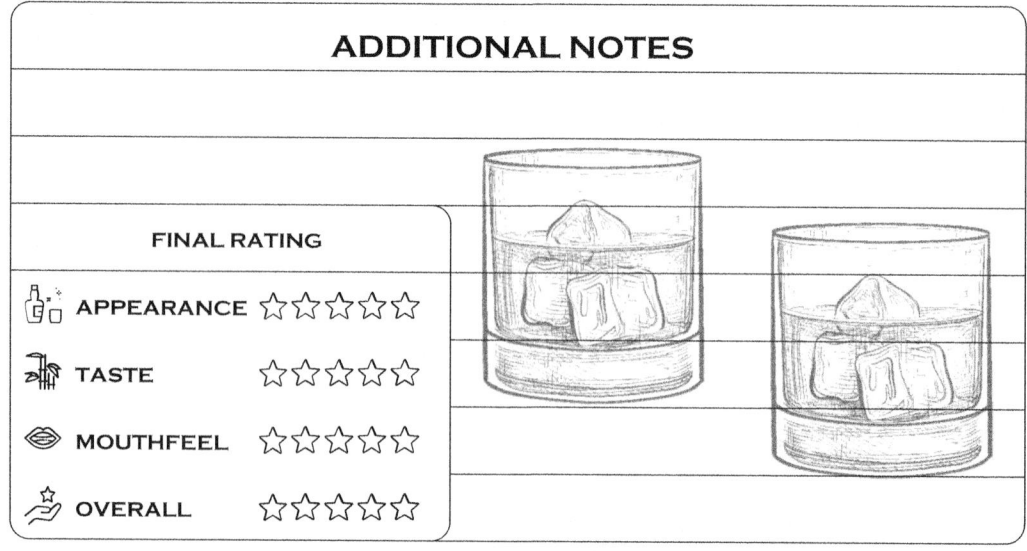

FINAL RATING

- APPEARANCE ☆☆☆☆☆
- TASTE ☆☆☆☆☆
- MOUTHFEEL ☆☆☆☆☆
- OVERALL ☆☆☆☆☆

NAME	
DISTILLERY	TYPE
ORIGIN	AGE
PRICE	SAMPLED

COLOR METER

- CLEAR
- STRAW
- HONEY
- GOLD
- AMBER
- MAHOGANY
- BLACK

FLAVOR WHEEL

SMOKY, WOODY, EARTHY, LEATHER, VEGETAL, HERBAL, CITRUS, TROPICAL, DRIED FRUIT, BITTER, SPICY, SWEET, CHOCOLATE, CARAMEL, COFFEE, NUTTY

ADDITIONAL NOTES

FINAL RATING

- APPEARANCE ☆☆☆☆☆
- TASTE ☆☆☆☆☆
- MOUTHFEEL ☆☆☆☆☆
- OVERALL ☆☆☆☆☆

🥃 NAME	
🛢️ DISTILLERY	🍾 TYPE
🌍 ORIGIN	🛢️ AGE
💰 PRICE	📅 SAMPLED

COLOR METER

- CLEAR
- STRAW
- HONEY
- GOLD
- AMBER
- MAHOGANY
- BLACK

FLAVOR WHEEL

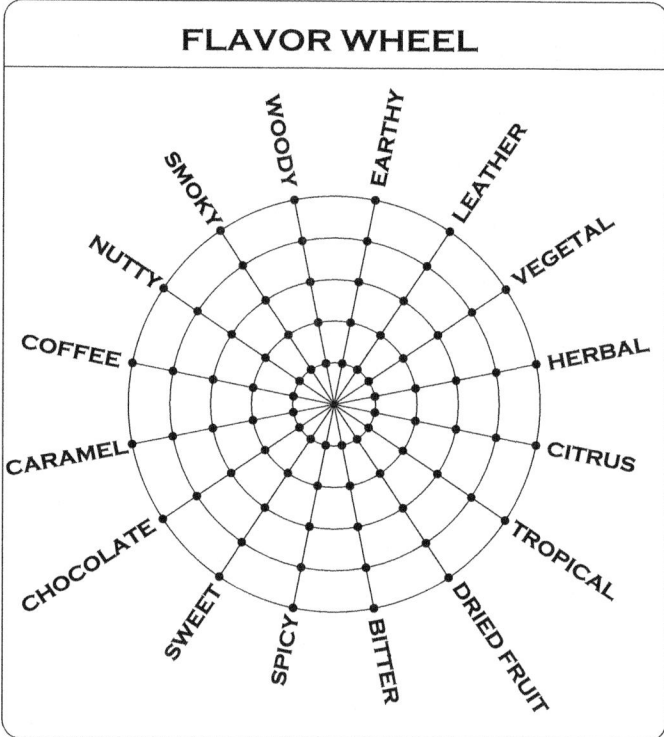

WOODY, EARTHY, LEATHER, VEGETAL, HERBAL, CITRUS, TROPICAL, DRIED FRUIT, BITTER, SPICY, SWEET, CHOCOLATE, CARAMEL, COFFEE, NUTTY, SMOKY

ADDITIONAL NOTES

FINAL RATING

- 🍾 APPEARANCE ☆☆☆☆☆
- 🌾 TASTE ☆☆☆☆☆
- 👄 MOUTHFEEL ☆☆☆☆☆
- 🖐️ OVERALL ☆☆☆☆☆

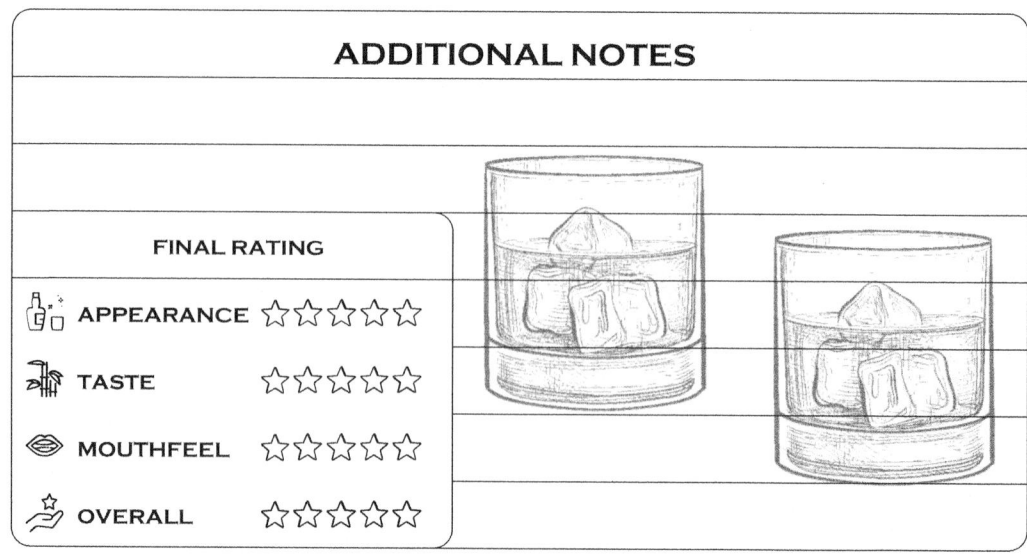

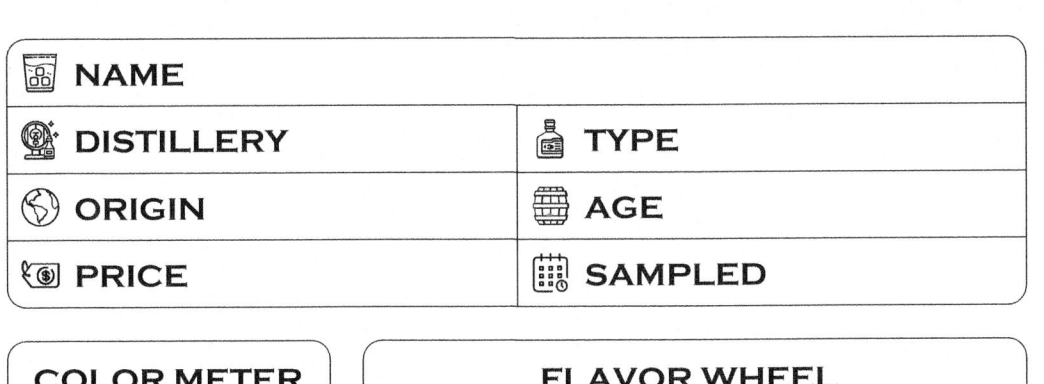
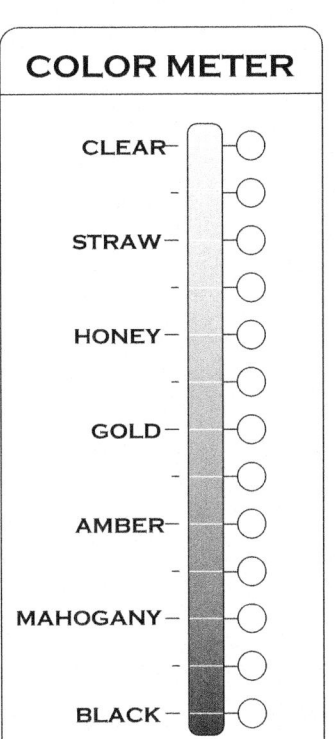
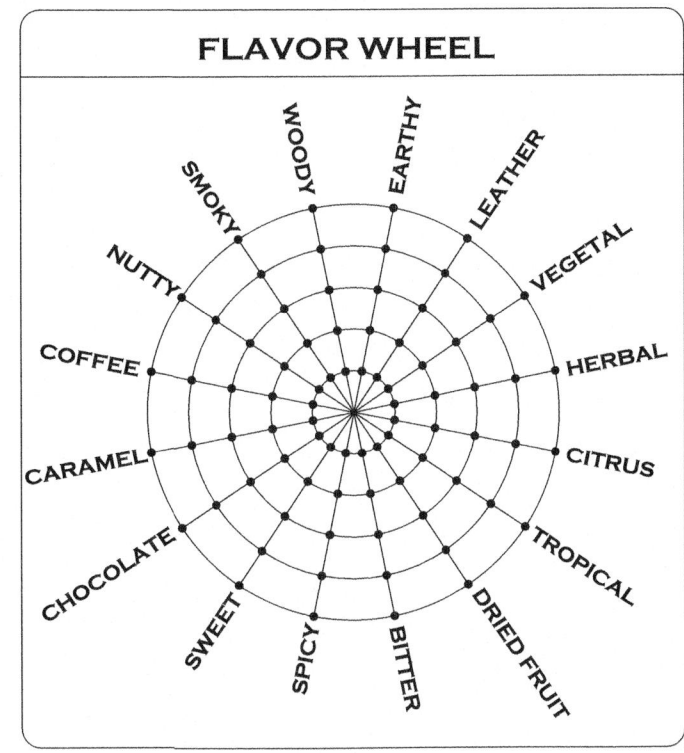
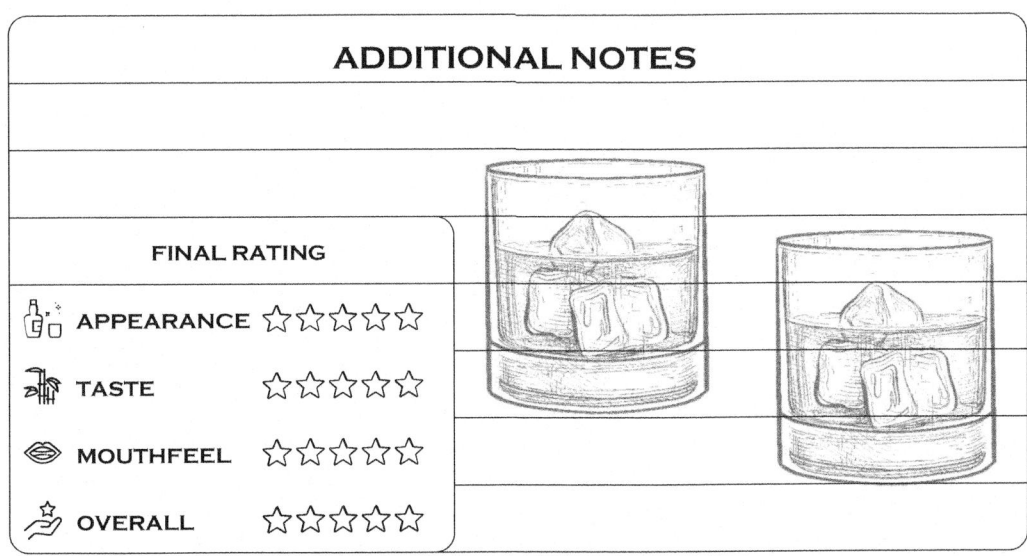

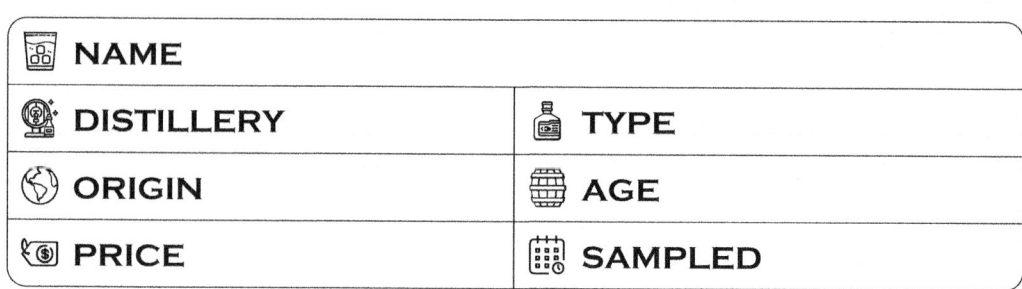
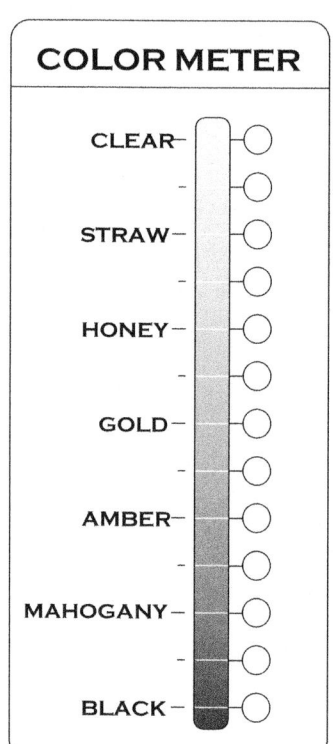
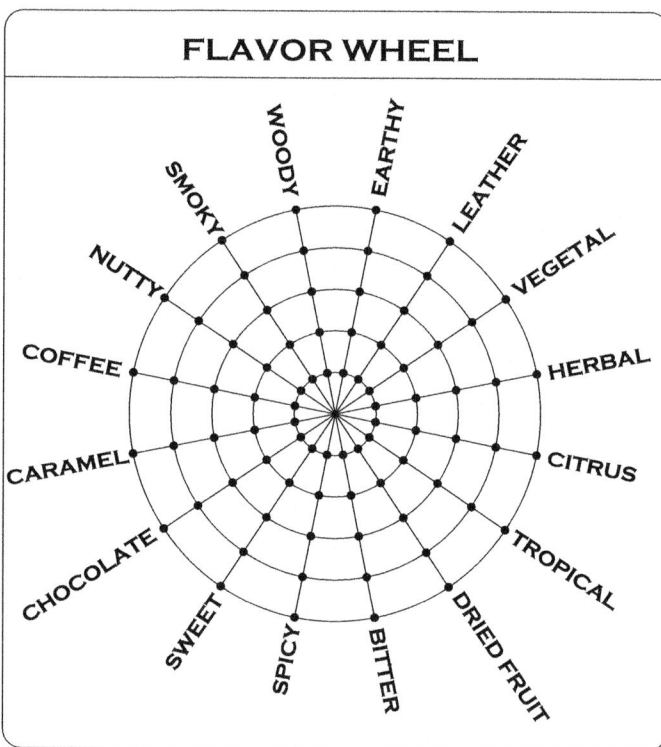
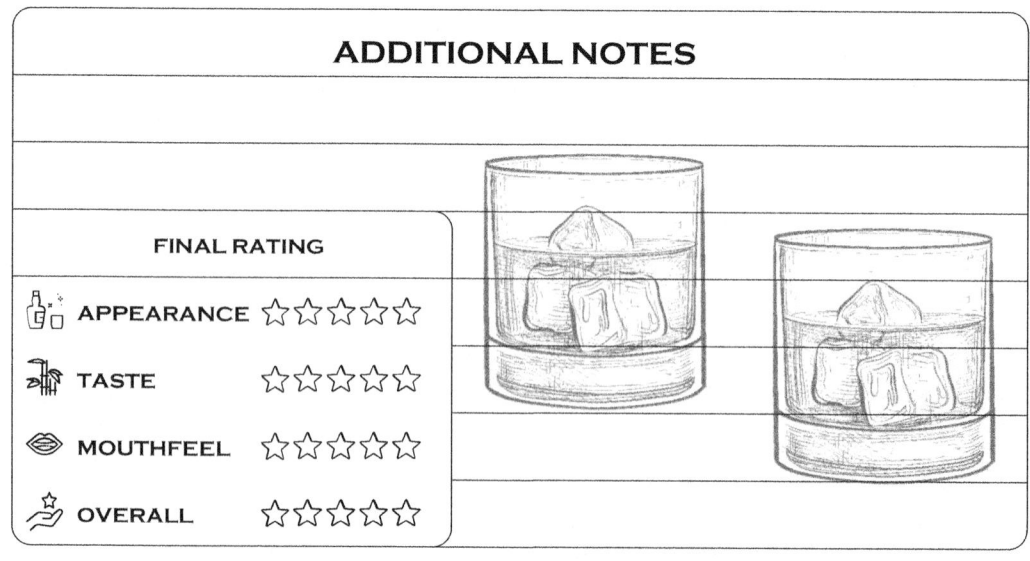

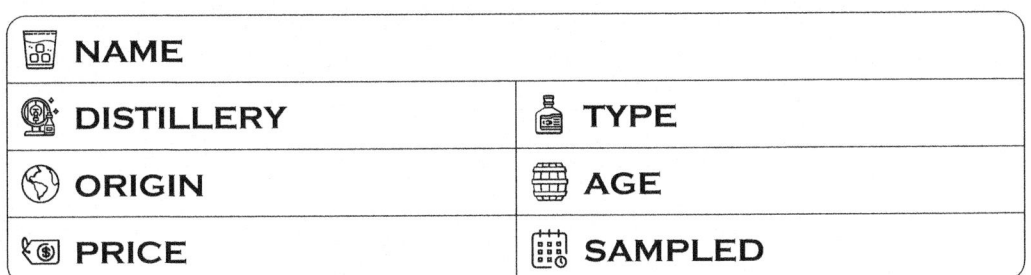

🥃 NAME	
🎡 DISTILLERY	🍾 TYPE
🌐 ORIGIN	🛢 AGE
💰 PRICE	📅 SAMPLED

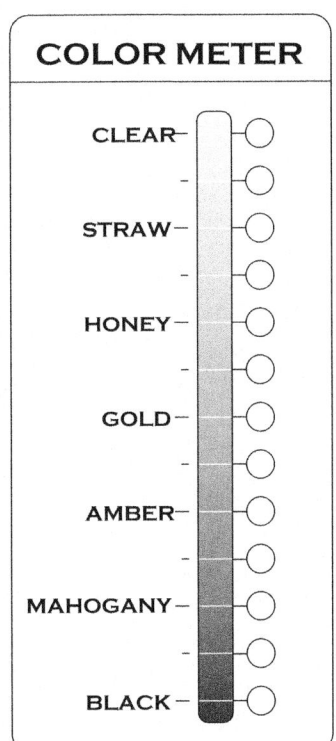

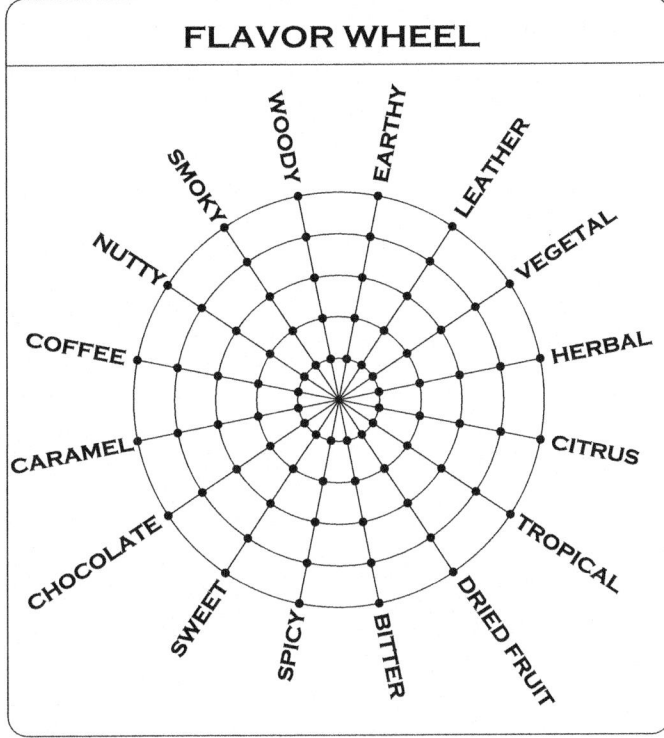

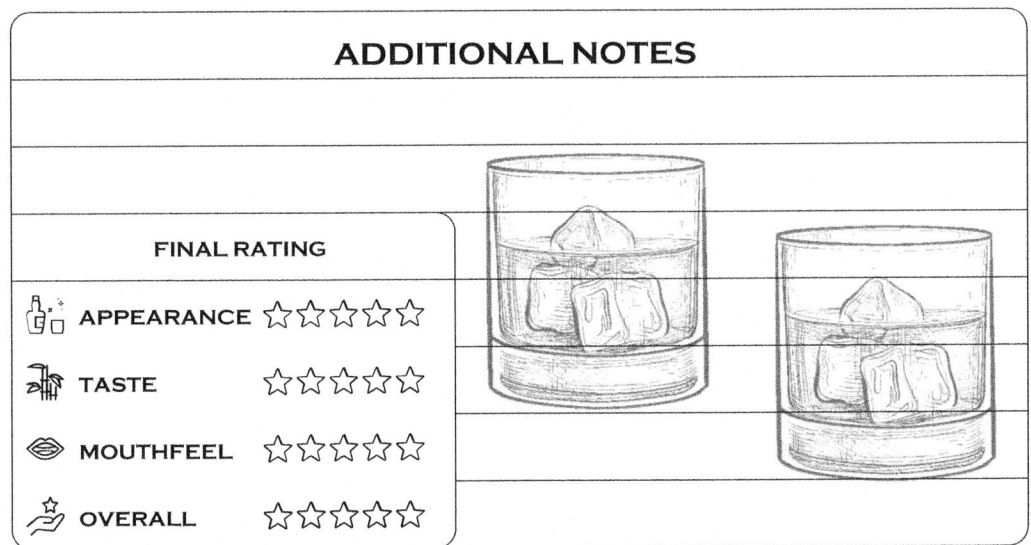

ADDITIONAL NOTES

FINAL RATING

- 🍾 APPEARANCE ☆☆☆☆☆
- 🥃 TASTE ☆☆☆☆☆
- 👄 MOUTHFEEL ☆☆☆☆☆
- 🤲 OVERALL ☆☆☆☆☆

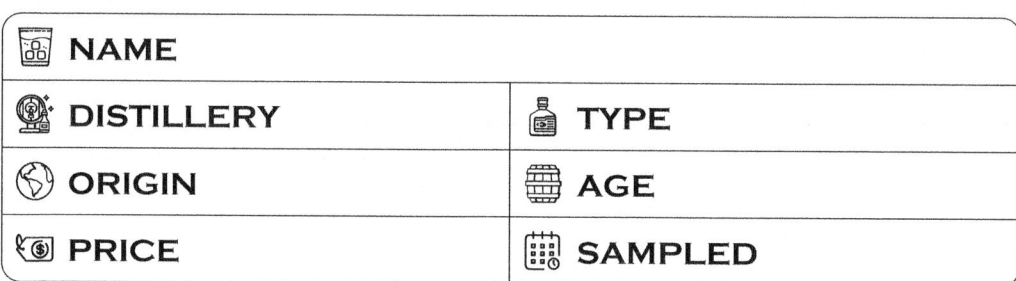

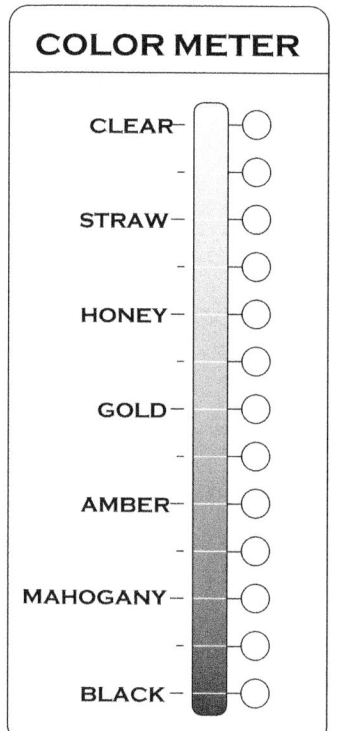

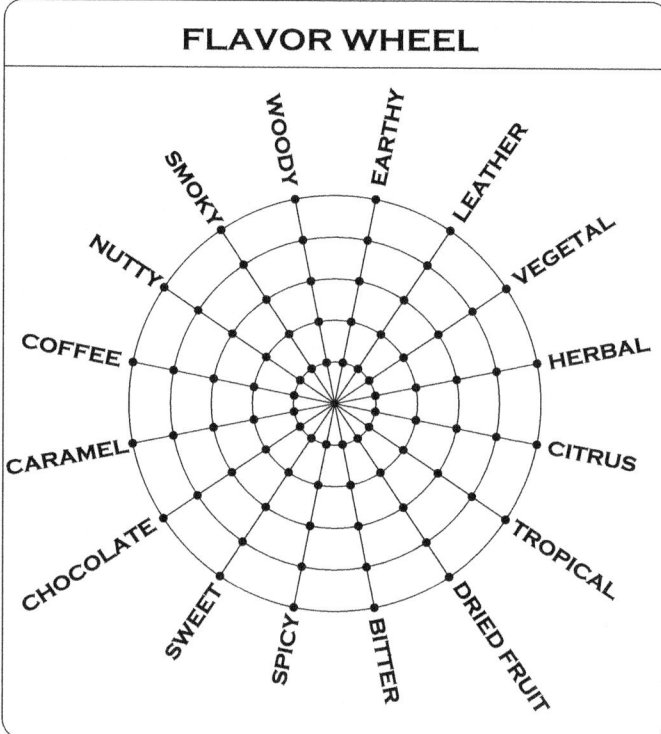

ADDITIONAL NOTES

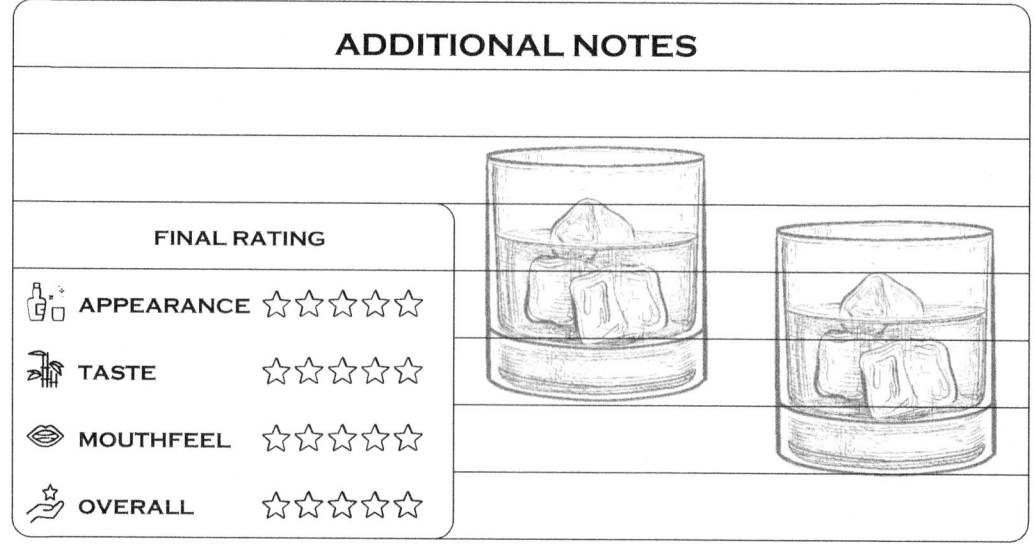

FINAL RATING

- APPEARANCE ☆☆☆☆☆
- TASTE ☆☆☆☆☆
- MOUTHFEEL ☆☆☆☆☆
- OVERALL ☆☆☆☆☆

🥃 NAME	
🏭 DISTILLERY	🍾 TYPE
🌐 ORIGIN	🛢 AGE
💵 PRICE	📅 SAMPLED

COLOR METER

- CLEAR
- –
- STRAW
- –
- HONEY
- –
- GOLD
- –
- AMBER
- –
- MAHOGANY
- –
- BLACK

FLAVOR WHEEL

WOODY, EARTHY, LEATHER, VEGETAL, HERBAL, CITRUS, TROPICAL, DRIED FRUIT, BITTER, SPICY, SWEET, CHOCOLATE, CARAMEL, COFFEE, NUTTY, SMOKY

ADDITIONAL NOTES

FINAL RATING

- 🍾 APPEARANCE ☆☆☆☆☆
- 🥃 TASTE ☆☆☆☆☆
- 👄 MOUTHFEEL ☆☆☆☆☆
- 🤲 OVERALL ☆☆☆☆☆

🥃 NAME	
🛢️ DISTILLERY	🍾 TYPE
🌐 ORIGIN	🛢️ AGE
💰 PRICE	📅 SAMPLED

COLOR METER

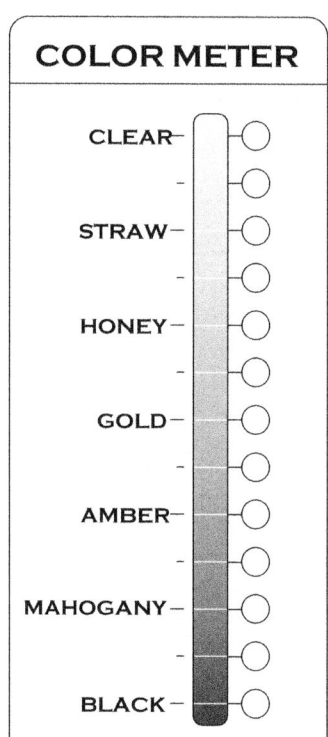

- CLEAR
- STRAW
- HONEY
- GOLD
- AMBER
- MAHOGANY
- BLACK

FLAVOR WHEEL

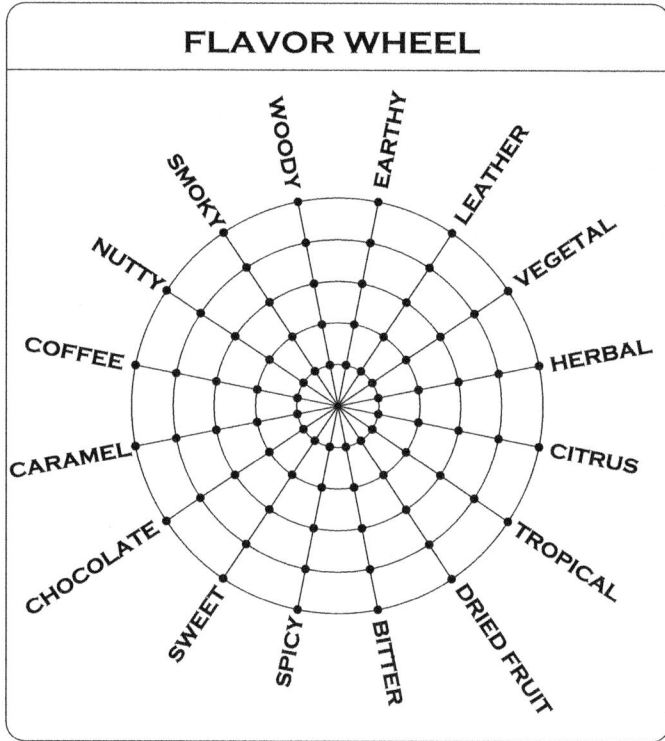

WOODY, EARTHY, LEATHER, VEGETAL, HERBAL, CITRUS, TROPICAL, DRIED FRUIT, BITTER, SPICY, SWEET, CHOCOLATE, CARAMEL, COFFEE, NUTTY, SMOKY

ADDITIONAL NOTES

FINAL RATING

- 🍾 APPEARANCE ☆☆☆☆☆
- 🥃 TASTE ☆☆☆☆☆
- 👄 MOUTHFEEL ☆☆☆☆☆
- 🤲 OVERALL ☆☆☆☆☆

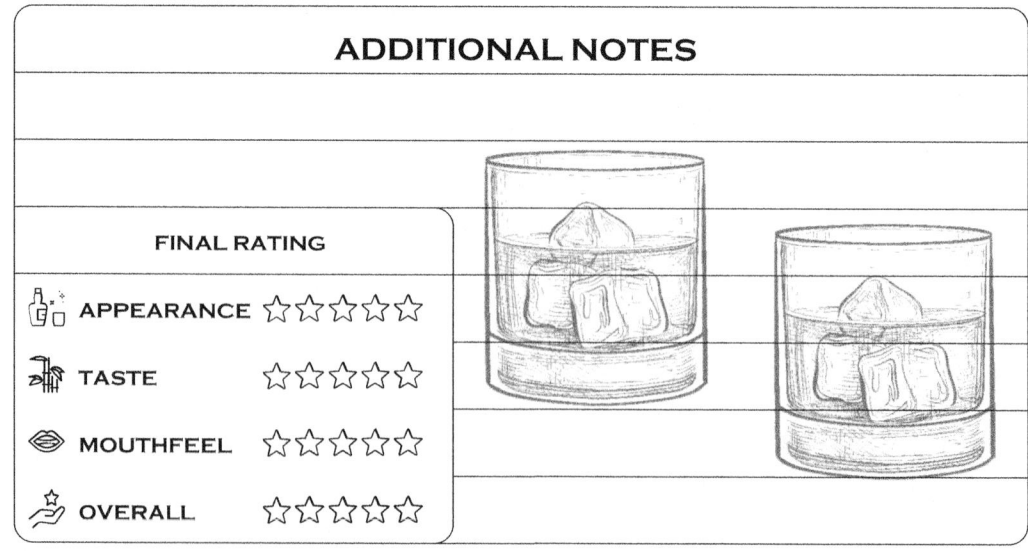

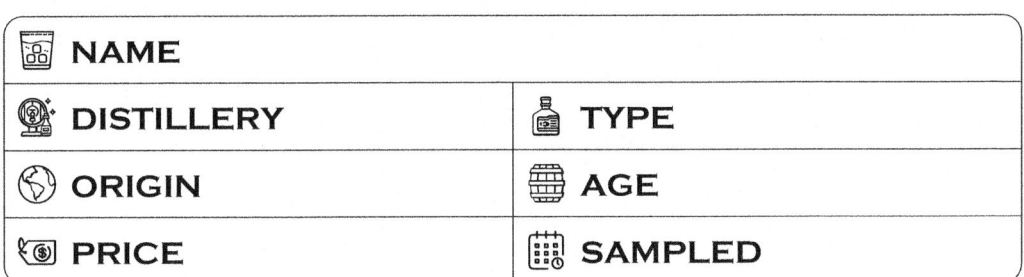

🥃 NAME	
🏭 DISTILLERY	🍾 TYPE
🌍 ORIGIN	🛢 AGE
💰 PRICE	📅 SAMPLED

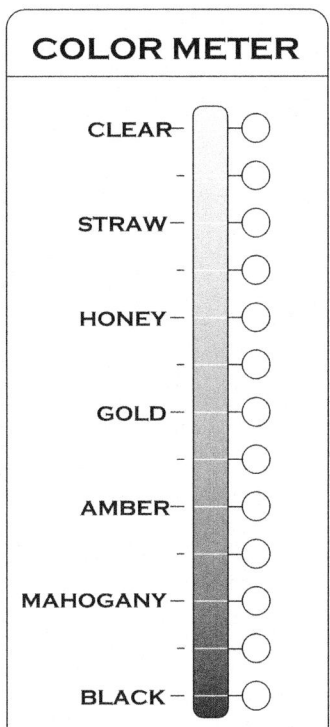

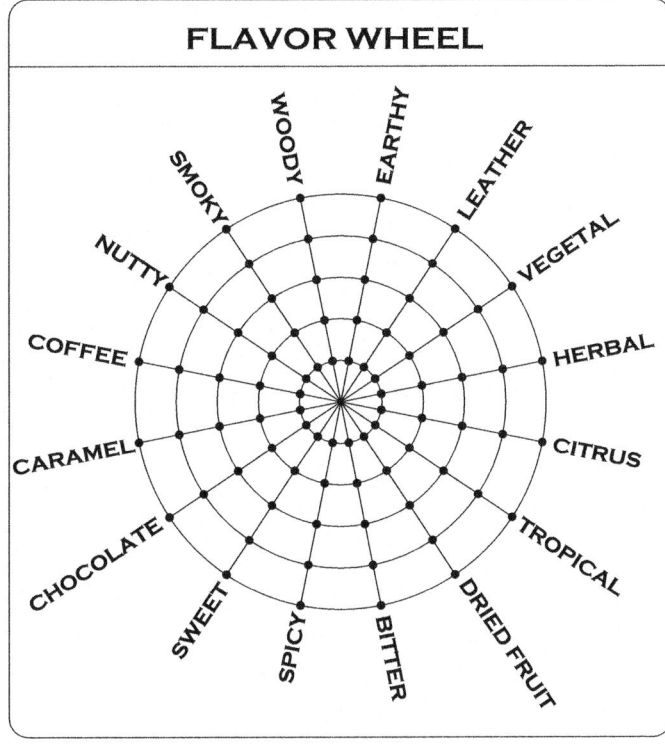

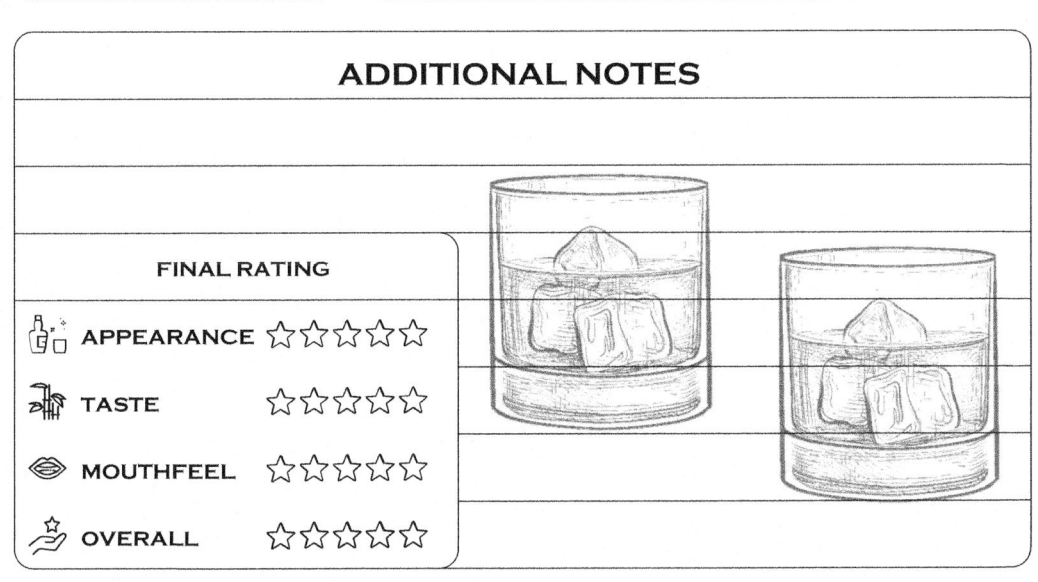

ADDITIONAL NOTES

FINAL RATING

- 🍾 APPEARANCE ☆☆☆☆☆
- 🥃 TASTE ☆☆☆☆☆
- 👄 MOUTHFEEL ☆☆☆☆☆
- 🤚 OVERALL ☆☆☆☆☆

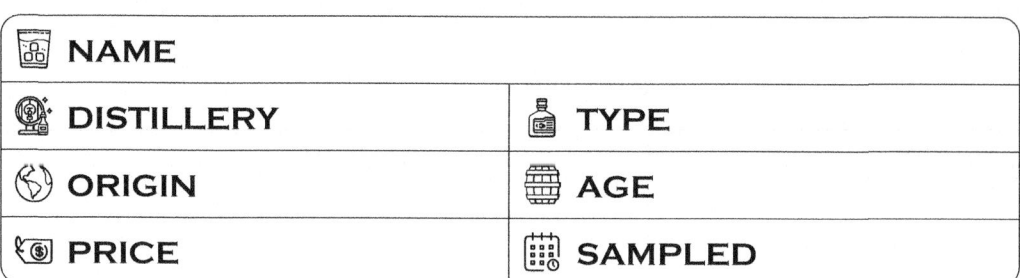

COLOR METER

- CLEAR
- STRAW
- HONEY
- GOLD
- AMBER
- MAHOGANY
- BLACK

FLAVOR WHEEL

SMOKY · WOODY · EARTHY · LEATHER · VEGETAL · NUTTY · HERBAL · COFFEE · CITRUS · CARAMEL · TROPICAL · CHOCOLATE · DRIED FRUIT · SWEET · SPICY · BITTER

ADDITIONAL NOTES

FINAL RATING

- APPEARANCE ☆☆☆☆☆
- TASTE ☆☆☆☆☆
- MOUTHFEEL ☆☆☆☆☆
- OVERALL ☆☆☆☆☆

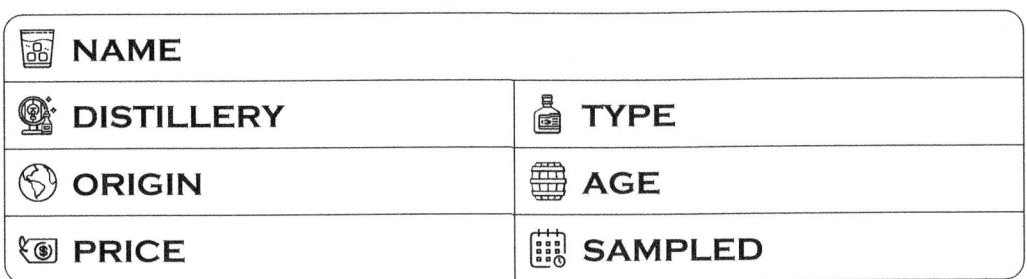

🥃 NAME	
🏭 DISTILLERY	🍾 TYPE
🌍 ORIGIN	🛢 AGE
💰 PRICE	📅 SAMPLED

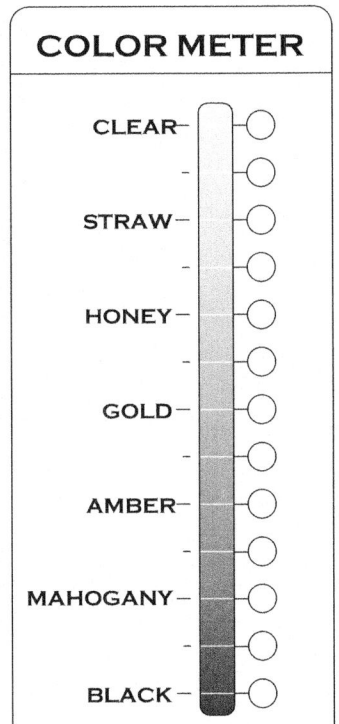

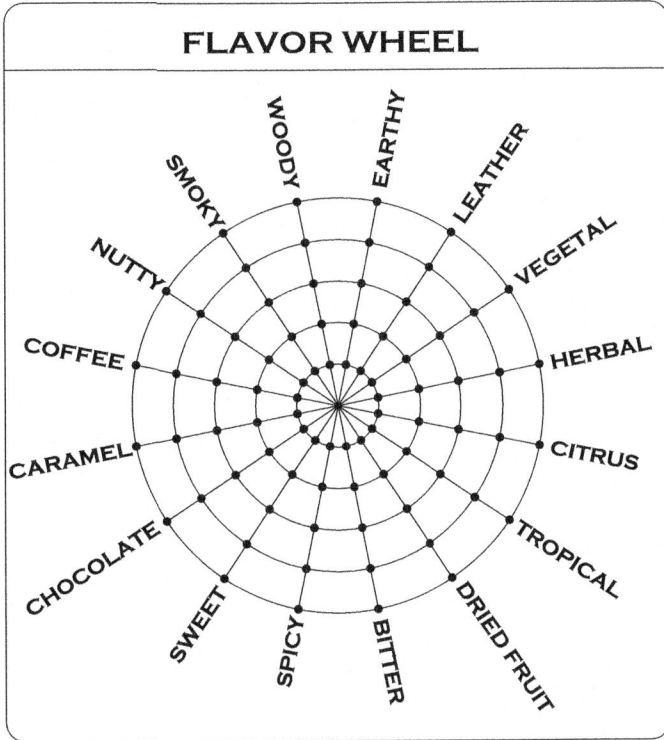

ADDITIONAL NOTES

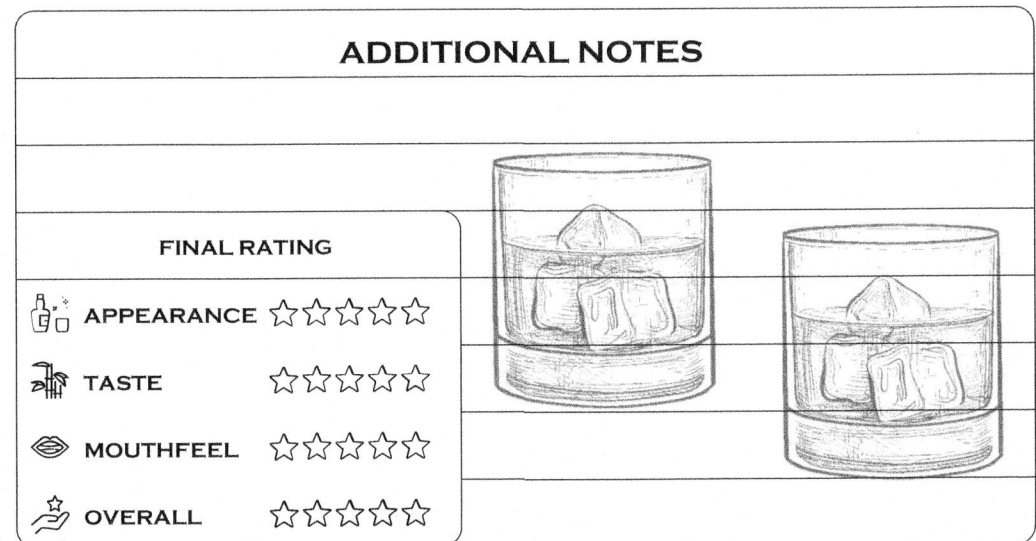

FINAL RATING

- 🍾 APPEARANCE ☆☆☆☆☆
- 🥃 TASTE ☆☆☆☆☆
- 👄 MOUTHFEEL ☆☆☆☆☆
- ⭐ OVERALL ☆☆☆☆☆

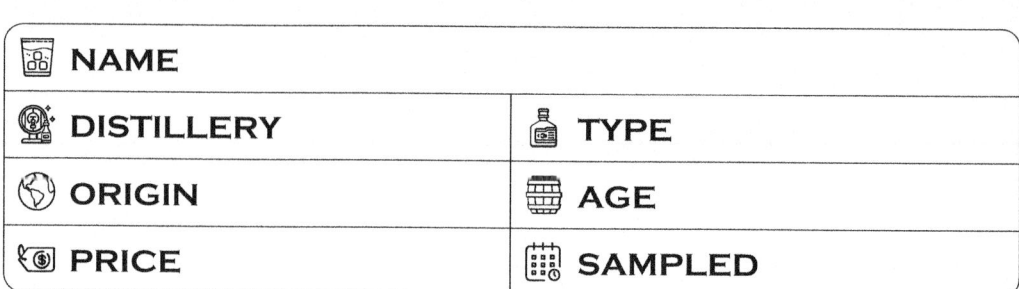

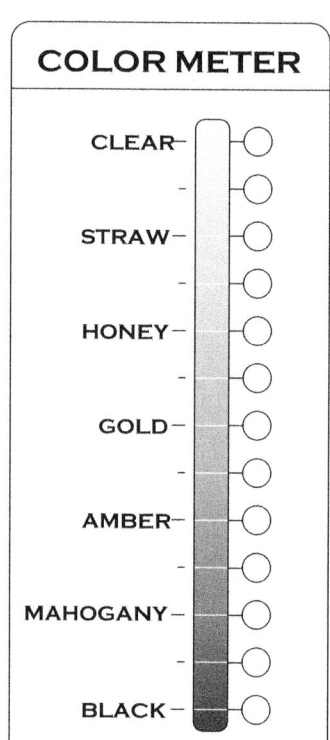

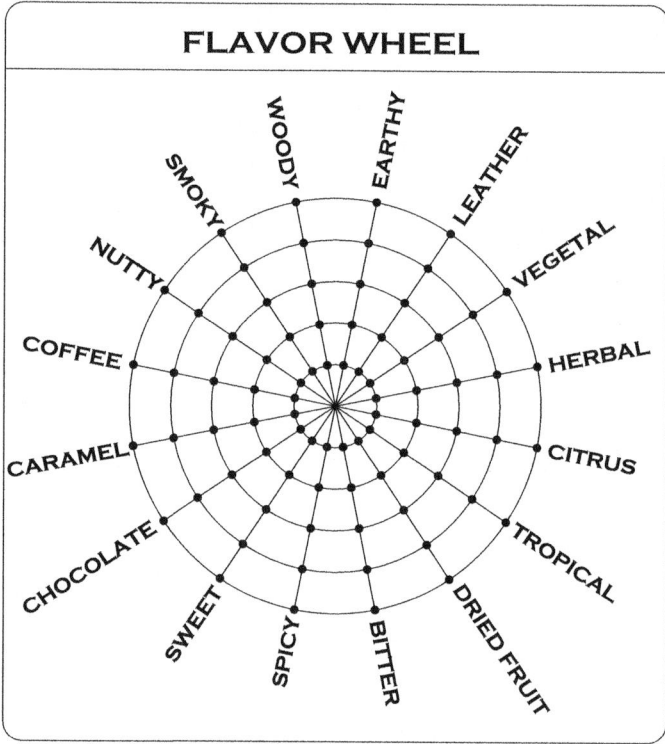

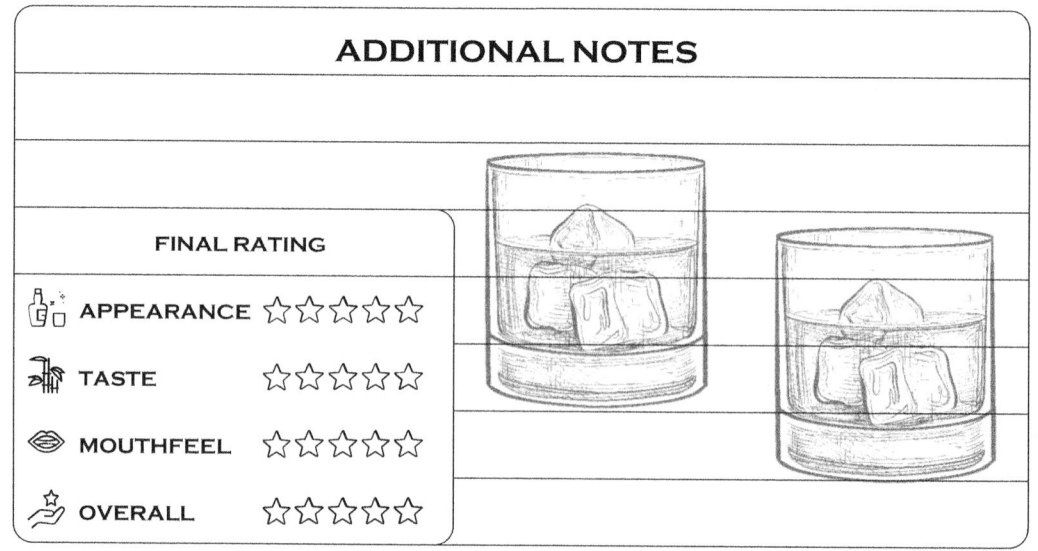

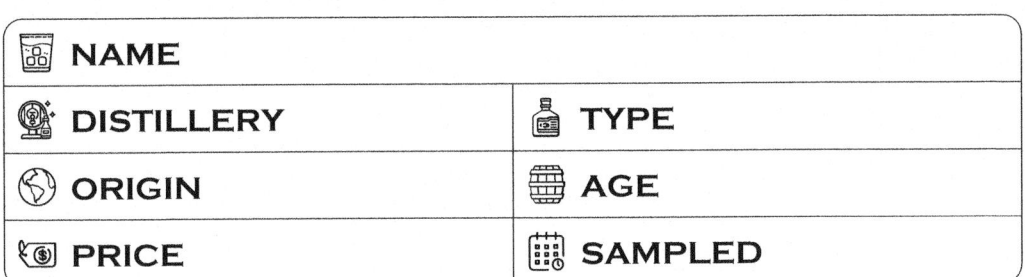

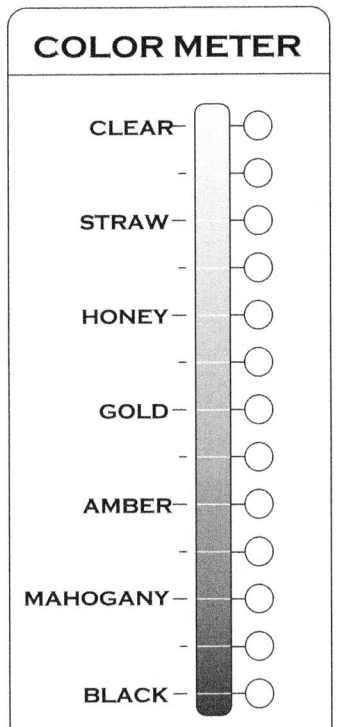

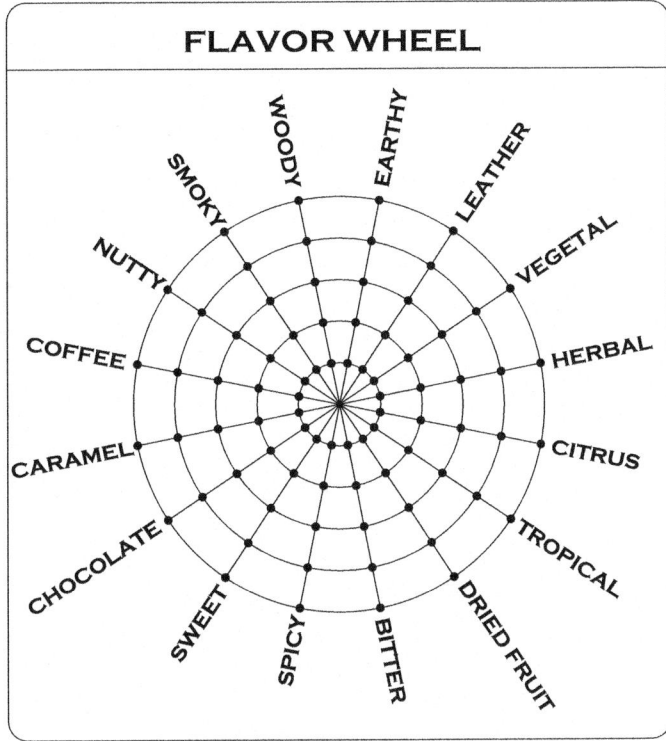

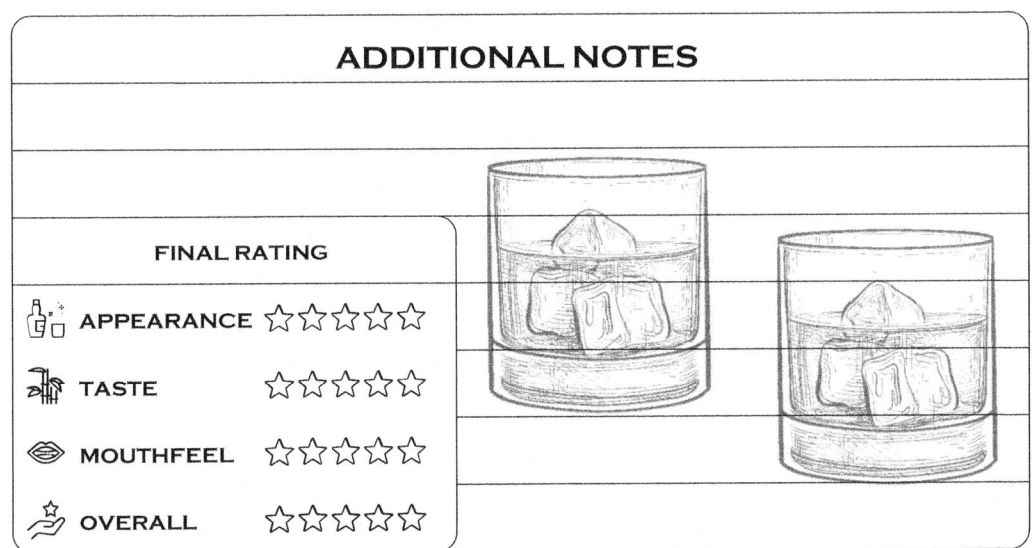

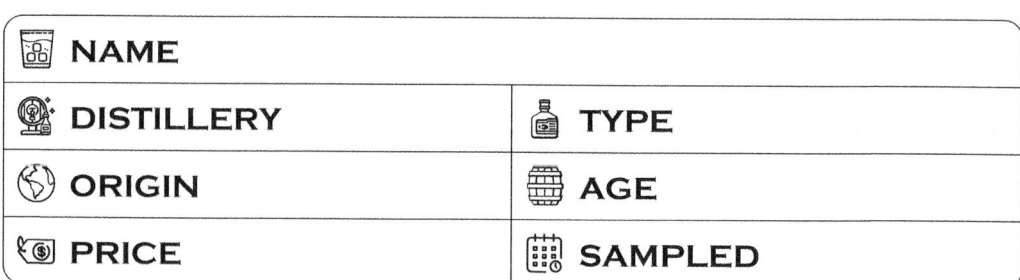

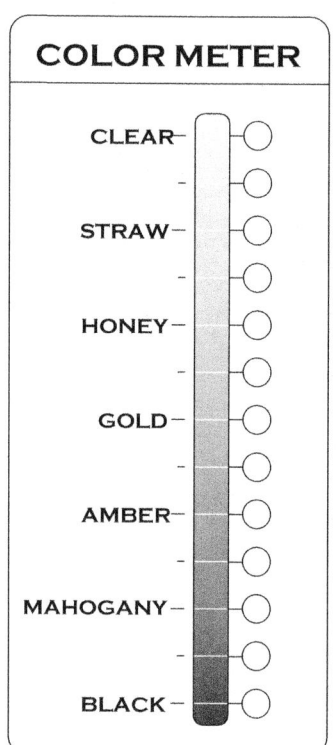

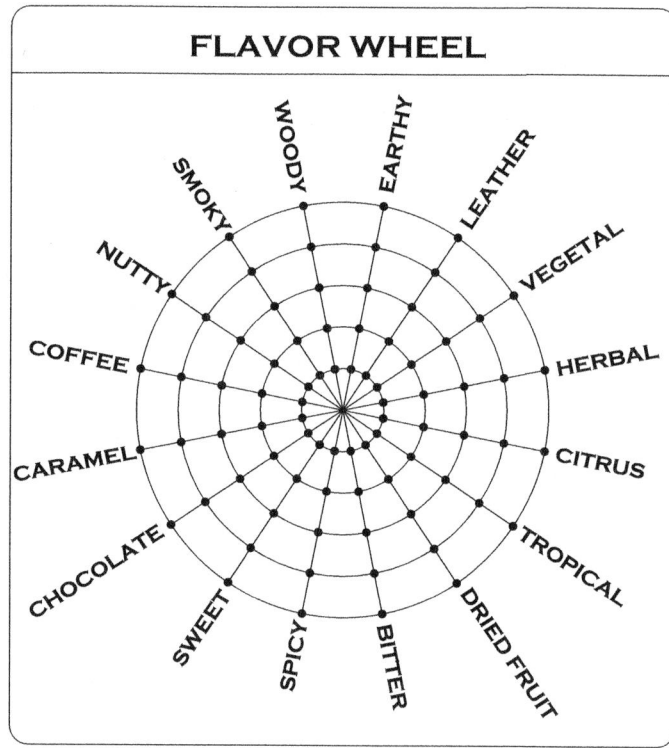

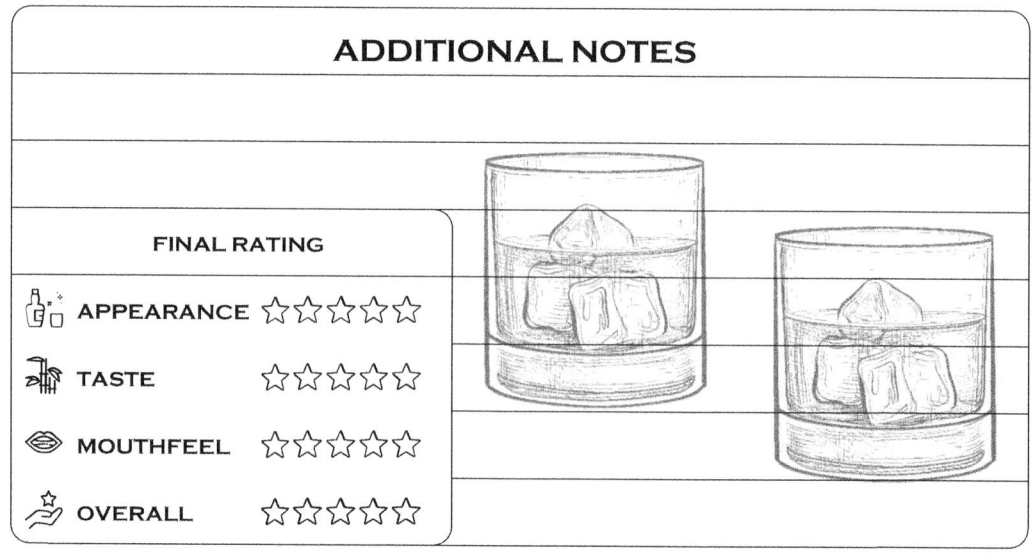

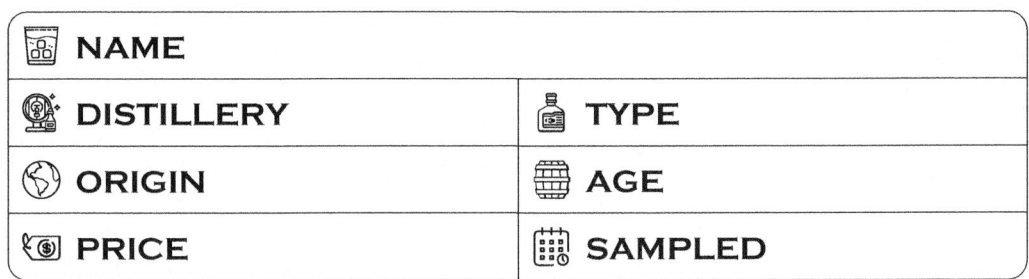

🥃 NAME	
🏭 DISTILLERY	🍾 TYPE
🌍 ORIGIN	🛢 AGE
💰 PRICE	📅 SAMPLED

COLOR METER

- CLEAR
- STRAW
- HONEY
- GOLD
- AMBER
- MAHOGANY
- BLACK

FLAVOR WHEEL

WOODY, EARTHY, LEATHER, VEGETAL, HERBAL, CITRUS, TROPICAL, DRIED FRUIT, BITTER, SPICY, SWEET, CHOCOLATE, CARAMEL, COFFEE, NUTTY, SMOKY

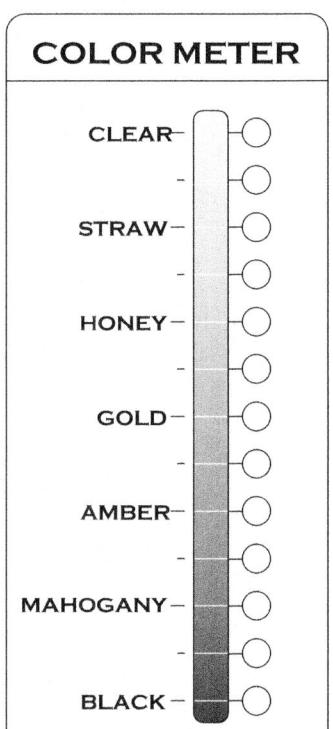
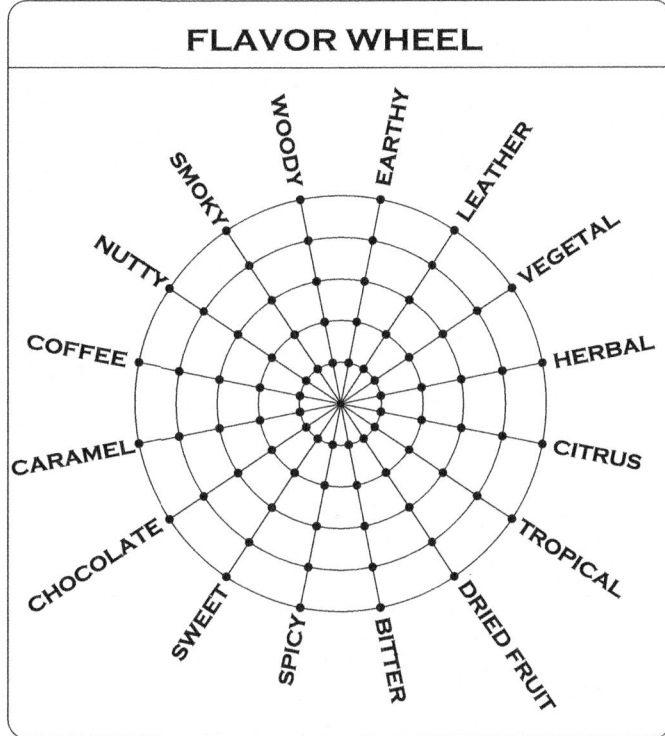

ADDITIONAL NOTES

FINAL RATING

- 🍾 APPEARANCE ☆☆☆☆☆
- 🥃 TASTE ☆☆☆☆☆
- 👄 MOUTHFEEL ☆☆☆☆☆
- 🌟 OVERALL ☆☆☆☆☆

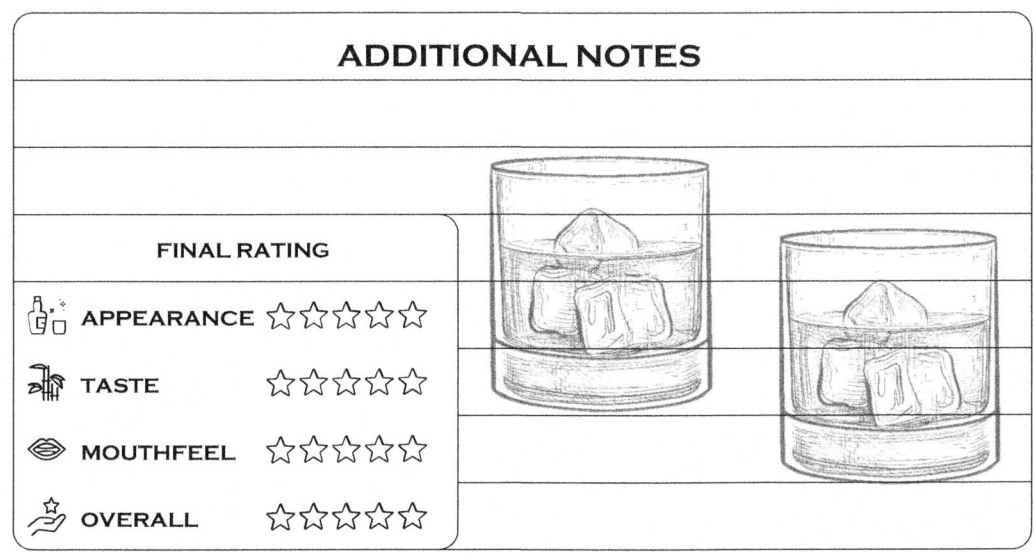

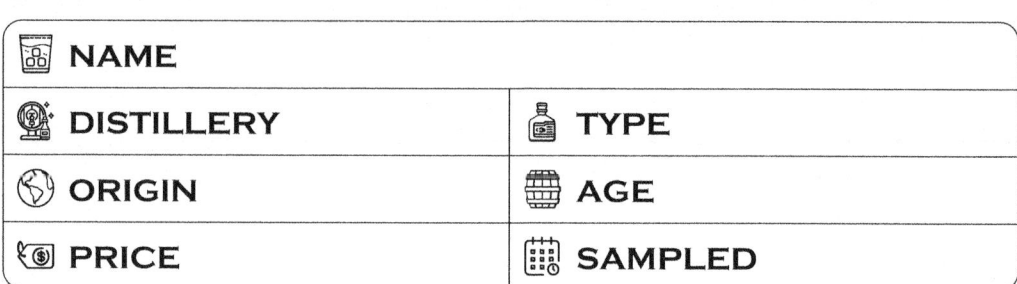	
🥃 NAME	
🛢️ DISTILLERY	🍾 TYPE
🌐 ORIGIN	🛢️ AGE
💰 PRICE	📅 SAMPLED

COLOR METER

- CLEAR
- STRAW
- HONEY
- GOLD
- AMBER
- MAHOGANY
- BLACK

FLAVOR WHEEL

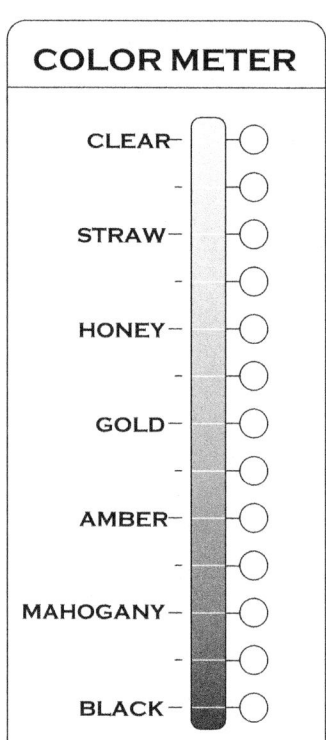
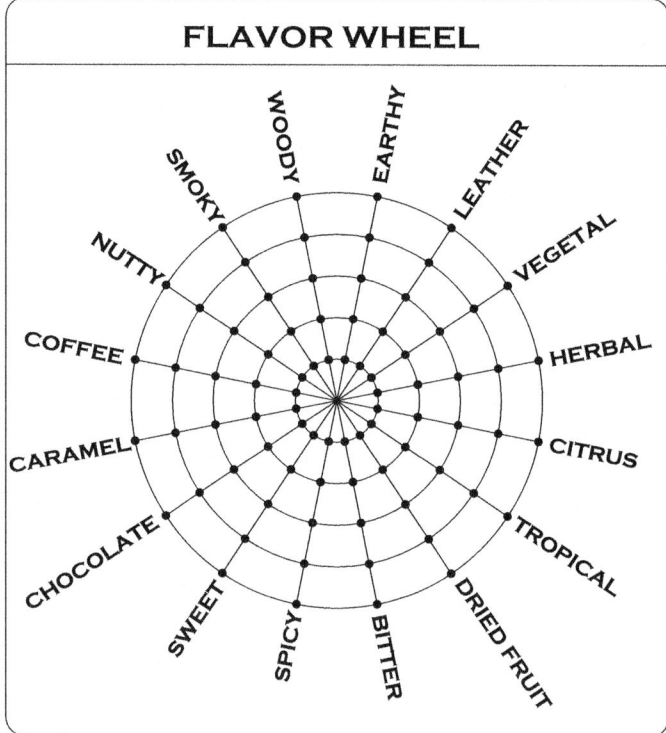

WOODY, EARTHY, LEATHER, VEGETAL, HERBAL, CITRUS, TROPICAL, DRIED FRUIT, BITTER, SPICY, SWEET, CHOCOLATE, CARAMEL, COFFEE, NUTTY, SMOKY

ADDITIONAL NOTES

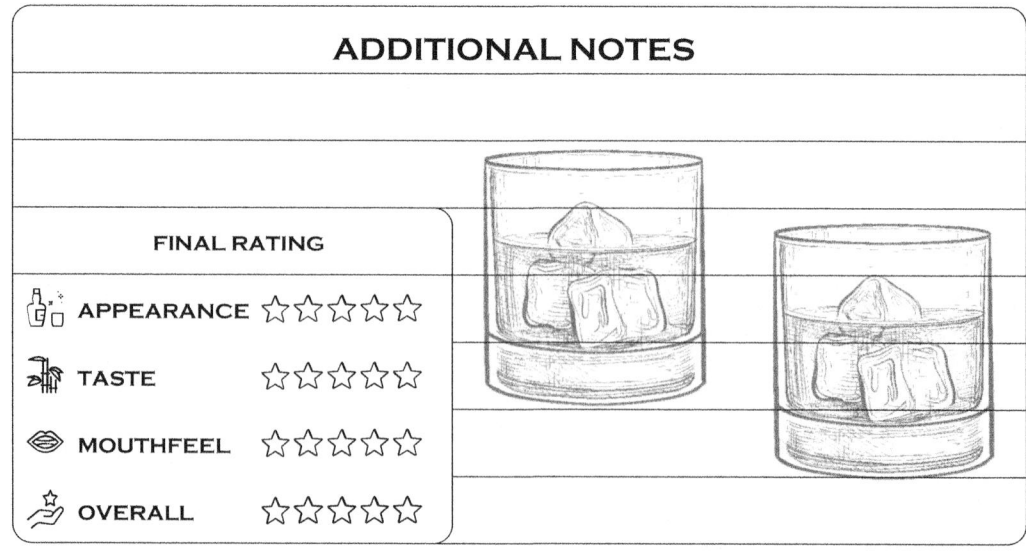

FINAL RATING

- 🍾 APPEARANCE ☆☆☆☆☆
- 🥃 TASTE ☆☆☆☆☆
- 👄 MOUTHFEEL ☆☆☆☆☆
- ✋ OVERALL ☆☆☆☆☆

🥃 **NAME**			
🏭 **DISTILLERY**		🍾 **TYPE**	
🌍 **ORIGIN**		🛢 **AGE**	
💰 **PRICE**		📅 **SAMPLED**	

COLOR METER

- CLEAR
- STRAW
- HONEY
- GOLD
- AMBER
- MAHOGANY
- BLACK

FLAVOR WHEEL

WOODY, EARTHY, LEATHER, VEGETAL, HERBAL, CITRUS, TROPICAL, DRIED FRUIT, BITTER, SPICY, SWEET, CHOCOLATE, CARAMEL, COFFEE, NUTTY, SMOKY

ADDITIONAL NOTES

FINAL RATING

- 🍾 APPEARANCE ☆☆☆☆☆
- 👅 TASTE ☆☆☆☆☆
- 👄 MOUTHFEEL ☆☆☆☆☆
- 🏆 OVERALL ☆☆☆☆☆

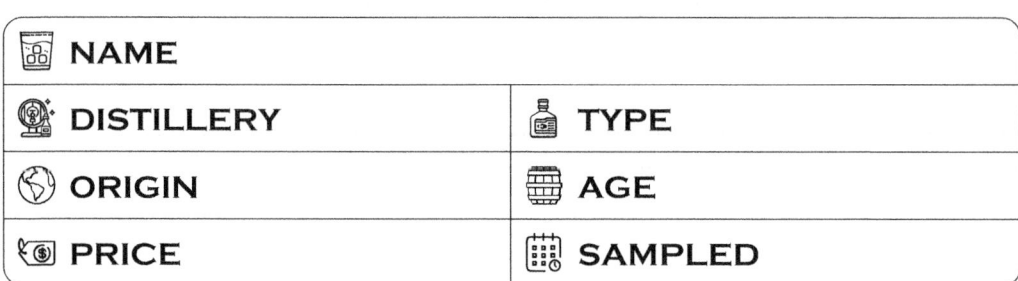

COLOR METER

- CLEAR
- STRAW
- HONEY
- GOLD
- AMBER
- MAHOGANY
- BLACK

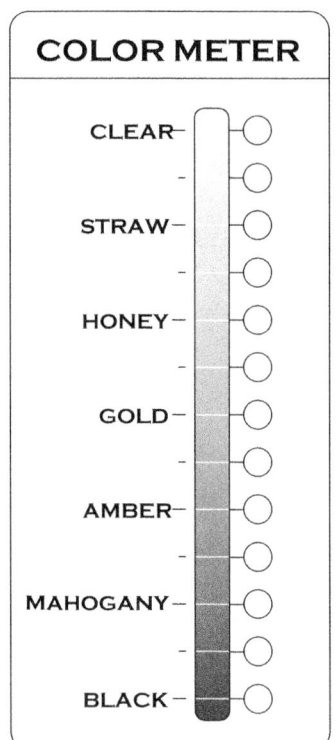

FLAVOR WHEEL

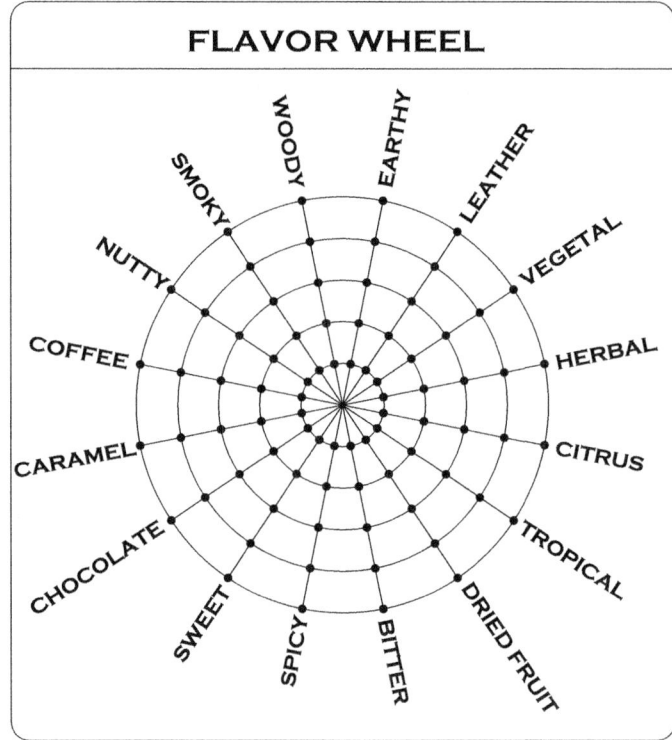

ADDITIONAL NOTES

FINAL RATING

- APPEARANCE ☆☆☆☆☆
- TASTE ☆☆☆☆☆
- MOUTHFEEL ☆☆☆☆☆
- OVERALL ☆☆☆☆☆

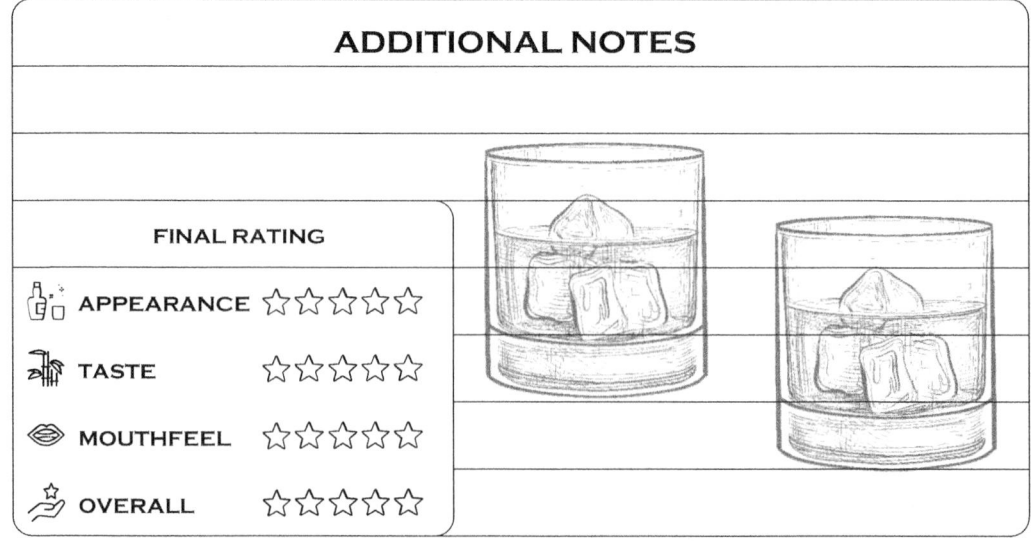

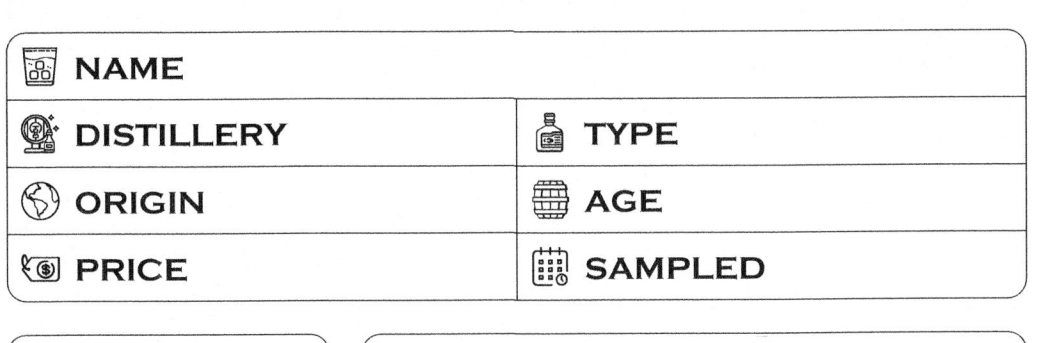

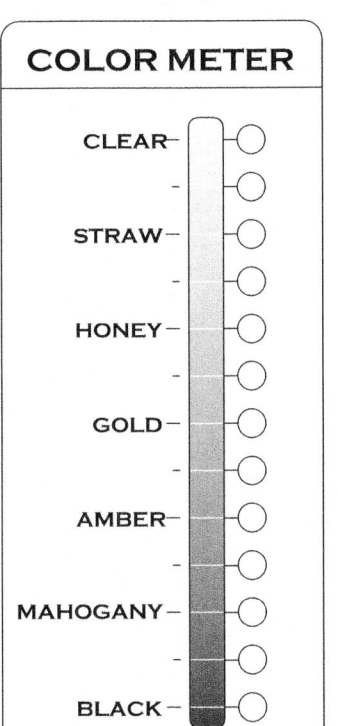

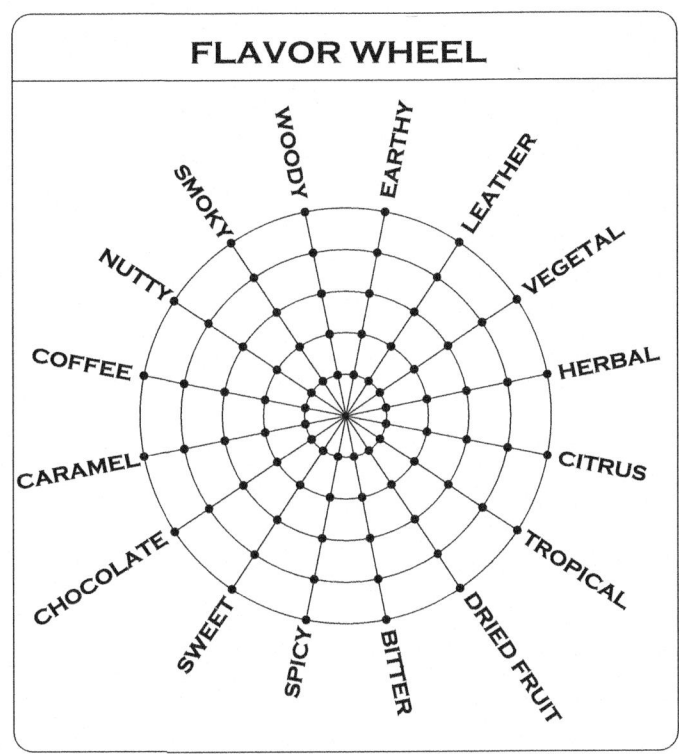

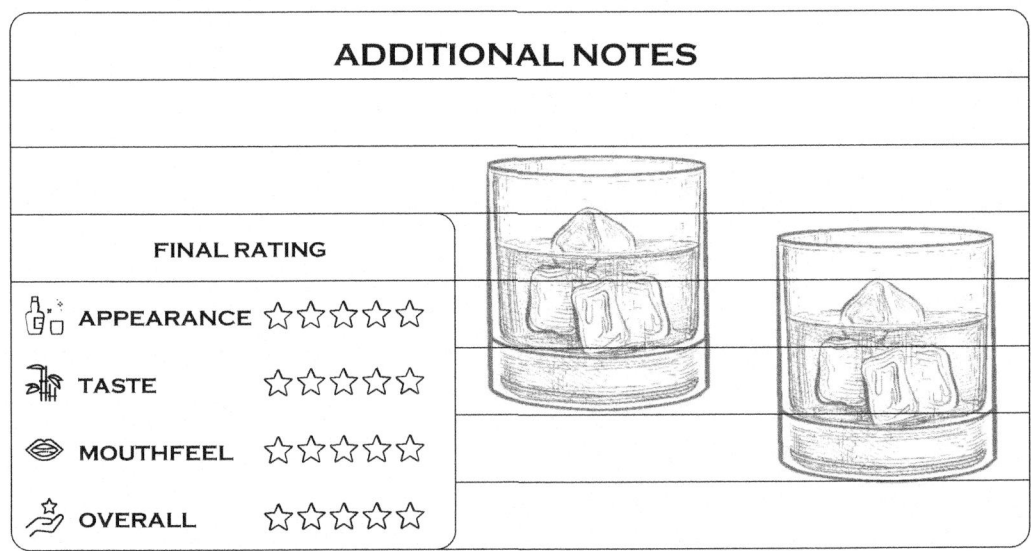

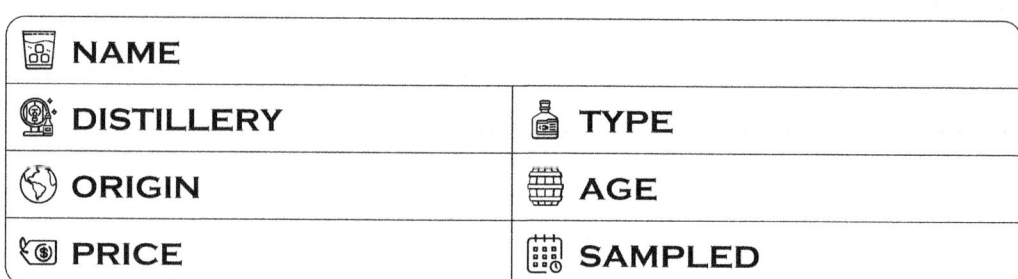

NAME	
DISTILLERY	TYPE
ORIGIN	AGE
PRICE	SAMPLED

COLOR METER

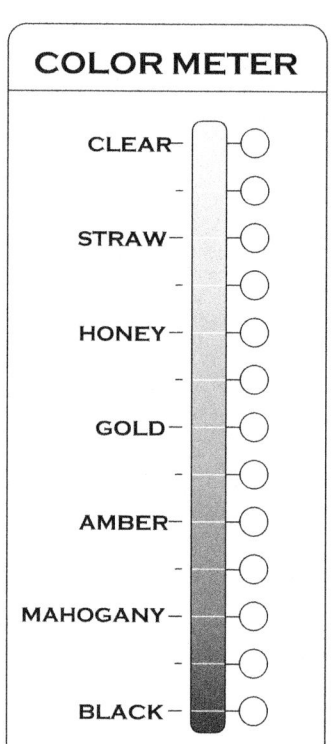

- CLEAR
- STRAW
- HONEY
- GOLD
- AMBER
- MAHOGANY
- BLACK

FLAVOR WHEEL

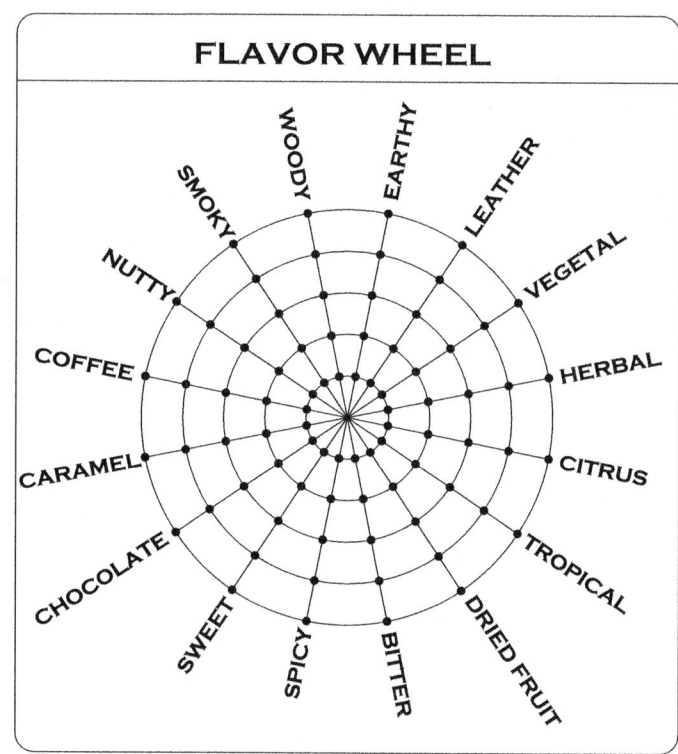

SMOKY, WOODY, EARTHY, LEATHER, NUTTY, VEGETAL, COFFEE, HERBAL, CARAMEL, CITRUS, CHOCOLATE, TROPICAL, SWEET, SPICY, BITTER, DRIED FRUIT

ADDITIONAL NOTES

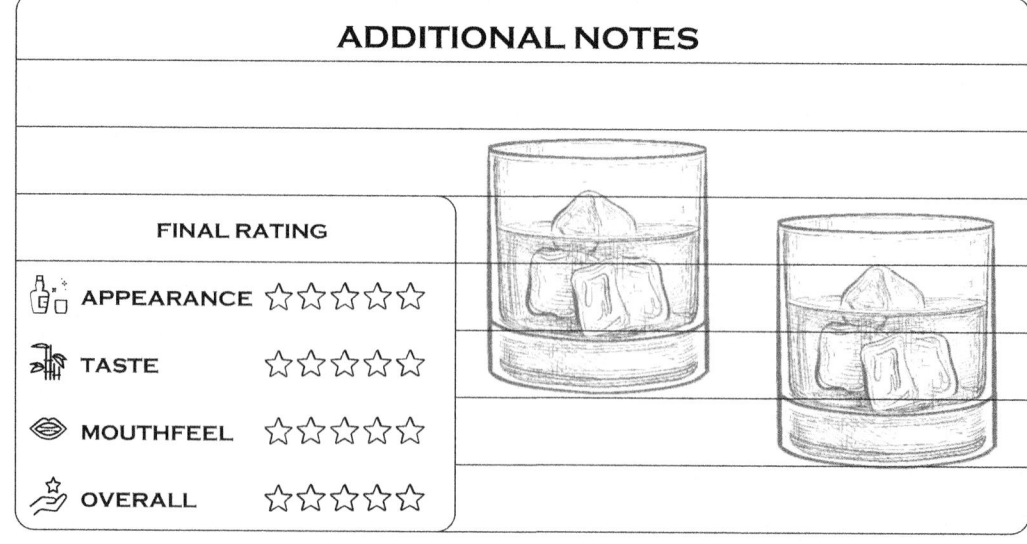

FINAL RATING

- APPEARANCE ☆☆☆☆☆
- TASTE ☆☆☆☆☆
- MOUTHFEEL ☆☆☆☆☆
- OVERALL ☆☆☆☆☆

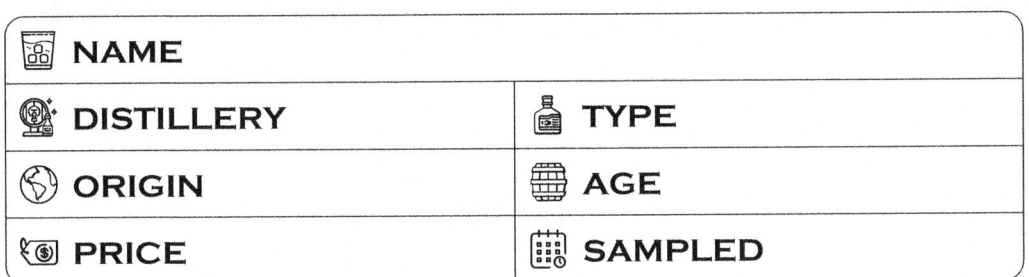

NAME	
DISTILLERY	TYPE
ORIGIN	AGE
PRICE	SAMPLED

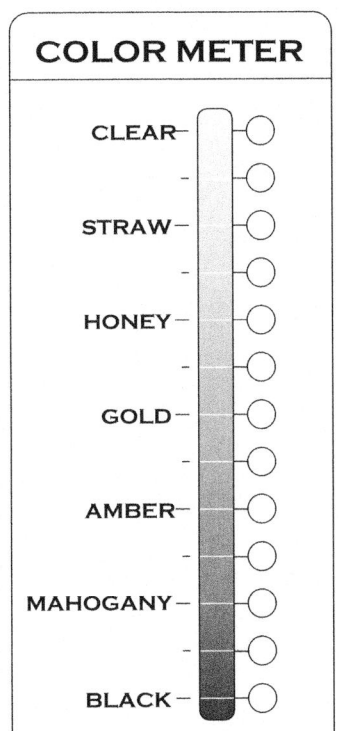

COLOR METER

- CLEAR
- STRAW
- HONEY
- GOLD
- AMBER
- MAHOGANY
- BLACK

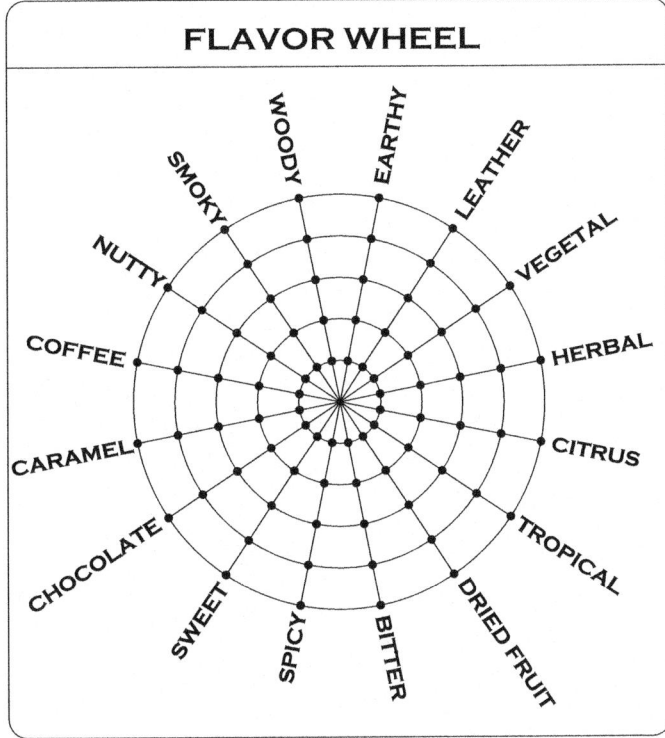

FLAVOR WHEEL

WOODY, EARTHY, LEATHER, VEGETAL, HERBAL, CITRUS, TROPICAL, DRIED FRUIT, BITTER, SPICY, SWEET, CHOCOLATE, CARAMEL, COFFEE, NUTTY, SMOKY

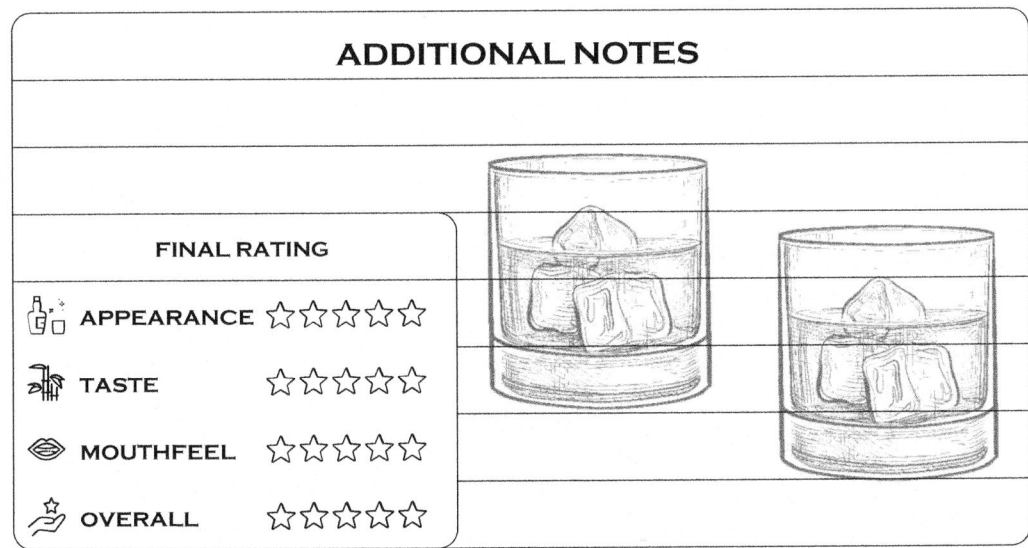

ADDITIONAL NOTES

FINAL RATING

- APPEARANCE ☆☆☆☆☆
- TASTE ☆☆☆☆☆
- MOUTHFEEL ☆☆☆☆☆
- OVERALL ☆☆☆☆☆

NAME	
DISTILLERY	TYPE
ORIGIN	AGE
PRICE	SAMPLED

COLOR METER

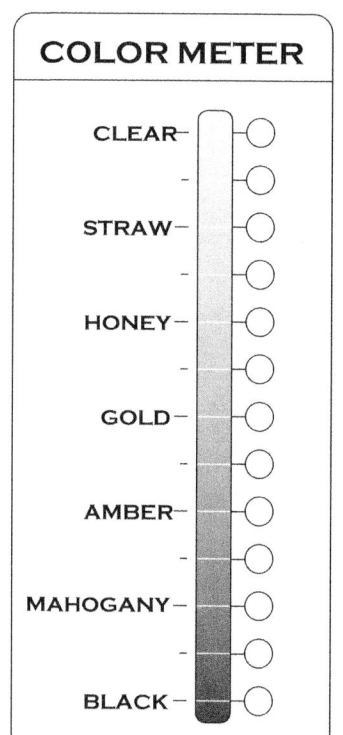

- CLEAR
- STRAW
- HONEY
- GOLD
- AMBER
- MAHOGANY
- BLACK

FLAVOR WHEEL

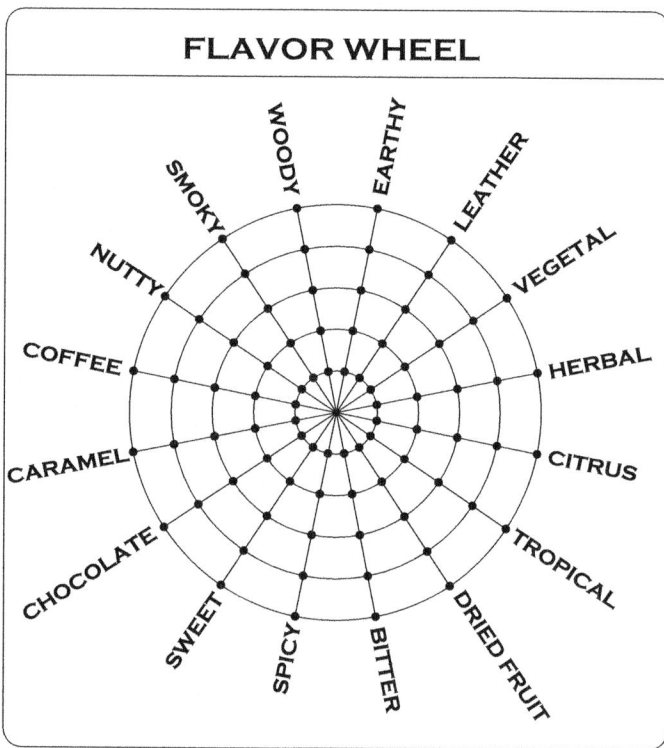

SMOKY, WOODY, EARTHY, LEATHER, NUTTY, VEGETAL, COFFEE, HERBAL, CARAMEL, CITRUS, CHOCOLATE, TROPICAL, SWEET, SPICY, BITTER, DRIED FRUIT

ADDITIONAL NOTES

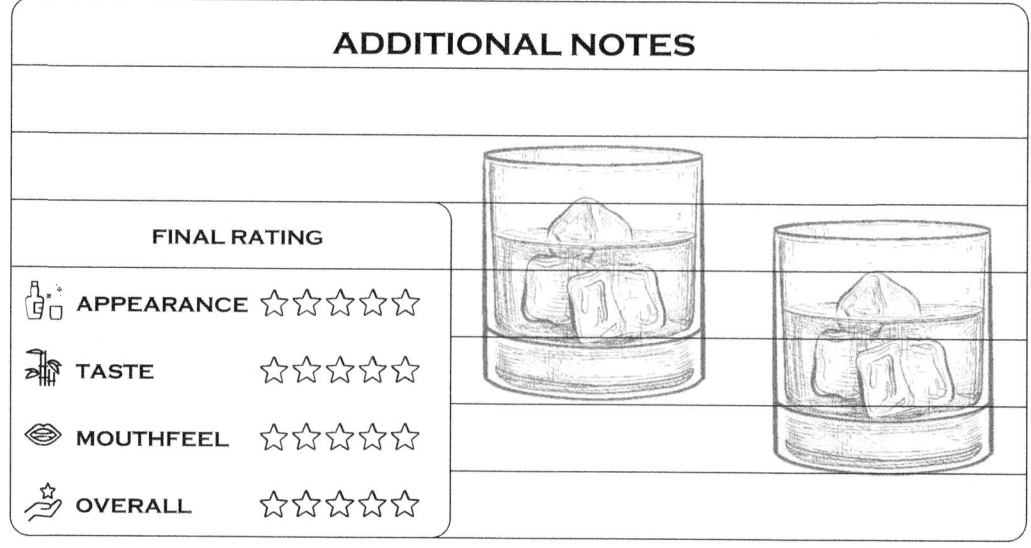

FINAL RATING

- APPEARANCE ☆☆☆☆☆
- TASTE ☆☆☆☆☆
- MOUTHFEEL ☆☆☆☆☆
- OVERALL ☆☆☆☆☆

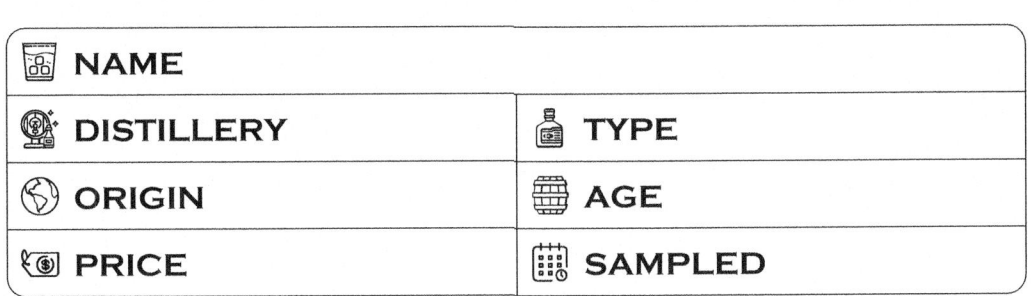

- NAME
- DISTILLERY
- TYPE
- ORIGIN
- AGE
- PRICE
- SAMPLED

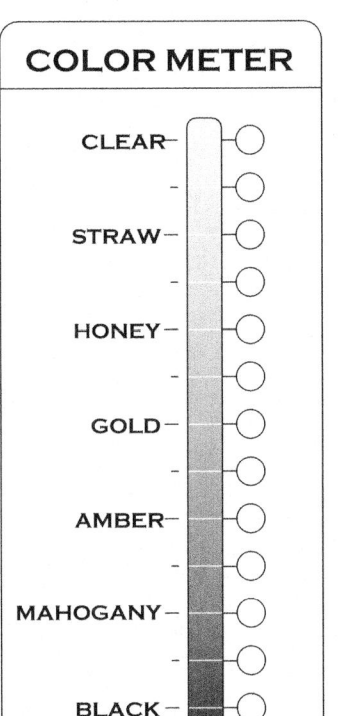

COLOR METER

- CLEAR
- STRAW
- HONEY
- GOLD
- AMBER
- MAHOGANY
- BLACK

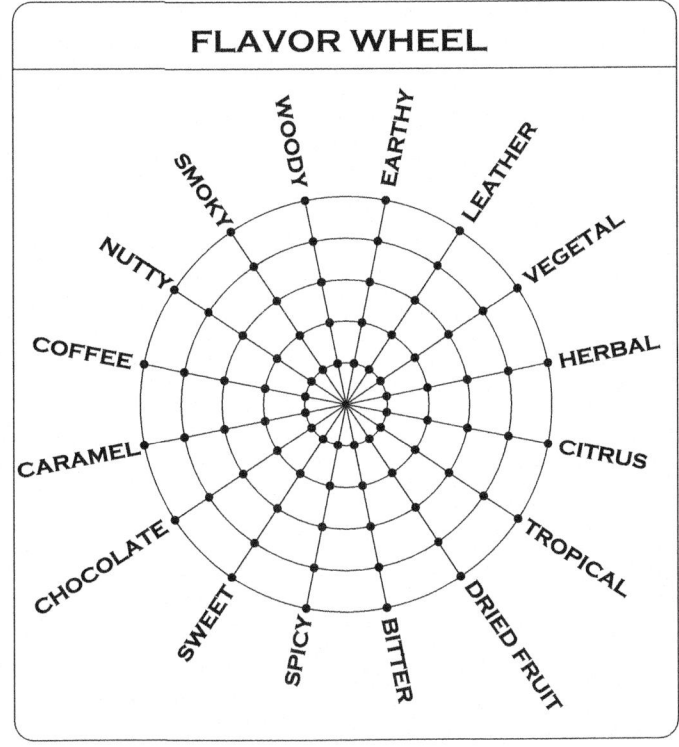

FLAVOR WHEEL

SMOKY, WOODY, EARTHY, LEATHER, VEGETAL, NUTTY, HERBAL, COFFEE, CITRUS, CARAMEL, TROPICAL, CHOCOLATE, DRIED FRUIT, SWEET, SPICY, BITTER

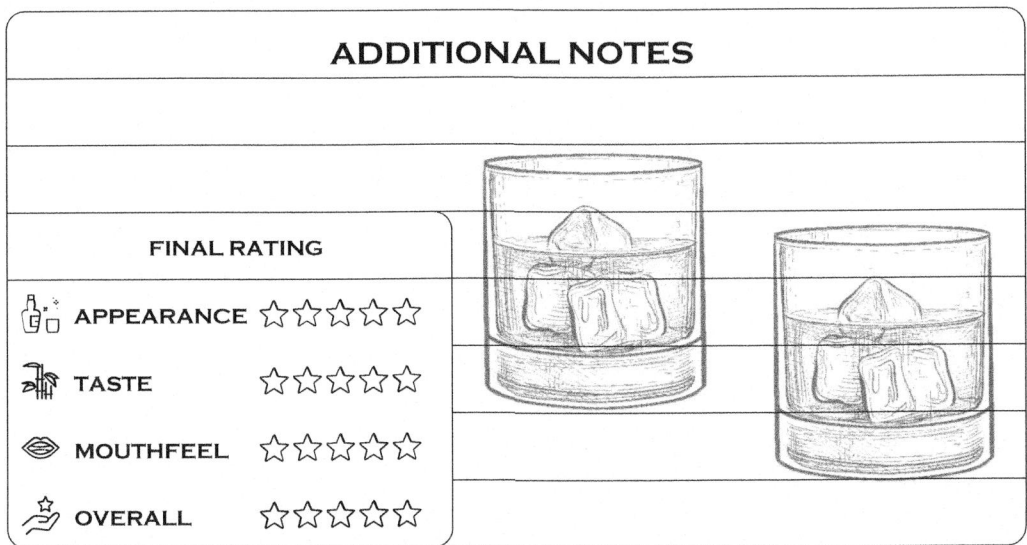

ADDITIONAL NOTES

FINAL RATING

- APPEARANCE ☆☆☆☆☆
- TASTE ☆☆☆☆☆
- MOUTHFEEL ☆☆☆☆☆
- OVERALL ☆☆☆☆☆

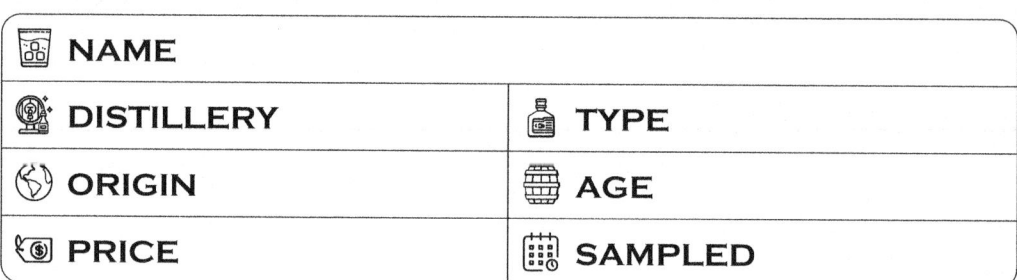

🥃 NAME	
🏭 DISTILLERY	🍾 TYPE
🌐 ORIGIN	🛢 AGE
💰 PRICE	📅 SAMPLED

COLOR METER

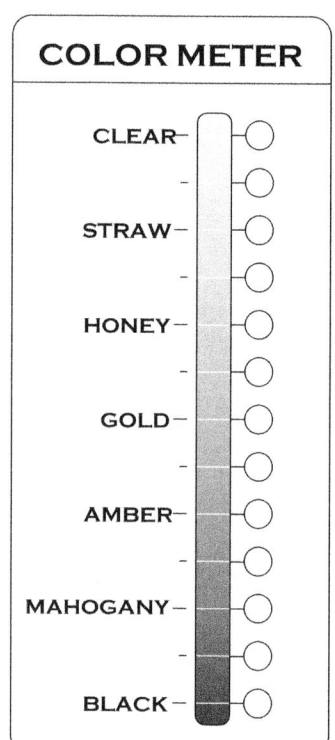

- CLEAR
- STRAW
- HONEY
- GOLD
- AMBER
- MAHOGANY
- BLACK

FLAVOR WHEEL

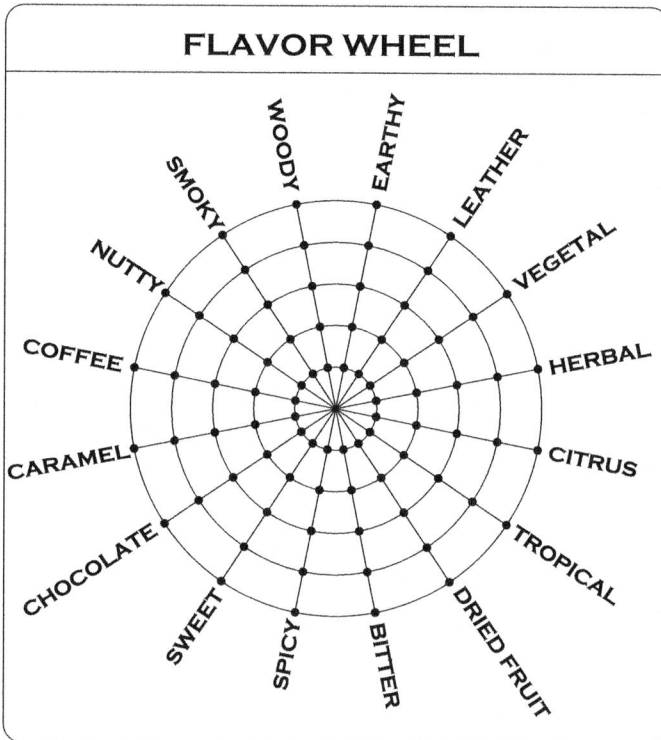

WOODY · EARTHY · LEATHER · VEGETAL · HERBAL · CITRUS · TROPICAL · DRIED FRUIT · BITTER · SPICY · SWEET · CHOCOLATE · CARAMEL · COFFEE · NUTTY · SMOKY

ADDITIONAL NOTES

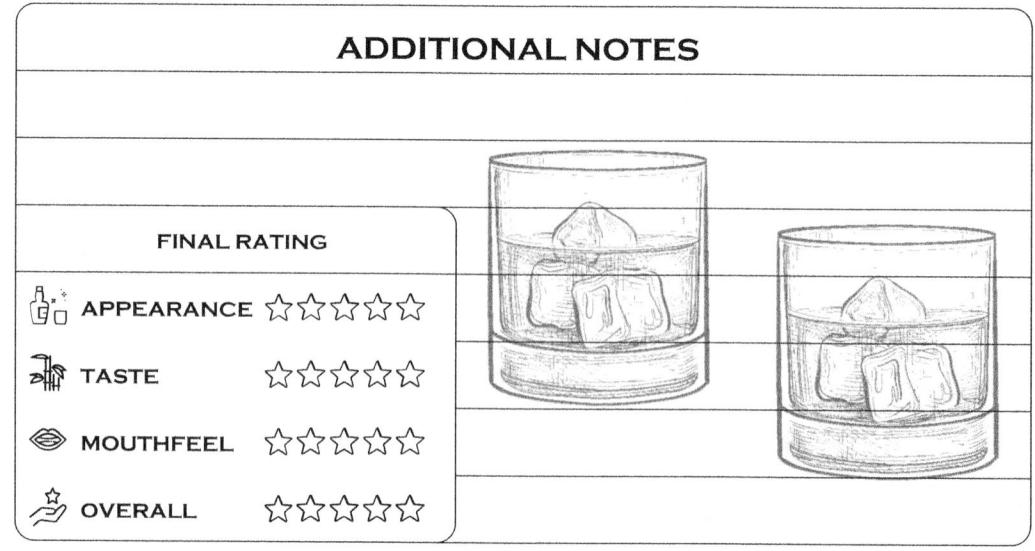

FINAL RATING

- 🍾 APPEARANCE ☆☆☆☆☆
- 🌾 TASTE ☆☆☆☆☆
- 👄 MOUTHFEEL ☆☆☆☆☆
- ✋ OVERALL ☆☆☆☆☆

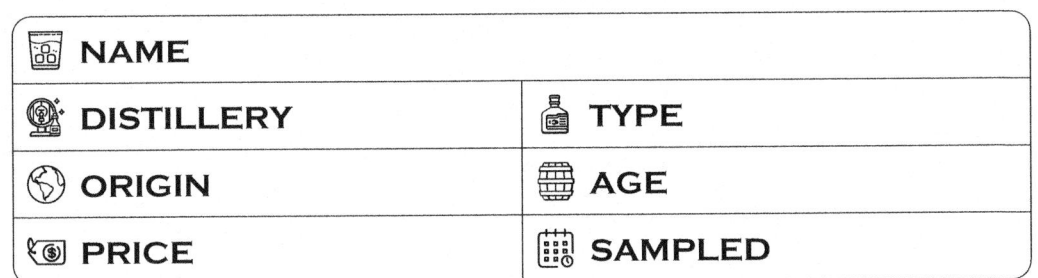

COLOR METER

- CLEAR
- STRAW
- HONEY
- GOLD
- AMBER
- MAHOGANY
- BLACK

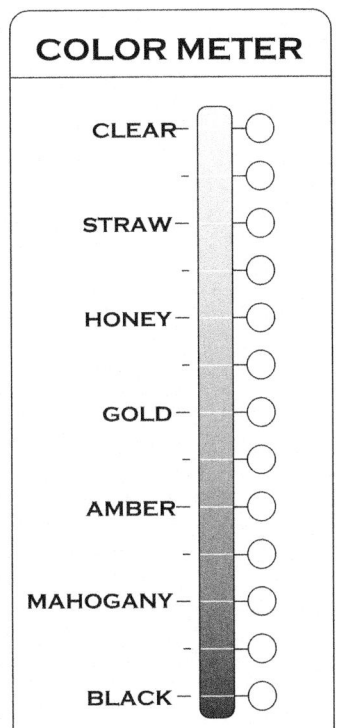

FLAVOR WHEEL

SMOKY, WOODY, EARTHY, LEATHER, NUTTY, VEGETAL, COFFEE, HERBAL, CARAMEL, CITRUS, CHOCOLATE, TROPICAL, SWEET, SPICY, BITTER, DRIED FRUIT

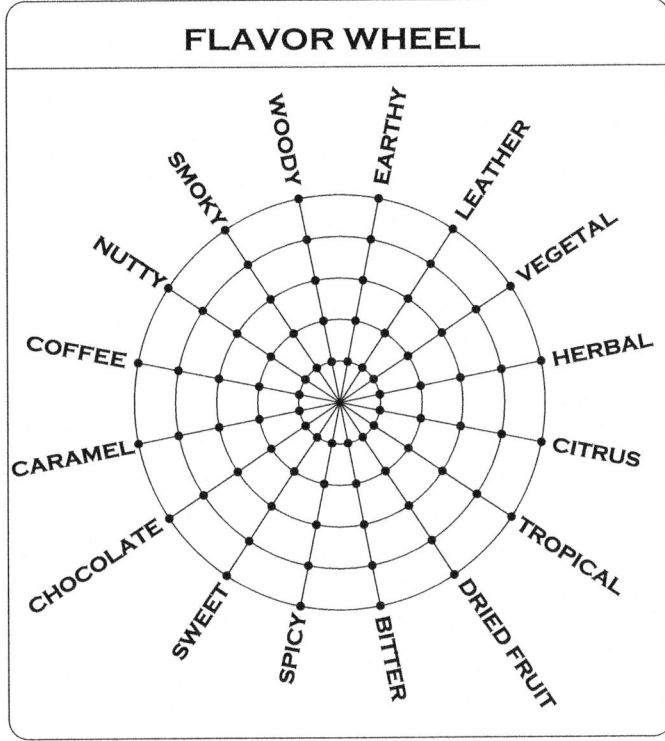

ADDITIONAL NOTES

FINAL RATING

- APPEARANCE ☆☆☆☆☆
- TASTE ☆☆☆☆☆
- MOUTHFEEL ☆☆☆☆☆
- OVERALL ☆☆☆☆☆

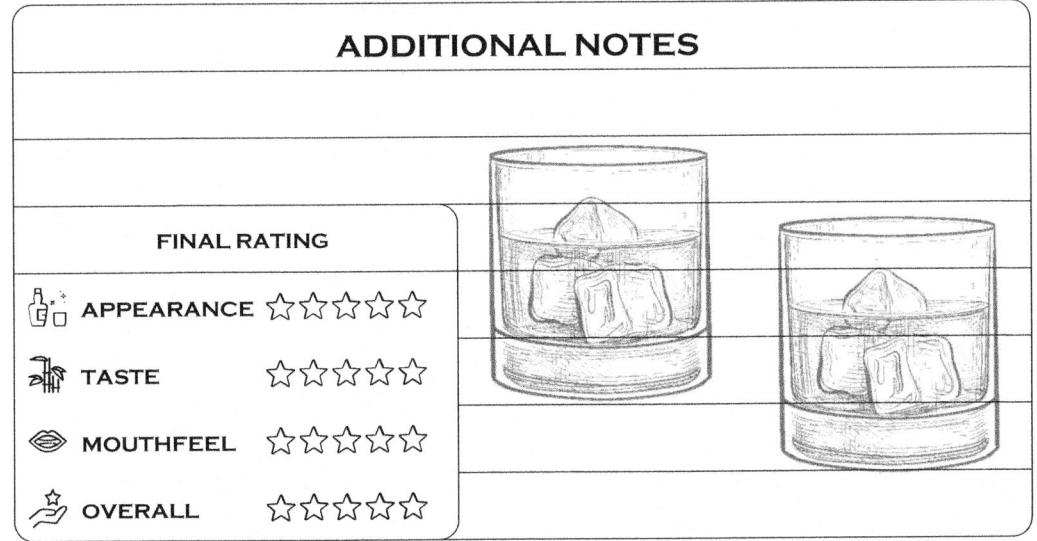

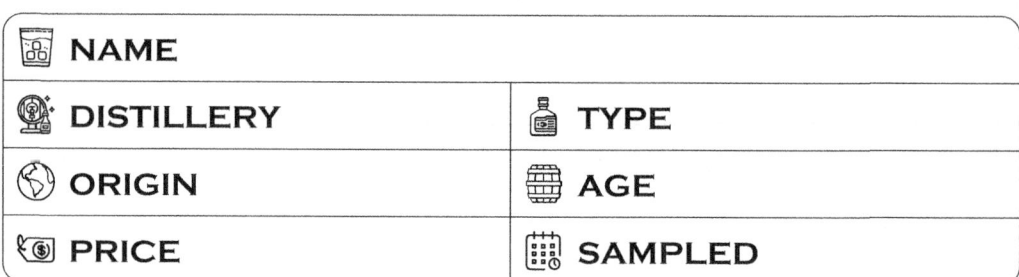

	NAME		
	DISTILLERY		TYPE
	ORIGIN		AGE
	PRICE		SAMPLED

COLOR METER

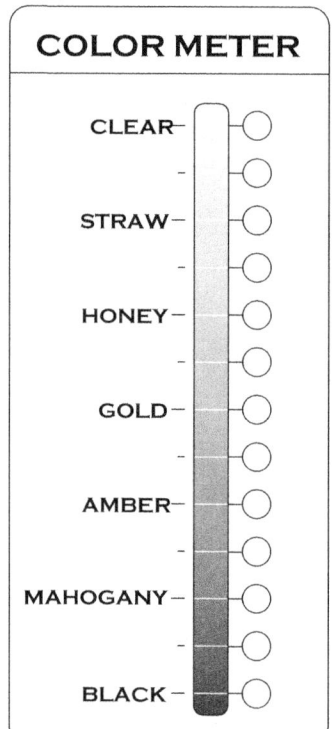

- CLEAR
- STRAW
- HONEY
- GOLD
- AMBER
- MAHOGANY
- BLACK

FLAVOR WHEEL

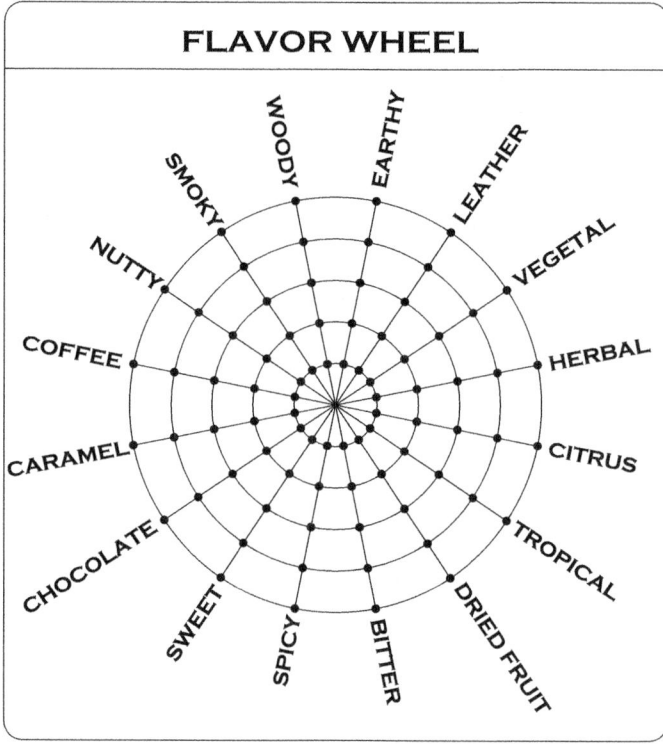

WOODY, EARTHY, LEATHER, VEGETAL, HERBAL, CITRUS, TROPICAL, DRIED FRUIT, BITTER, SPICY, SWEET, CHOCOLATE, CARAMEL, COFFEE, NUTTY, SMOKY

ADDITIONAL NOTES

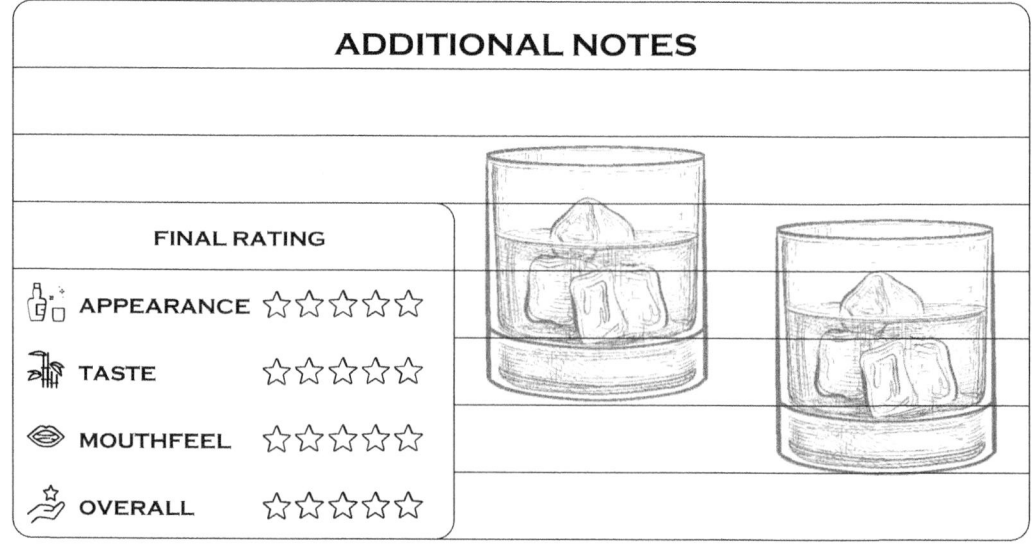

FINAL RATING

- APPEARANCE ☆☆☆☆☆
- TASTE ☆☆☆☆☆
- MOUTHFEEL ☆☆☆☆☆
- OVERALL ☆☆☆☆☆

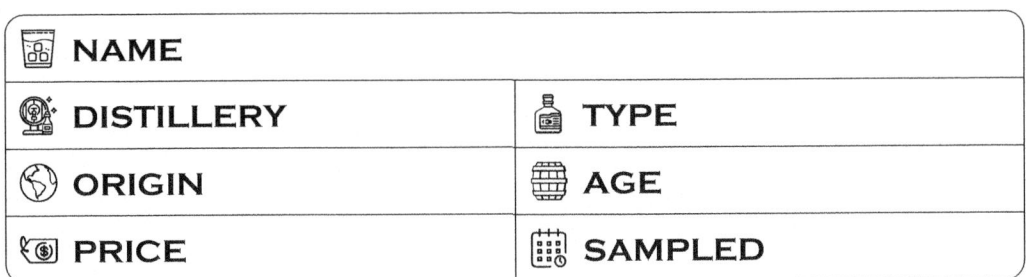
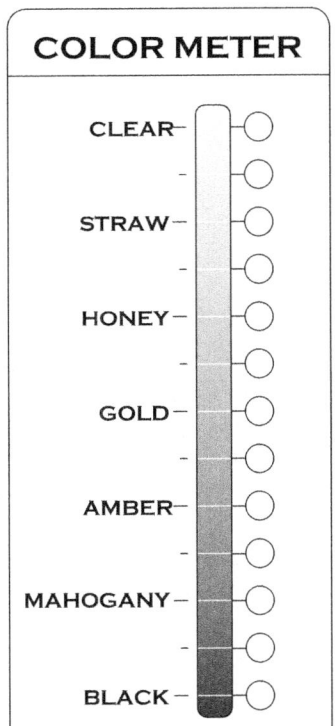
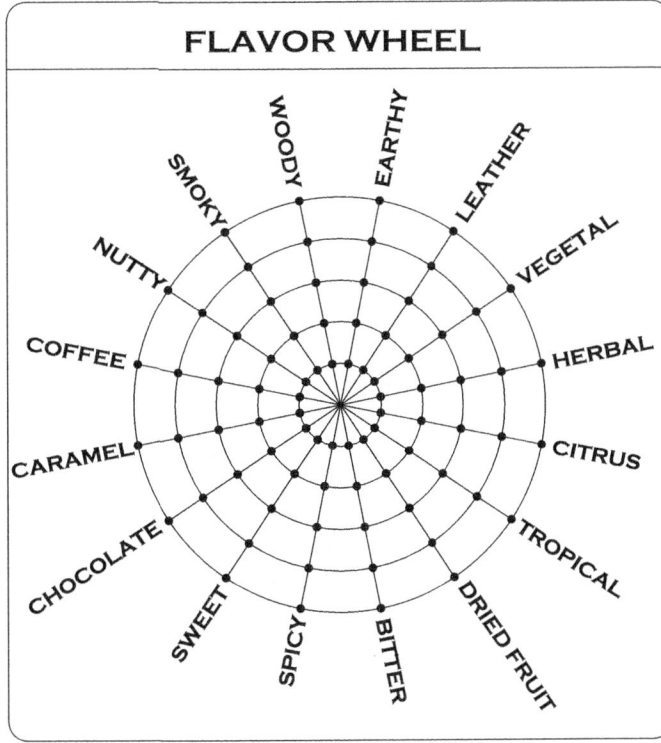
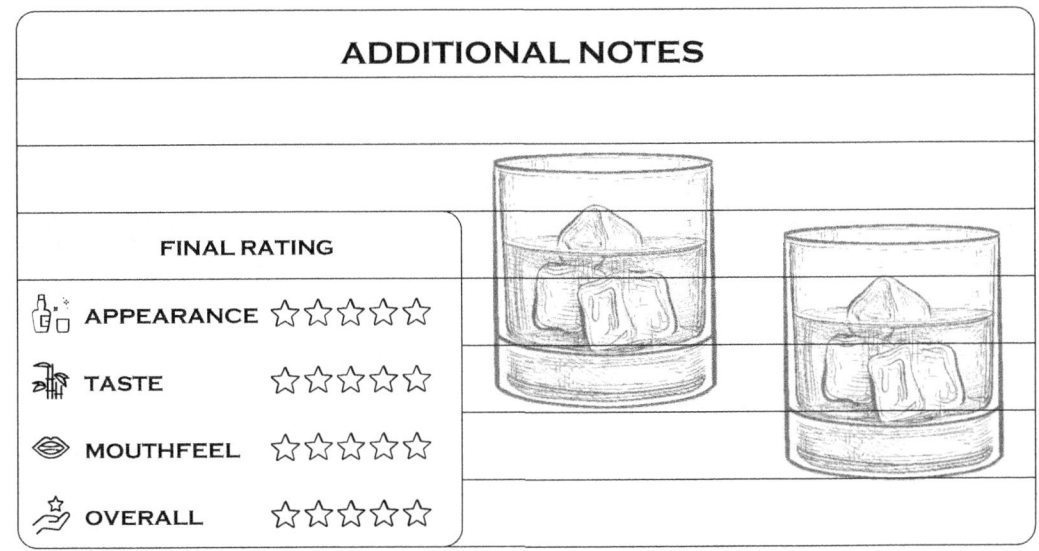

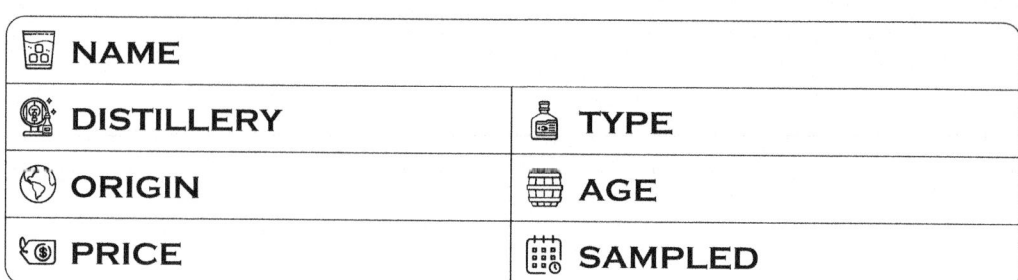

🥃 NAME	
🏭 DISTILLERY	🍾 TYPE
🌍 ORIGIN	🛢 AGE
💵 PRICE	📅 SAMPLED

COLOR METER

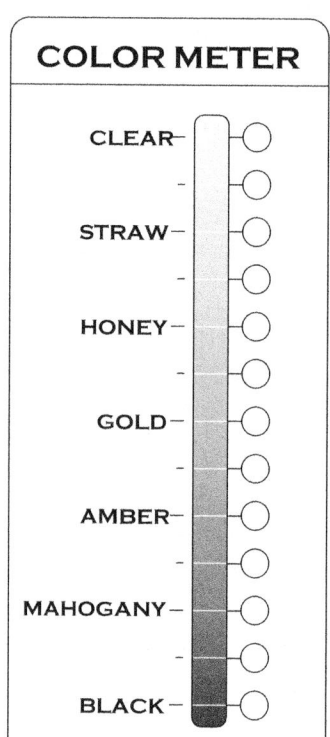

- CLEAR
- STRAW
- HONEY
- GOLD
- AMBER
- MAHOGANY
- BLACK

FLAVOR WHEEL

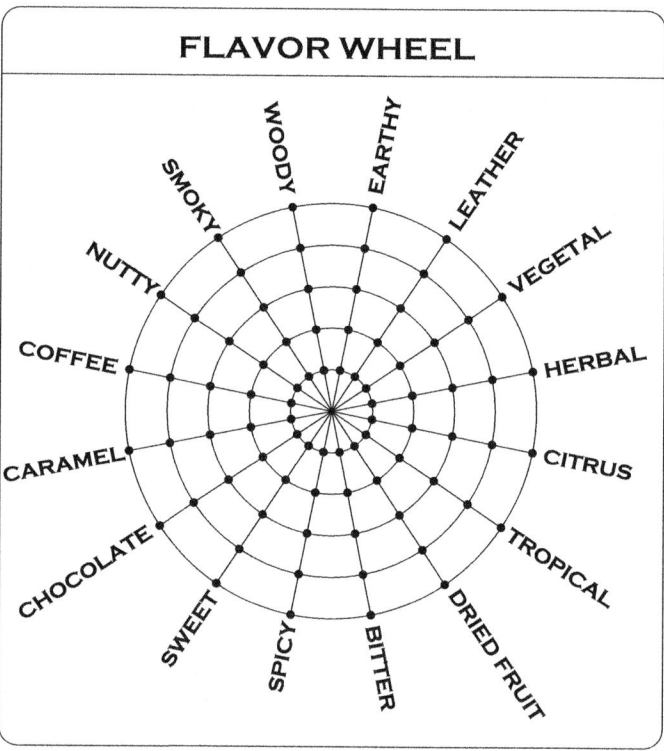

WOODY, EARTHY, LEATHER, VEGETAL, HERBAL, CITRUS, TROPICAL, DRIED FRUIT, BITTER, SPICY, SWEET, CHOCOLATE, CARAMEL, COFFEE, NUTTY, SMOKY

ADDITIONAL NOTES

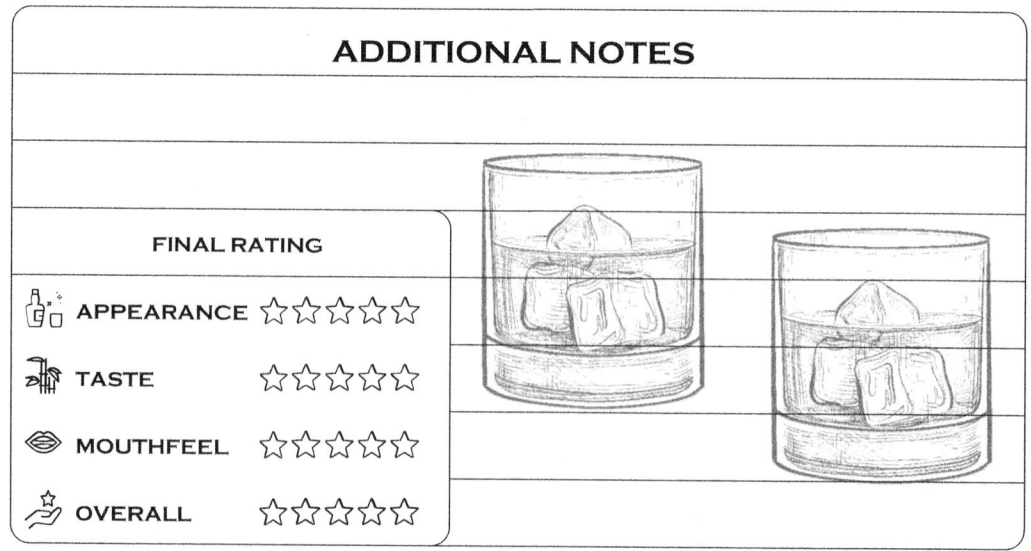

FINAL RATING

- 🍾 APPEARANCE ☆☆☆☆☆
- 👅 TASTE ☆☆☆☆☆
- 👄 MOUTHFEEL ☆☆☆☆☆
- 🖐 OVERALL ☆☆☆☆☆

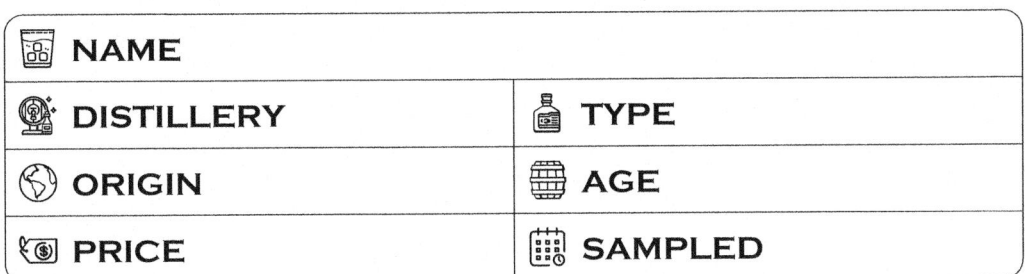
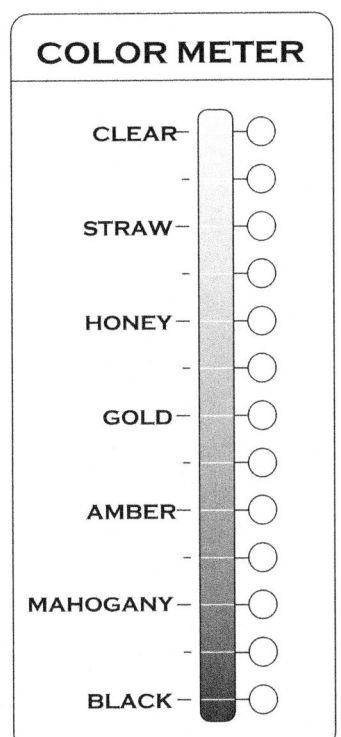
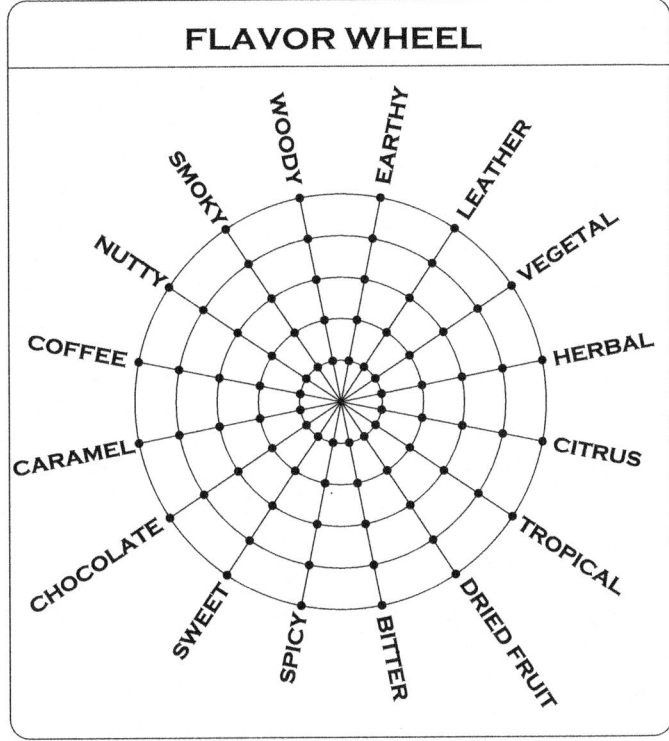
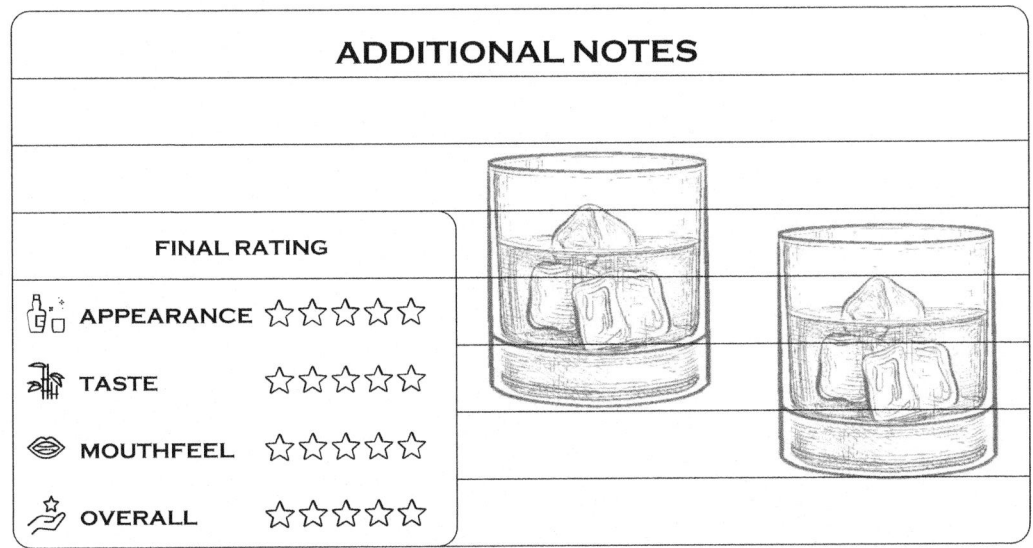

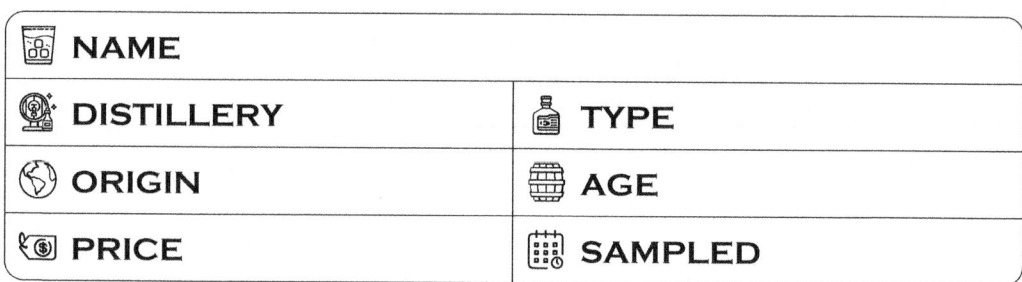

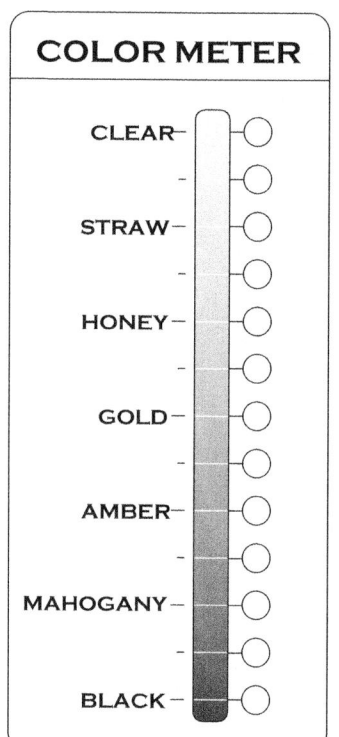

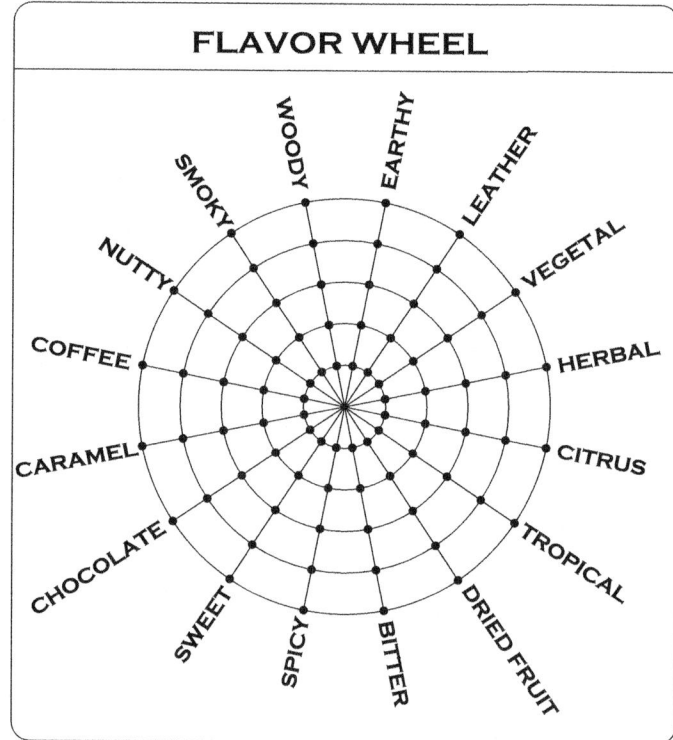

ADDITIONAL NOTES

FINAL RATING

- APPEARANCE ☆☆☆☆☆
- TASTE ☆☆☆☆☆
- MOUTHFEEL ☆☆☆☆☆
- OVERALL ☆☆☆☆☆

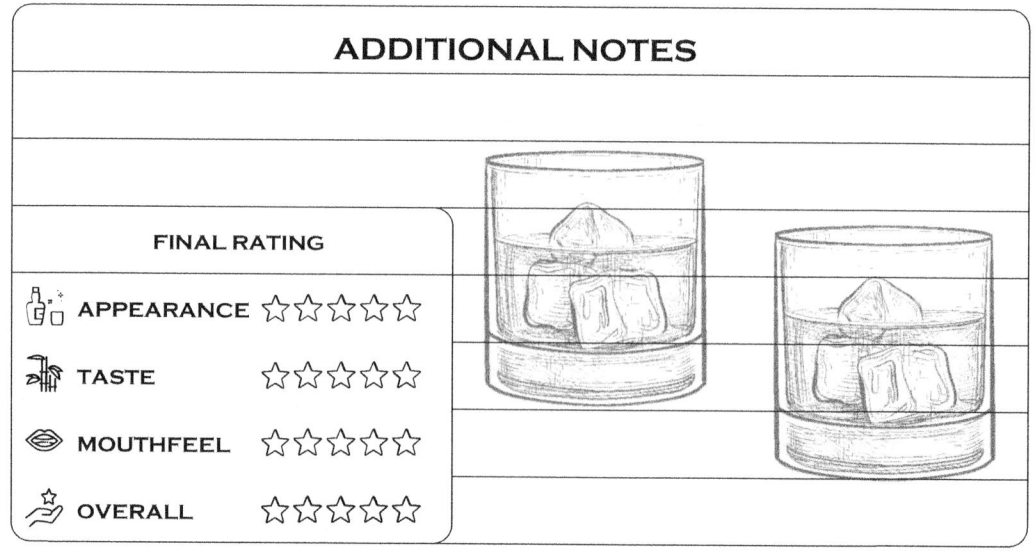

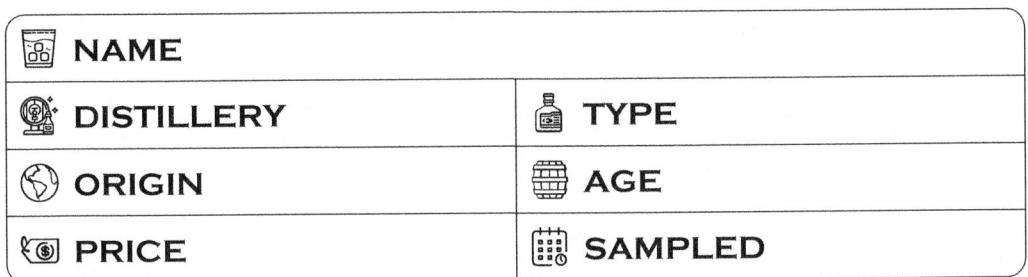

NAME	
DISTILLERY	TYPE
ORIGIN	AGE
PRICE	SAMPLED

COLOR METER

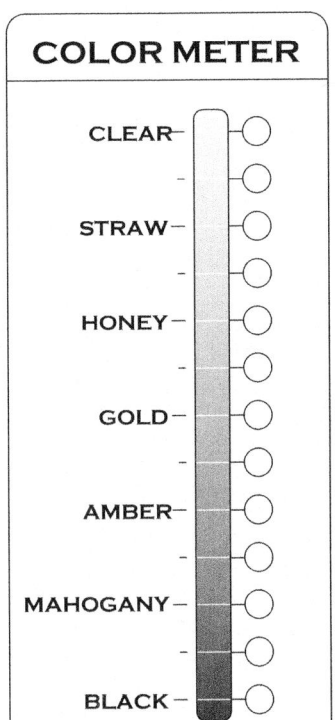

- CLEAR
- STRAW
- HONEY
- GOLD
- AMBER
- MAHOGANY
- BLACK

FLAVOR WHEEL

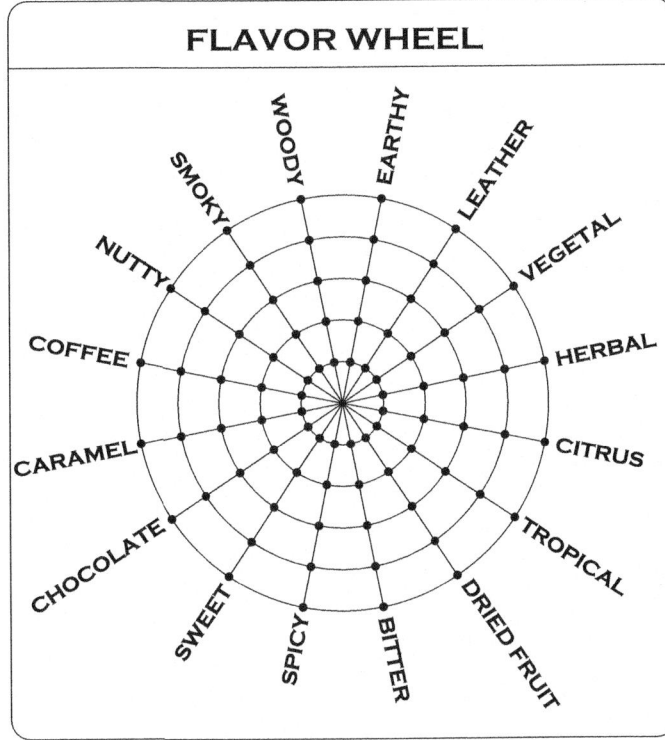

ADDITIONAL NOTES

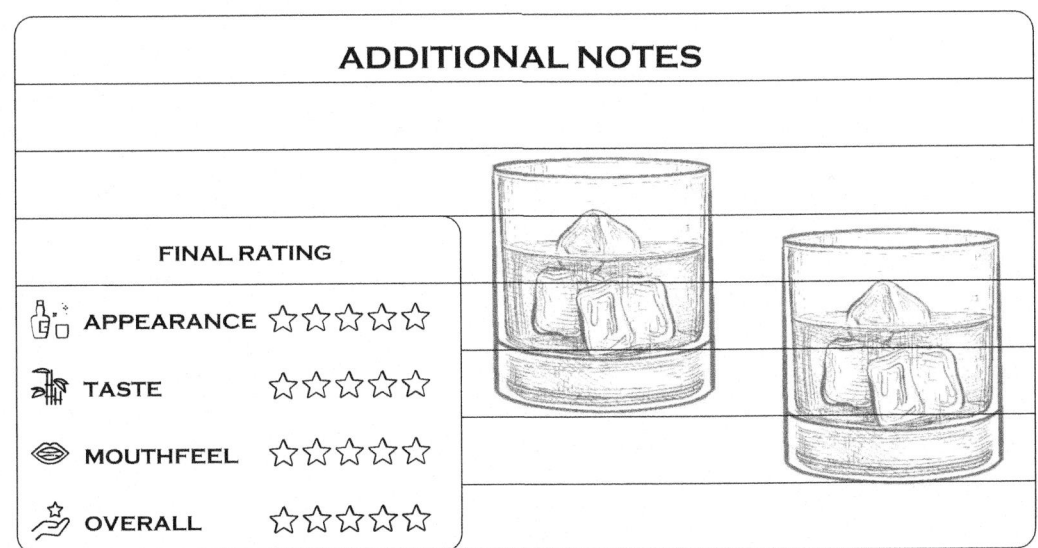

FINAL RATING

- APPEARANCE ☆☆☆☆☆
- TASTE ☆☆☆☆☆
- MOUTHFEEL ☆☆☆☆☆
- OVERALL ☆☆☆☆☆

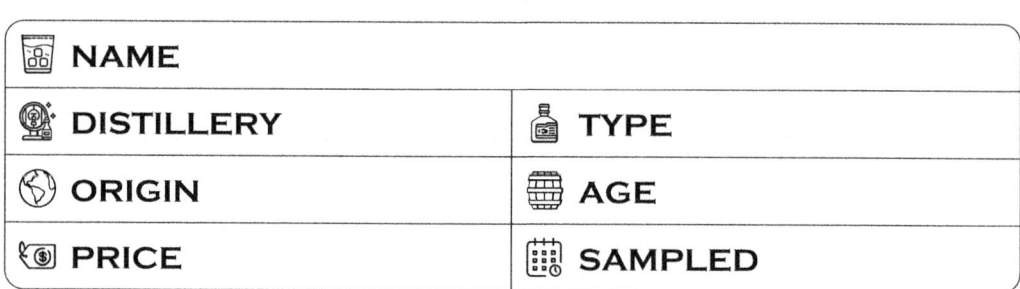

NAME	
DISTILLERY	TYPE
ORIGIN	AGE
PRICE	SAMPLED

COLOR METER

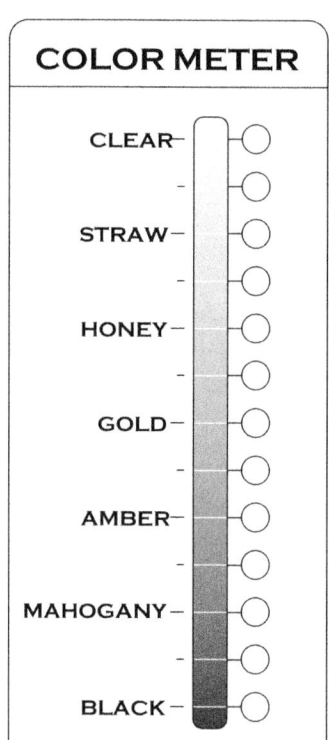

- CLEAR
- STRAW
- HONEY
- GOLD
- AMBER
- MAHOGANY
- BLACK

FLAVOR WHEEL

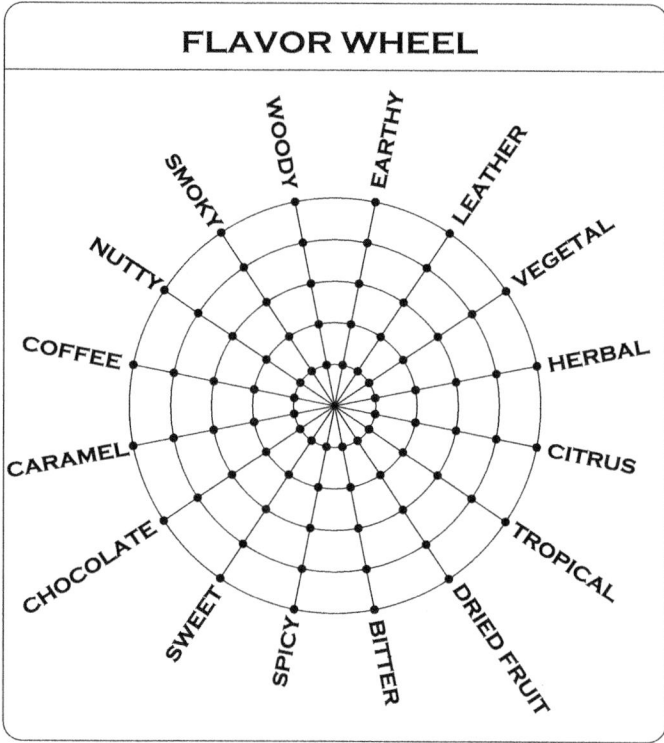

WOODY · EARTHY · LEATHER · VEGETAL · HERBAL · CITRUS · TROPICAL · DRIED FRUIT · BITTER · SPICY · SWEET · CHOCOLATE · CARAMEL · COFFEE · NUTTY · SMOKY

ADDITIONAL NOTES

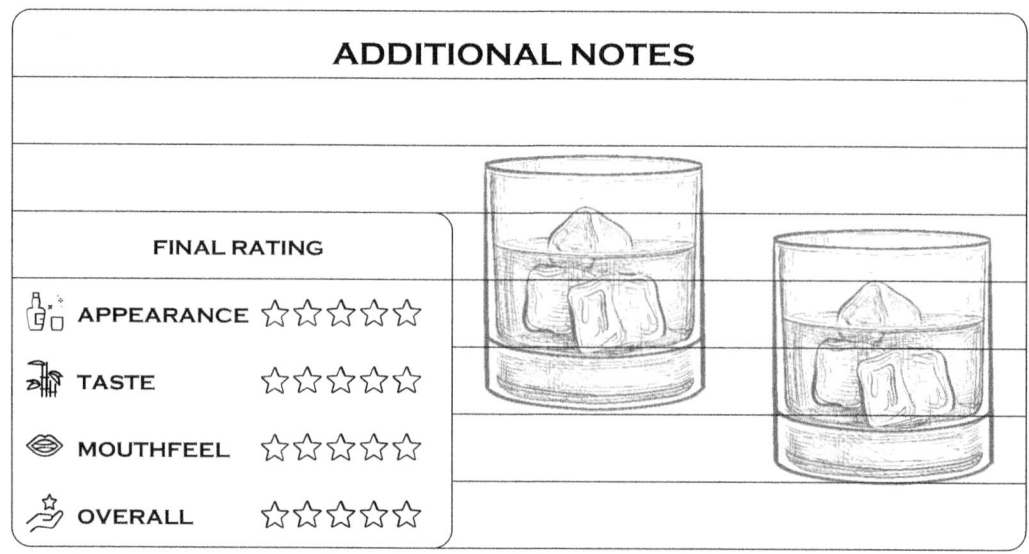

FINAL RATING

- APPEARANCE ☆☆☆☆☆
- TASTE ☆☆☆☆☆
- MOUTHFEEL ☆☆☆☆☆
- OVERALL ☆☆☆☆☆

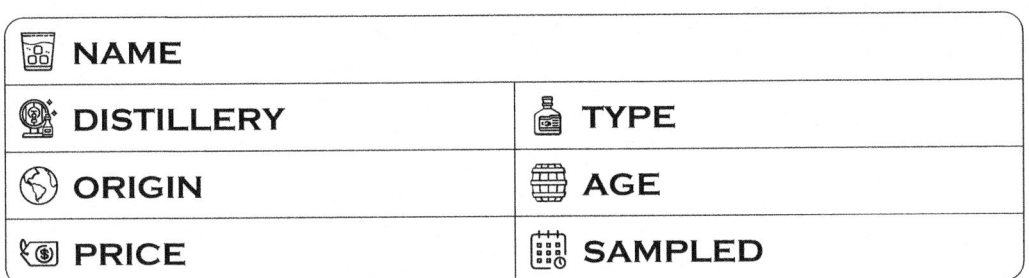

COLOR METER

- CLEAR
- STRAW
- HONEY
- GOLD
- AMBER
- MAHOGANY
- BLACK

FLAVOR WHEEL

SMOKY, WOODY, EARTHY, LEATHER, VEGETAL, NUTTY, HERBAL, COFFEE, CITRUS, CARAMEL, TROPICAL, CHOCOLATE, DRIED FRUIT, SWEET, SPICY, BITTER

ADDITIONAL NOTES

FINAL RATING

- APPEARANCE ☆☆☆☆☆
- TASTE ☆☆☆☆☆
- MOUTHFEEL ☆☆☆☆☆
- OVERALL ☆☆☆☆☆

🥃 NAME	
🏭 DISTILLERY	🍾 TYPE
🌎 ORIGIN	🛢 AGE
💰 PRICE	📅 SAMPLED

COLOR METER

- CLEAR
- STRAW
- HONEY
- GOLD
- AMBER
- MAHOGANY
- BLACK

FLAVOR WHEEL

SMOKY · WOODY · EARTHY · LEATHER · NUTTY · VEGETAL · COFFEE · HERBAL · CARAMEL · CITRUS · CHOCOLATE · TROPICAL · SWEET · SPICY · BITTER · DRIED FRUIT

ADDITIONAL NOTES

FINAL RATING

- 🍾 APPEARANCE ☆☆☆☆☆
- 🥃 TASTE ☆☆☆☆☆
- 👄 MOUTHFEEL ☆☆☆☆☆
- 🤲 OVERALL ☆☆☆☆☆

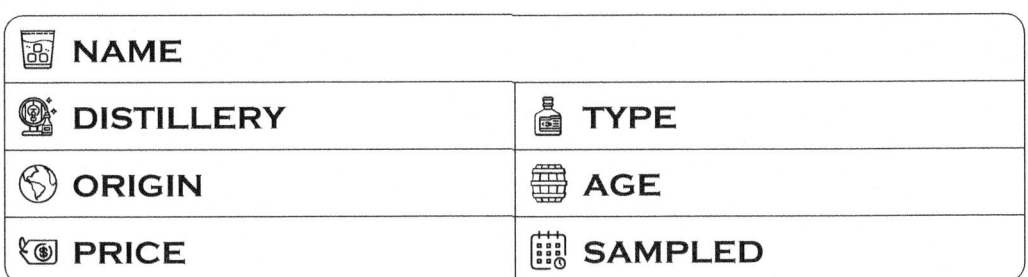

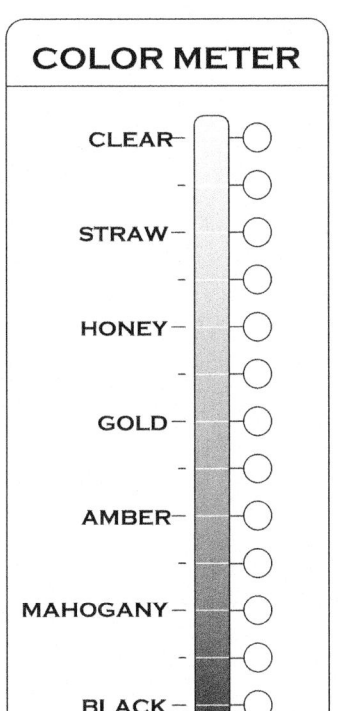

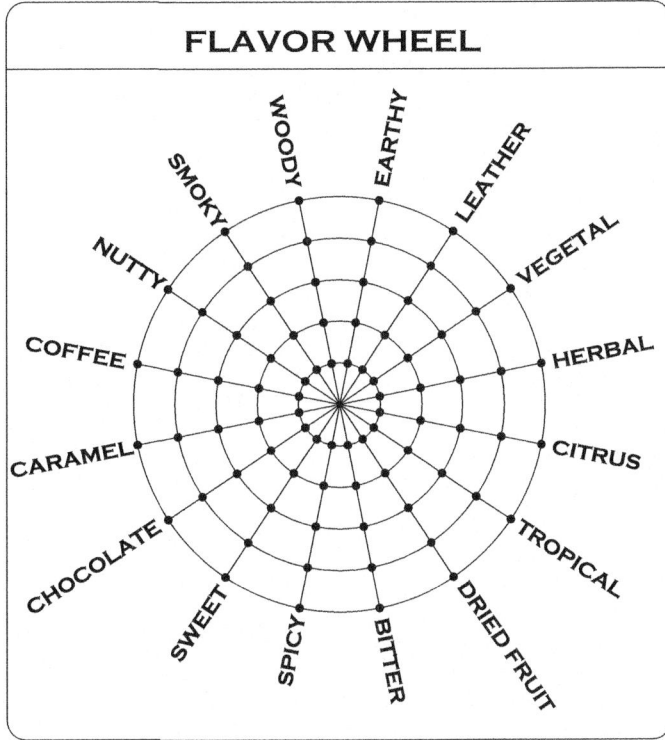

ADDITIONAL NOTES

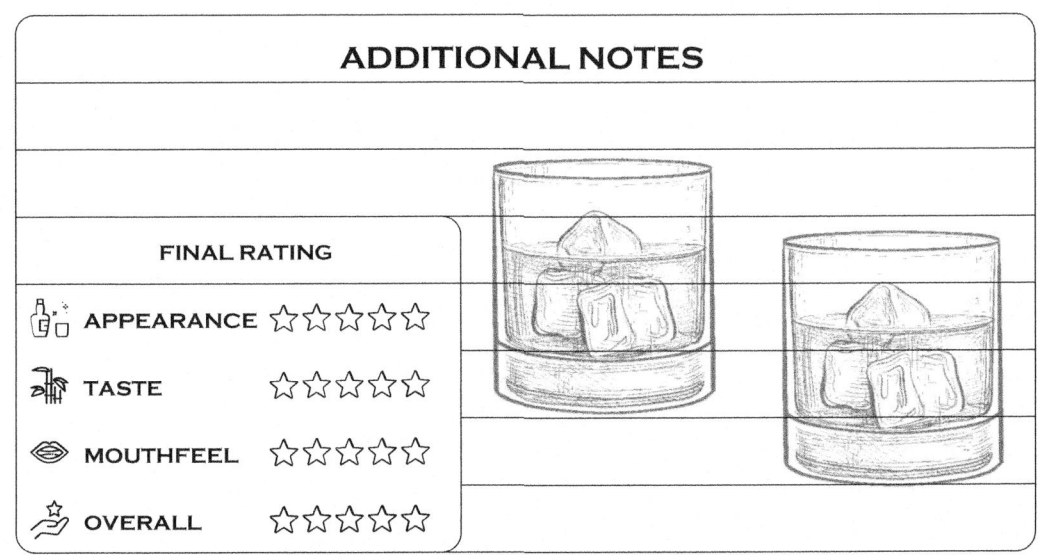

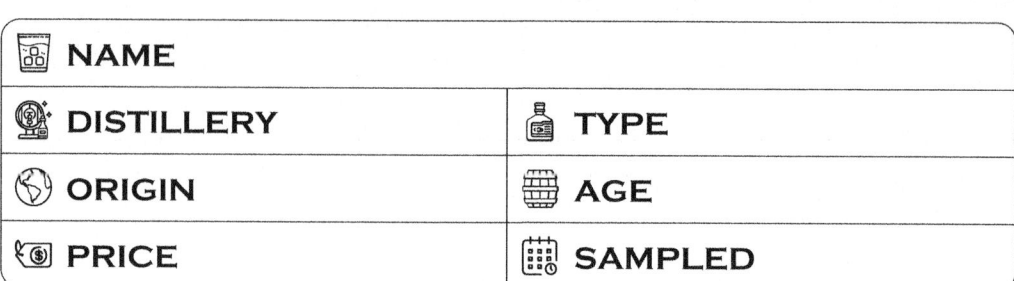

NAME	
DISTILLERY	TYPE
ORIGIN	AGE
PRICE	SAMPLED

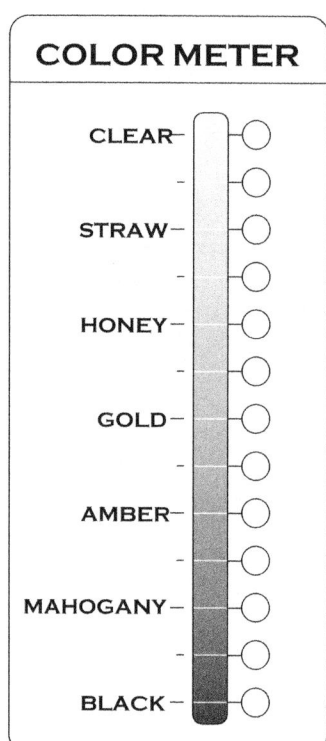

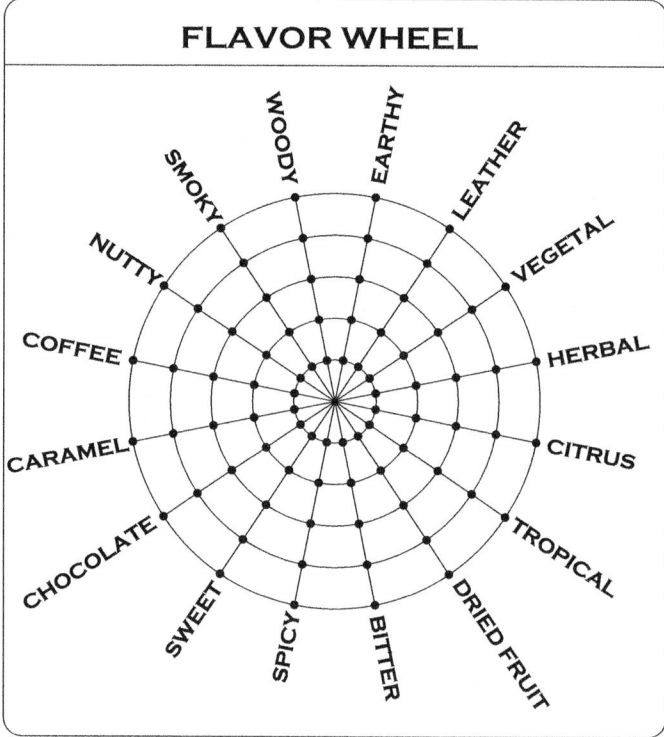

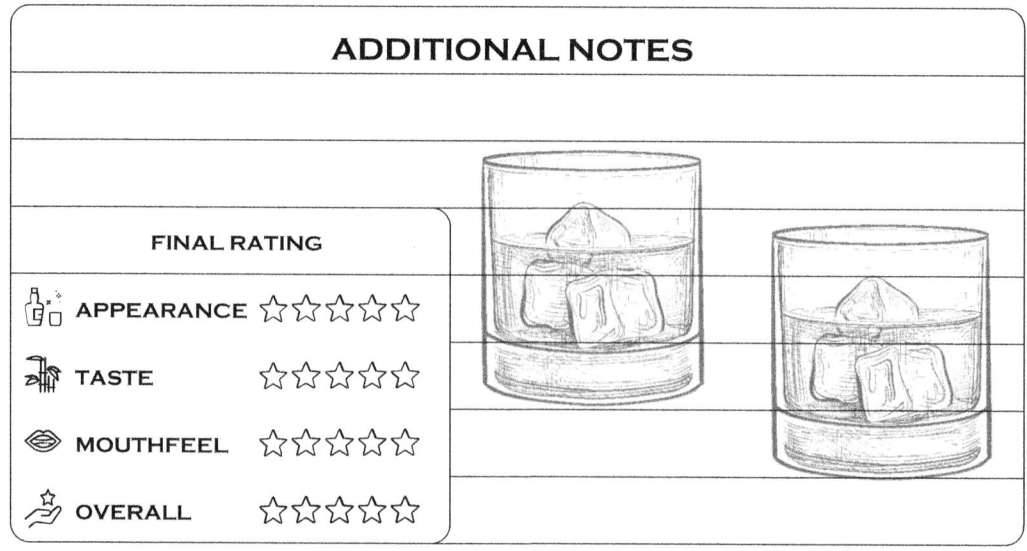

ADDITIONAL NOTES

FINAL RATING

- APPEARANCE ☆☆☆☆☆
- TASTE ☆☆☆☆☆
- MOUTHFEEL ☆☆☆☆☆
- OVERALL ☆☆☆☆☆

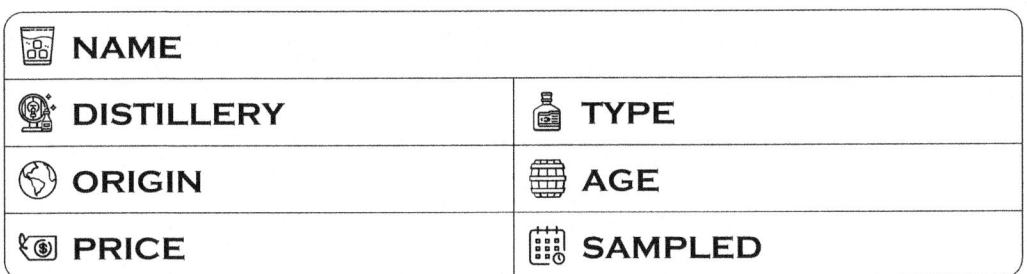

🥃 NAME	
🌀 DISTILLERY	🍾 TYPE
🌍 ORIGIN	🛢 AGE
💰 PRICE	📅 SAMPLED

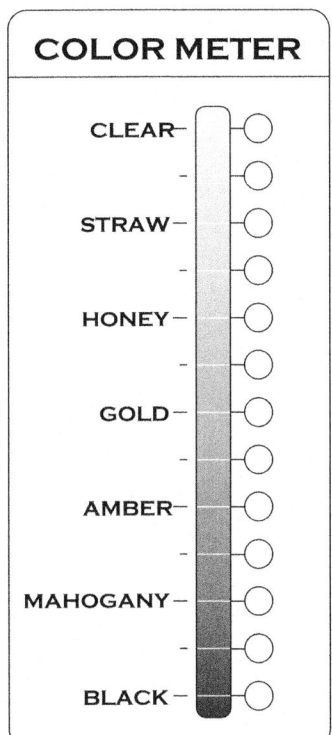

COLOR METER

- CLEAR
- STRAW
- HONEY
- GOLD
- AMBER
- MAHOGANY
- BLACK

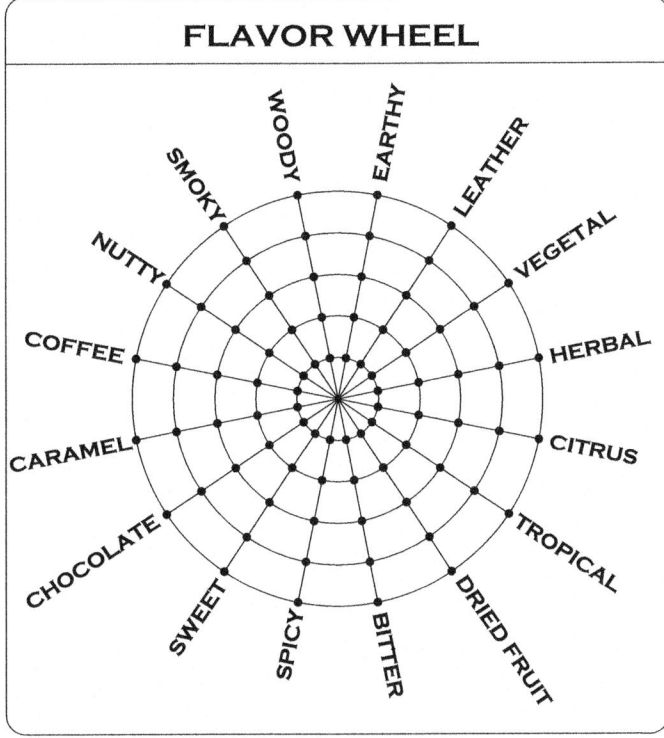

FLAVOR WHEEL

WOODY, EARTHY, LEATHER, VEGETAL, HERBAL, CITRUS, TROPICAL, DRIED FRUIT, BITTER, SPICY, SWEET, CHOCOLATE, CARAMEL, COFFEE, NUTTY, SMOKY

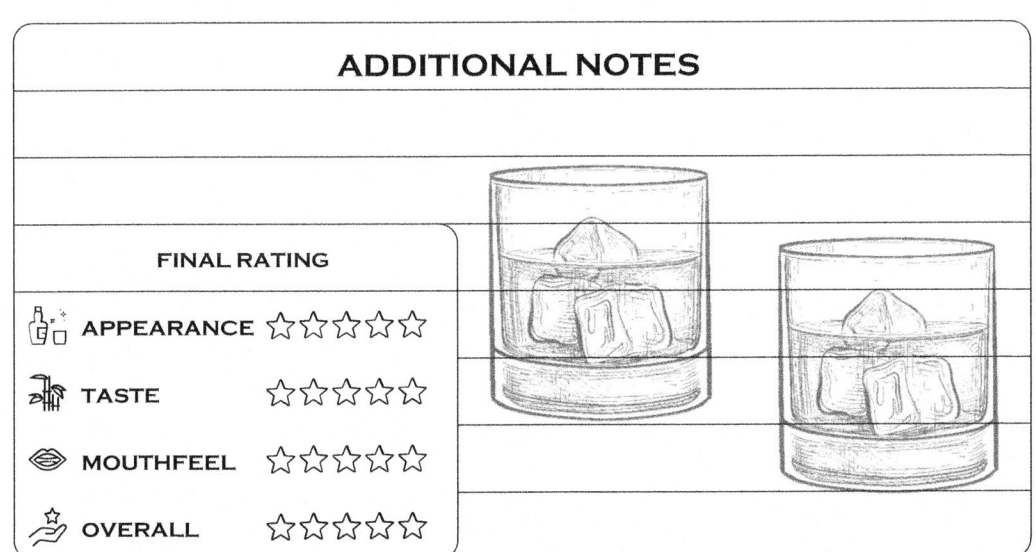

ADDITIONAL NOTES

FINAL RATING

- 🍾 APPEARANCE ☆☆☆☆☆
- 👅 TASTE ☆☆☆☆☆
- 👄 MOUTHFEEL ☆☆☆☆☆
- ⭐ OVERALL ☆☆☆☆☆

🥃 NAME	

🧴 DISTILLERY		🍾 TYPE	
🌍 ORIGIN		🛢 AGE	
💵 PRICE		📅 SAMPLED	

COLOR METER

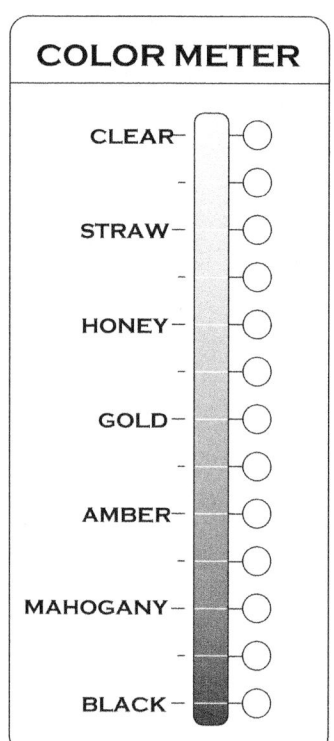

- CLEAR
- STRAW
- HONEY
- GOLD
- AMBER
- MAHOGANY
- BLACK

FLAVOR WHEEL

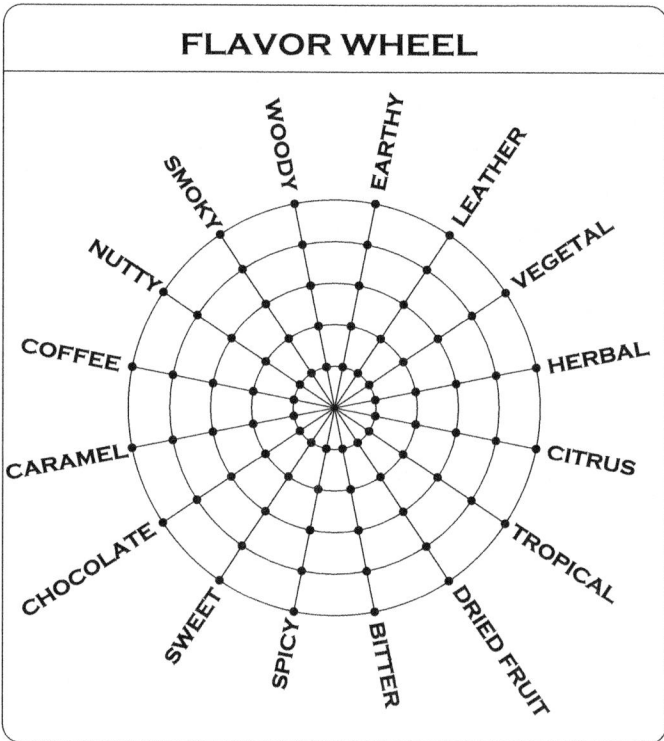

WOODY, EARTHY, LEATHER, SMOKY, VEGETAL, NUTTY, HERBAL, COFFEE, CITRUS, CARAMEL, TROPICAL, CHOCOLATE, DRIED FRUIT, SWEET, SPICY, BITTER

ADDITIONAL NOTES

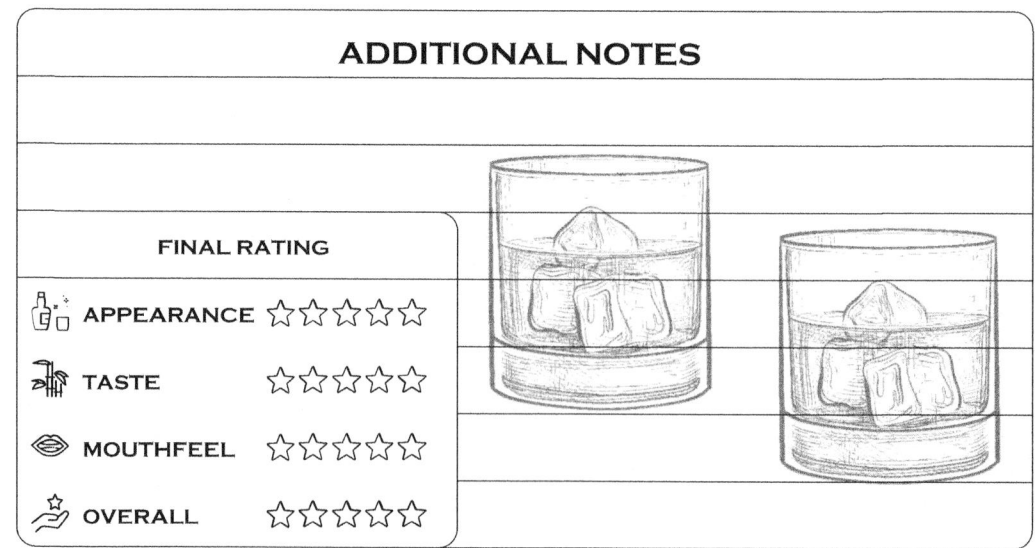

FINAL RATING

- 🍾 APPEARANCE ☆☆☆☆☆
- 👅 TASTE ☆☆☆☆☆
- 👄 MOUTHFEEL ☆☆☆☆☆
- 🖐 OVERALL ☆☆☆☆☆

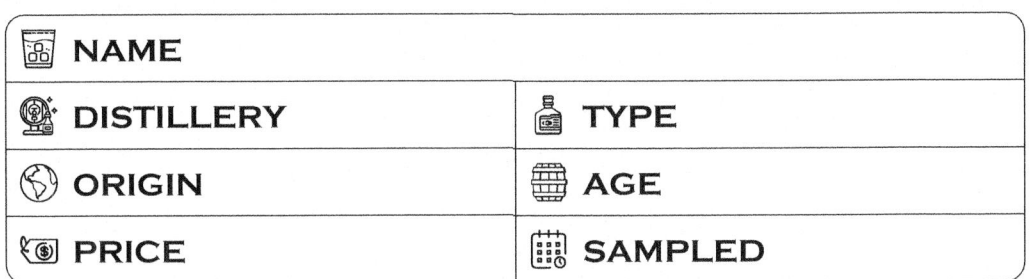

🥃 NAME	
🎯 DISTILLERY	🍾 TYPE
🌐 ORIGIN	🛢 AGE
💰 PRICE	📅 SAMPLED

COLOR METER

- CLEAR ○
- ○
- STRAW ○
- ○
- HONEY ○
- ○
- GOLD ○
- ○
- AMBER ○
- ○
- MAHOGANY ○
- ○
- BLACK ○

FLAVOR WHEEL

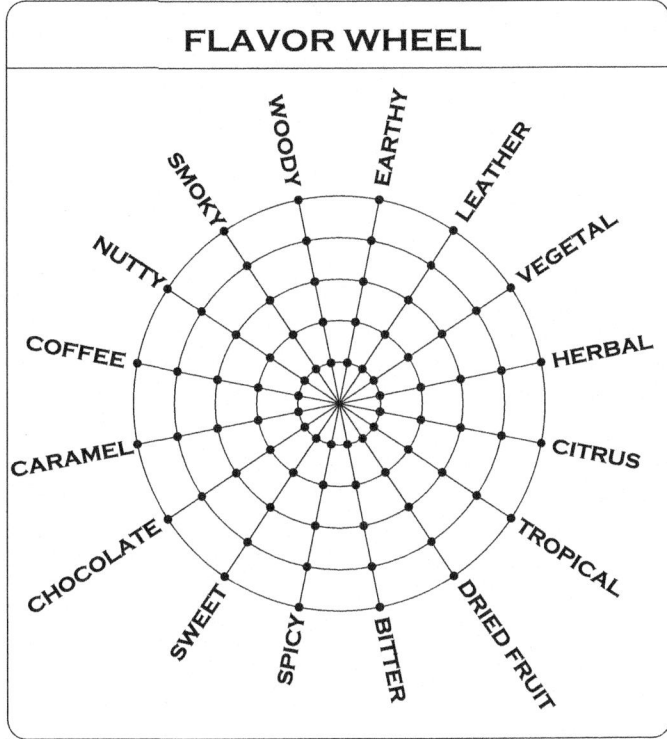

Categories: SMOKY, WOODY, EARTHY, LEATHER, NUTTY, VEGETAL, COFFEE, HERBAL, CARAMEL, CITRUS, CHOCOLATE, TROPICAL, SWEET, SPICY, BITTER, DRIED FRUIT

ADDITIONAL NOTES

FINAL RATING

- 🍾 APPEARANCE ☆☆☆☆☆
- 🥃 TASTE ☆☆☆☆☆
- 👄 MOUTHFEEL ☆☆☆☆☆
- 🤲 OVERALL ☆☆☆☆☆

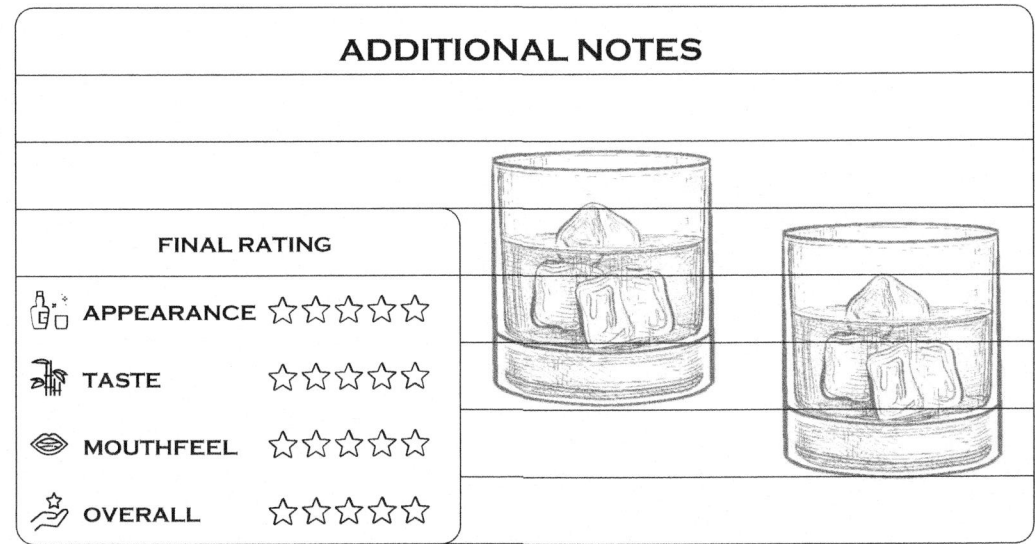

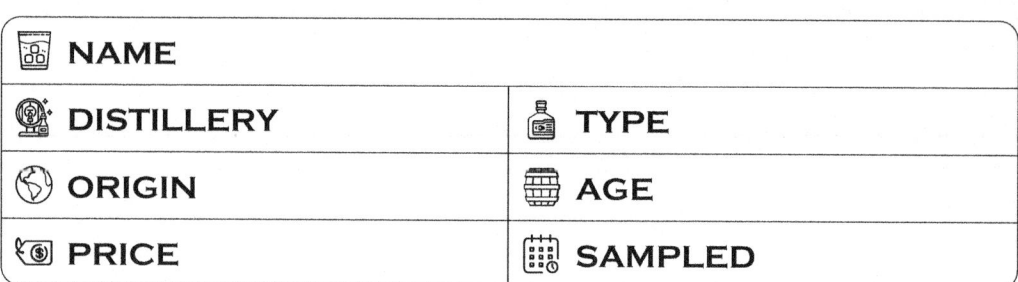

COLOR METER

- CLEAR
- STRAW
- HONEY
- GOLD
- AMBER
- MAHOGANY
- BLACK

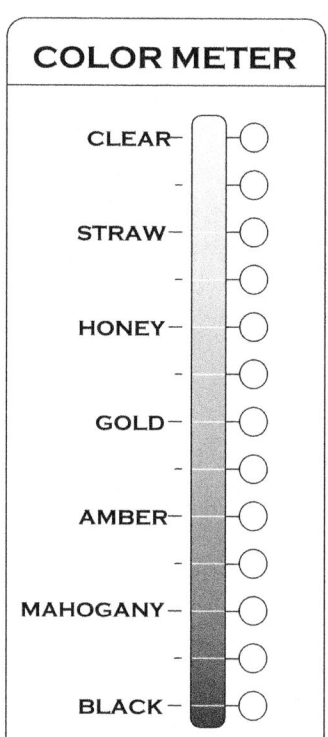

FLAVOR WHEEL

WOODY · EARTHY · LEATHER · VEGETAL · HERBAL · CITRUS · TROPICAL · DRIED FRUIT · BITTER · SPICY · SWEET · CHOCOLATE · CARAMEL · COFFEE · NUTTY · SMOKY

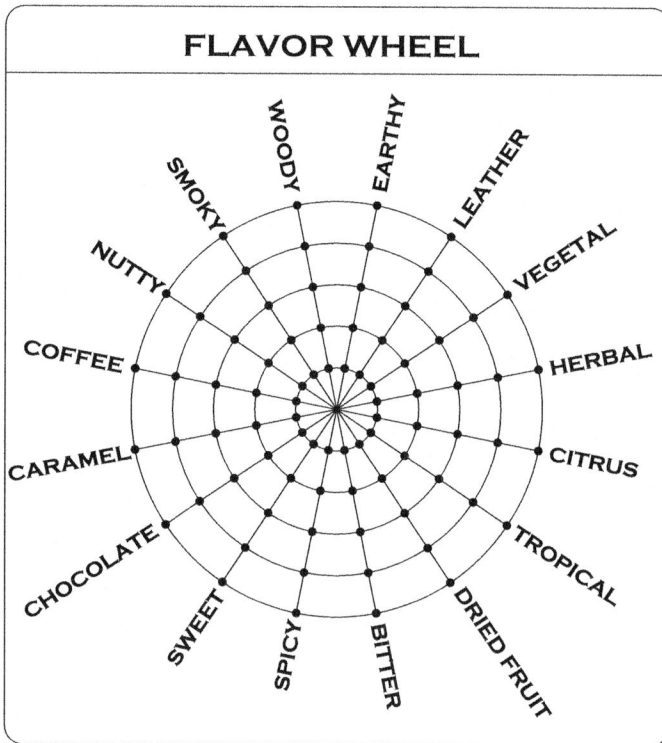

ADDITIONAL NOTES

FINAL RATING

- APPEARANCE ☆☆☆☆☆
- TASTE ☆☆☆☆☆
- MOUTHFEEL ☆☆☆☆☆
- OVERALL ☆☆☆☆☆

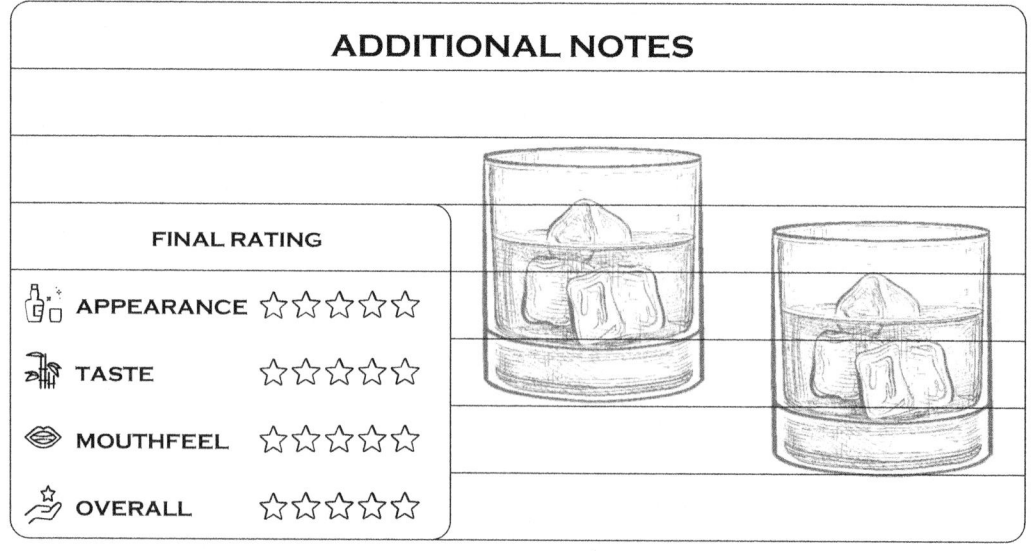

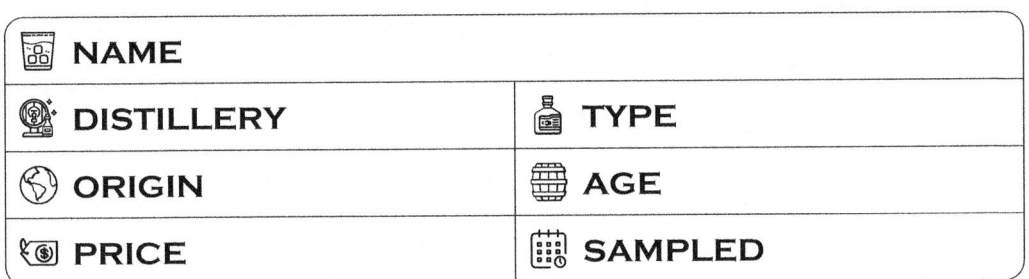

- NAME
- DISTILLERY
- ORIGIN
- PRICE
- TYPE
- AGE
- SAMPLED

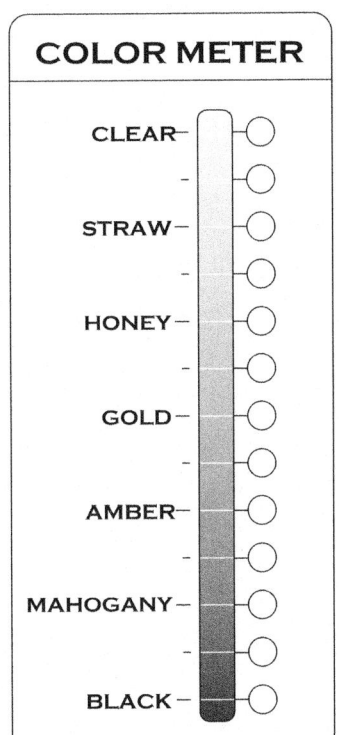

COLOR METER

- CLEAR
- STRAW
- HONEY
- GOLD
- AMBER
- MAHOGANY
- BLACK

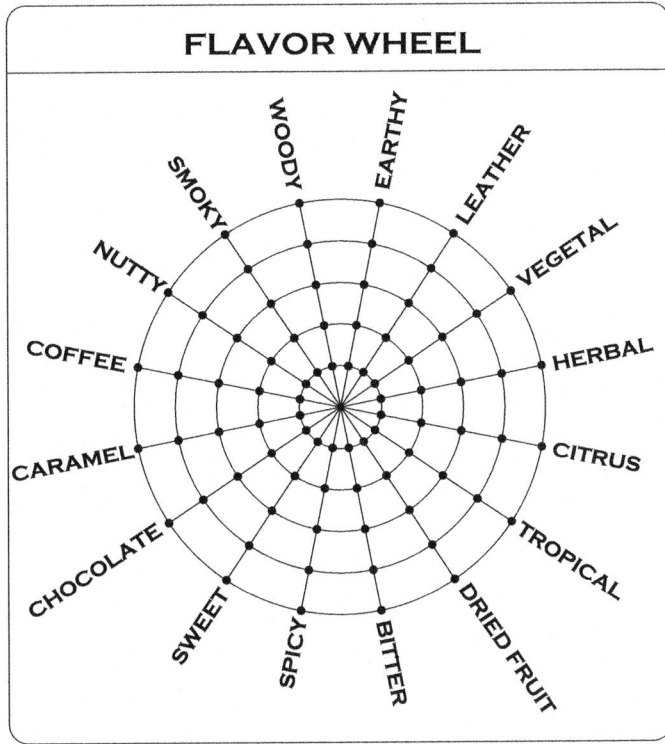

FLAVOR WHEEL

WOODY, EARTHY, LEATHER, VEGETAL, HERBAL, CITRUS, TROPICAL, DRIED FRUIT, BITTER, SPICY, SWEET, CHOCOLATE, CARAMEL, COFFEE, NUTTY, SMOKY

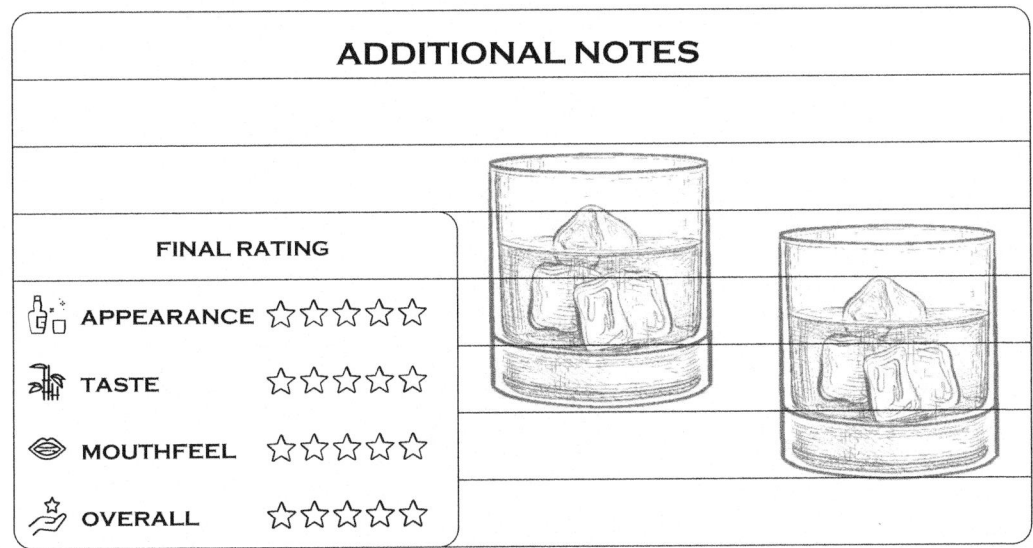

ADDITIONAL NOTES

FINAL RATING

- APPEARANCE ☆☆☆☆☆
- TASTE ☆☆☆☆☆
- MOUTHFEEL ☆☆☆☆☆
- OVERALL ☆☆☆☆☆

🥃 **NAME**	
🌐 **DISTILLERY**	🍾 **TYPE**
🌎 **ORIGIN**	🛢 **AGE**
💰 **PRICE**	📅 **SAMPLED**

COLOR METER

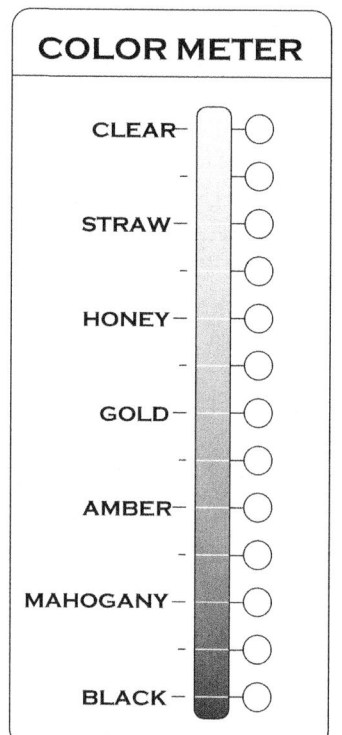

- CLEAR
- STRAW
- HONEY
- GOLD
- AMBER
- MAHOGANY
- BLACK

FLAVOR WHEEL

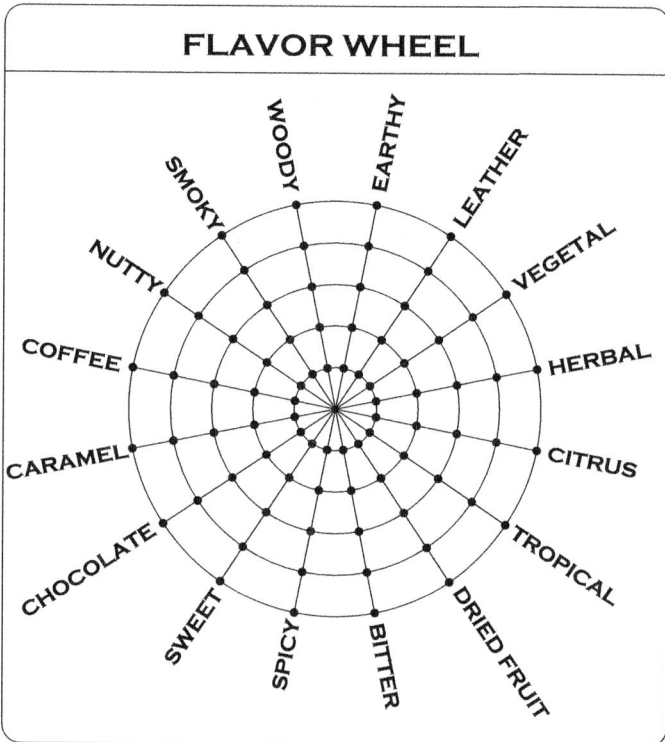

SMOKY, WOODY, EARTHY, LEATHER, NUTTY, VEGETAL, COFFEE, HERBAL, CARAMEL, CITRUS, CHOCOLATE, TROPICAL, SWEET, SPICY, BITTER, DRIED FRUIT

ADDITIONAL NOTES

FINAL RATING

- 🍾 APPEARANCE ☆☆☆☆☆
- 🌾 TASTE ☆☆☆☆☆
- 👄 MOUTHFEEL ☆☆☆☆☆
- 🖐 OVERALL ☆☆☆☆☆

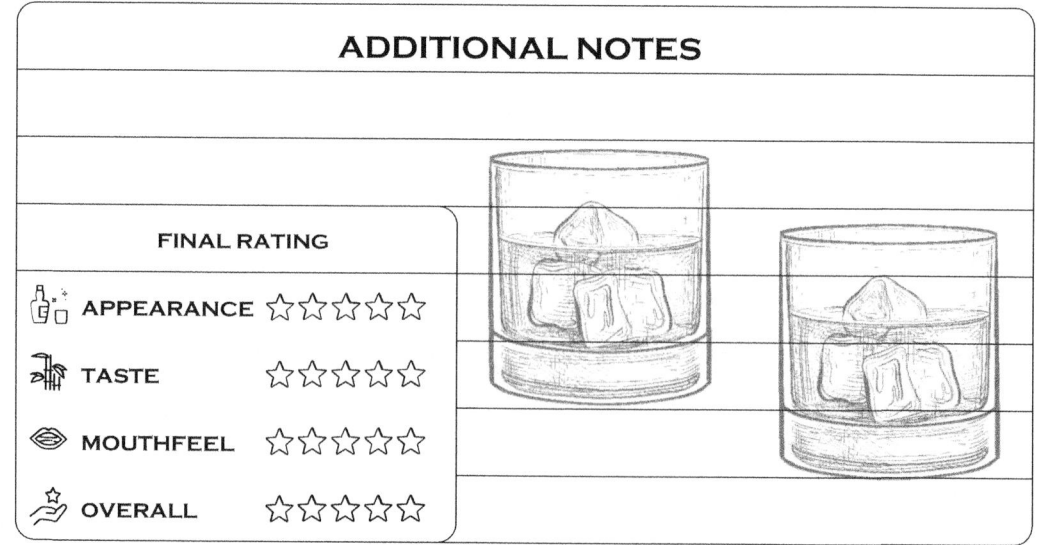

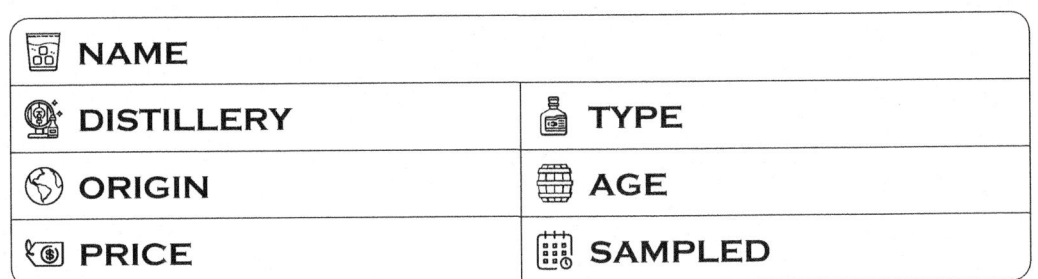

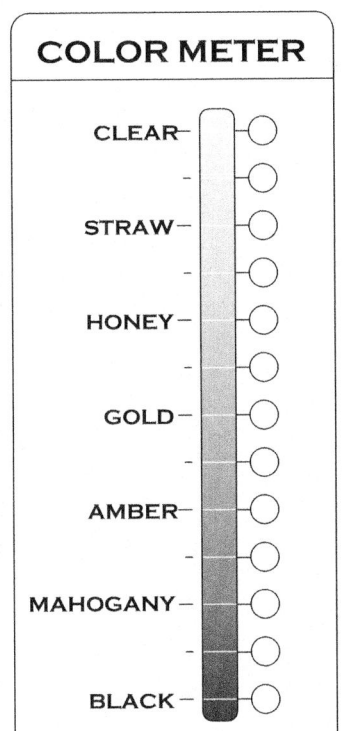

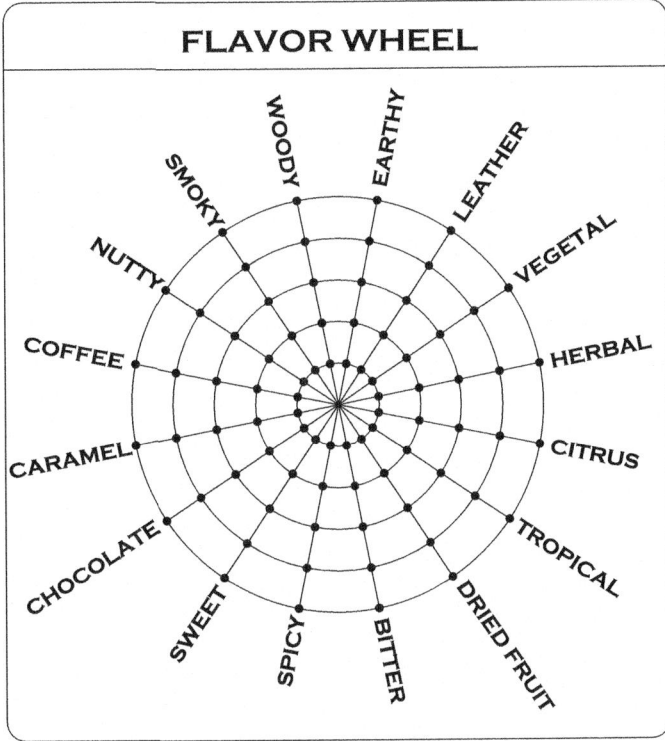

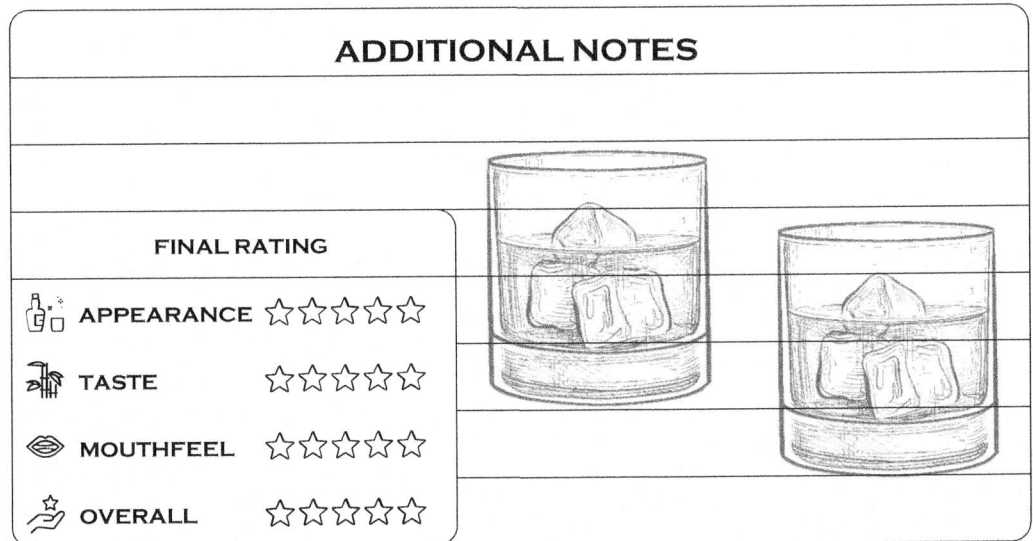

NAME	
DISTILLERY	TYPE
ORIGIN	AGE
PRICE	SAMPLED

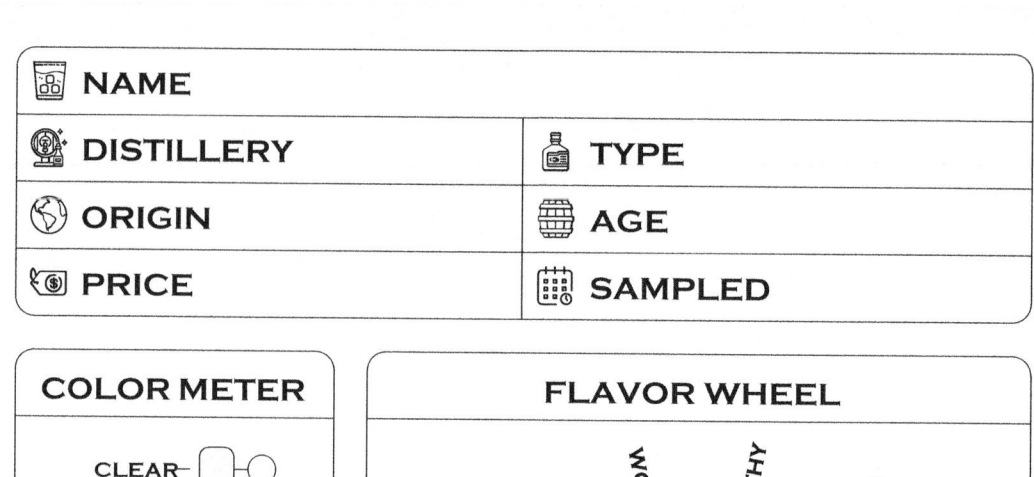

COLOR METER

- CLEAR ○
- ○
- STRAW ○
- ○
- HONEY ○
- ○
- GOLD ○
- ○
- AMBER ○
- ○
- MAHOGANY ○
- ○
- BLACK ○

FLAVOR WHEEL

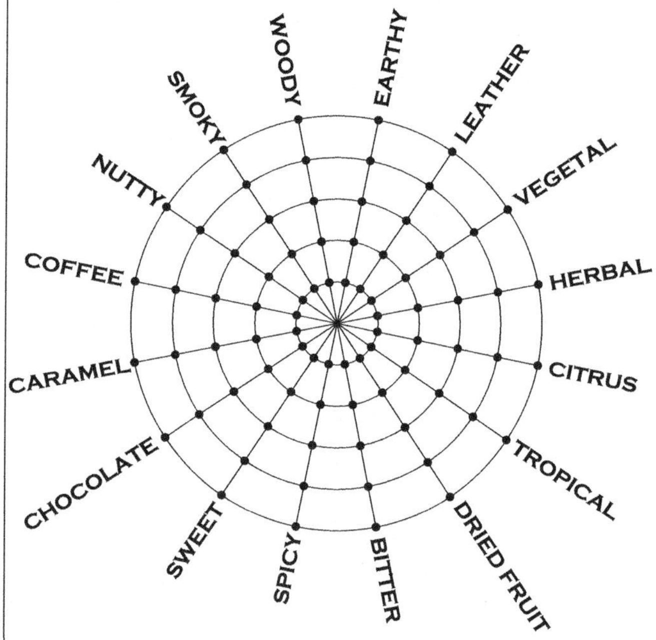
WOODY
EARTHY
LEATHER
VEGETAL
HERBAL
CITRUS
TROPICAL
DRIED FRUIT
BITTER
SPICY
SWEET
CHOCOLATE
CARAMEL
COFFEE
NUTTY
SMOKY

ADDITIONAL NOTES

FINAL RATING

APPEARANCE	☆☆☆☆☆
TASTE	☆☆☆☆☆
MOUTHFEEL	☆☆☆☆☆
OVERALL	☆☆☆☆☆

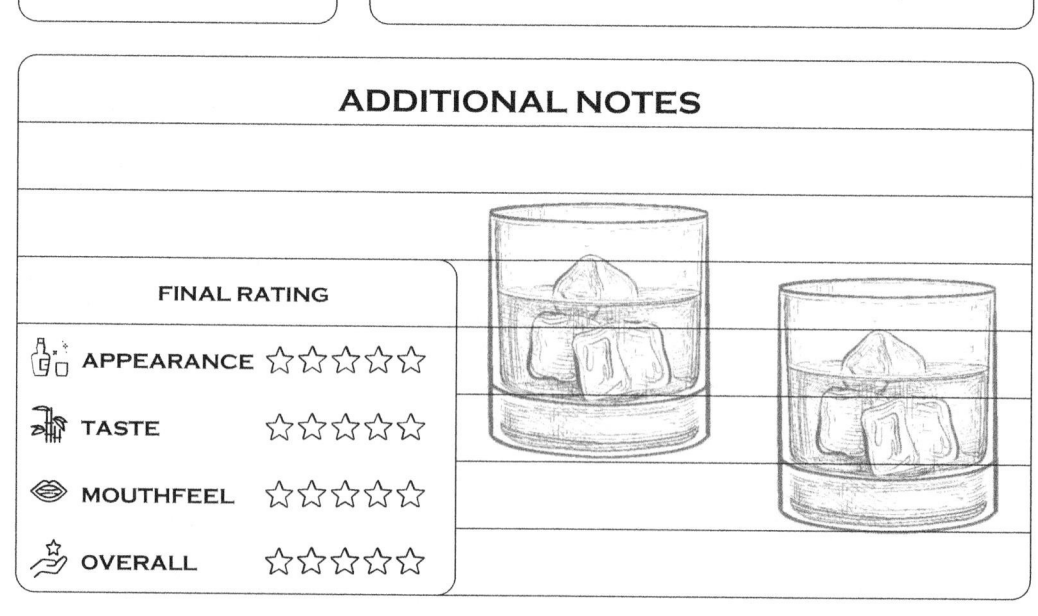

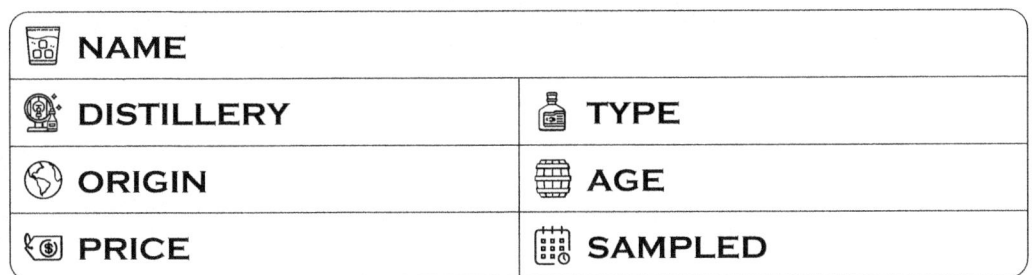
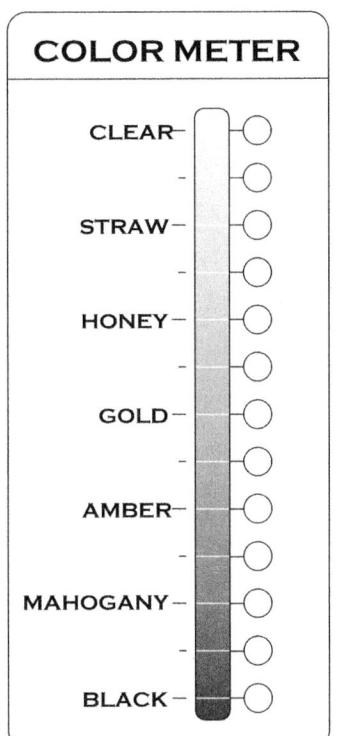
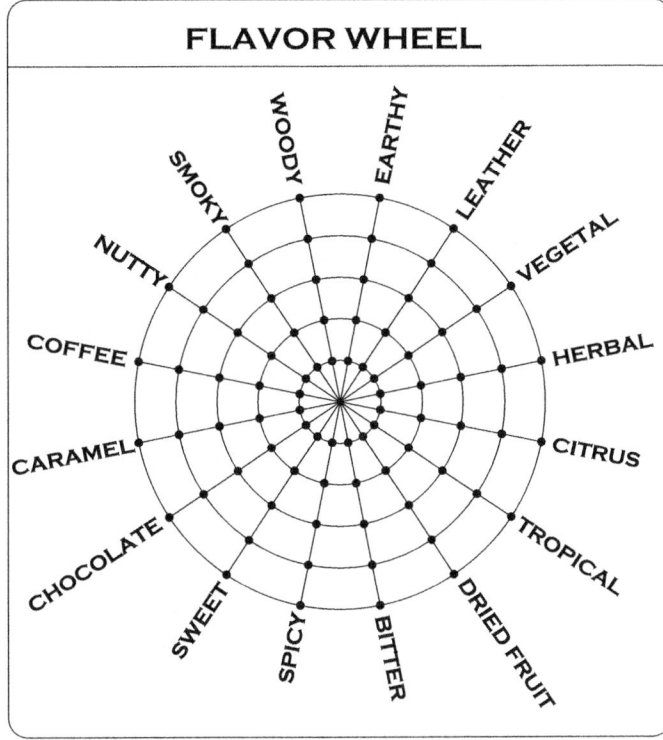
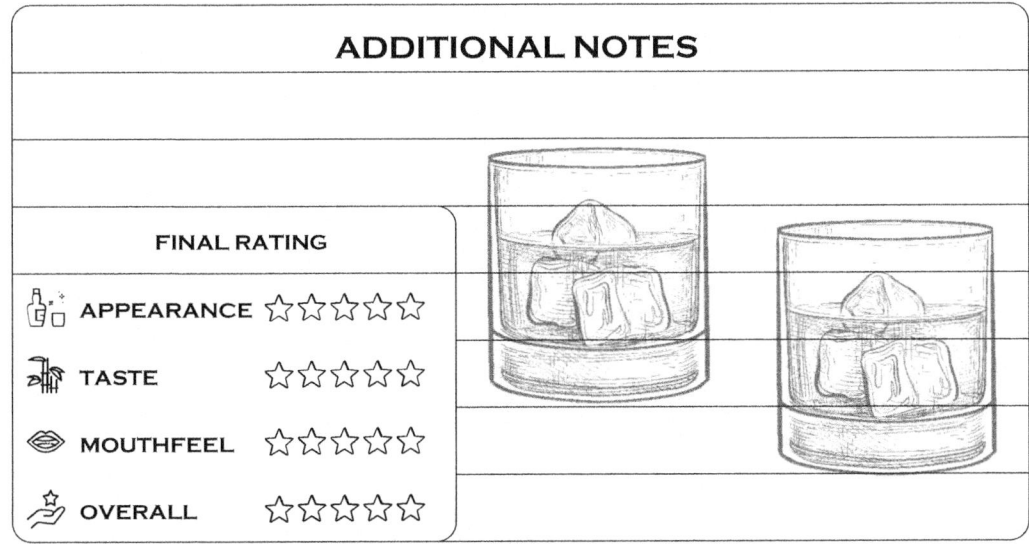

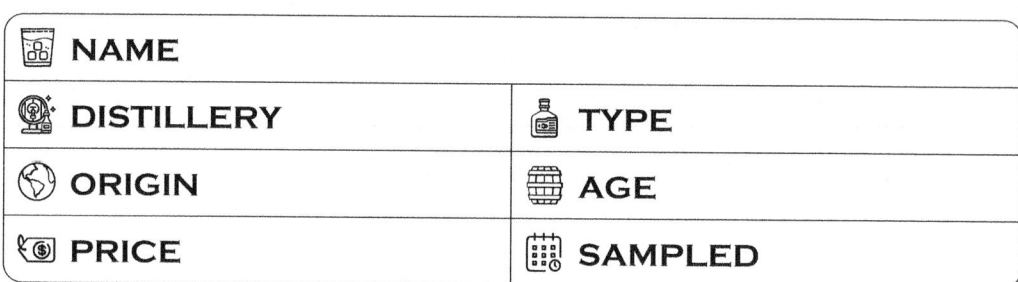

- NAME
- DISTILLERY
- TYPE
- ORIGIN
- AGE
- PRICE
- SAMPLED

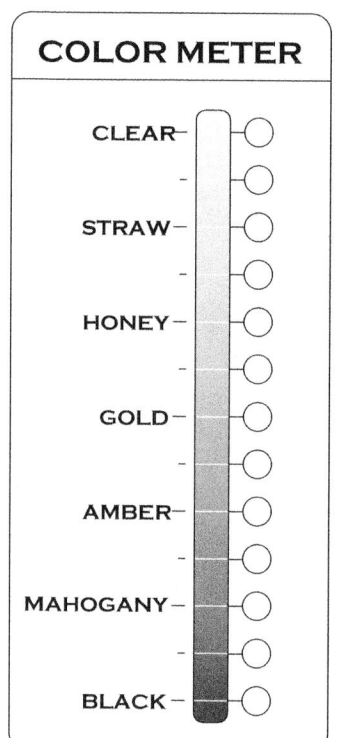

COLOR METER

- CLEAR
- STRAW
- HONEY
- GOLD
- AMBER
- MAHOGANY
- BLACK

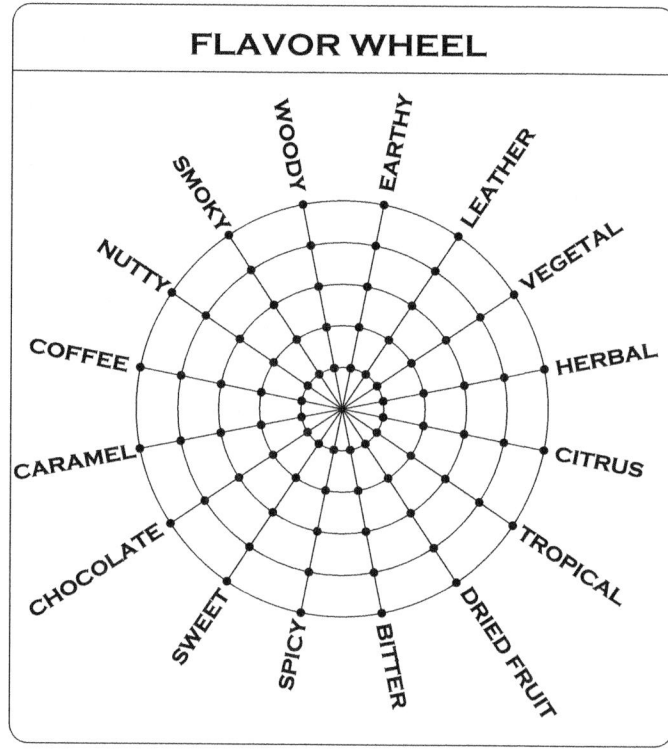

FLAVOR WHEEL

SMOKY, WOODY, EARTHY, LEATHER, NUTTY, VEGETAL, COFFEE, HERBAL, CARAMEL, CITRUS, CHOCOLATE, TROPICAL, SWEET, SPICY, BITTER, DRIED FRUIT

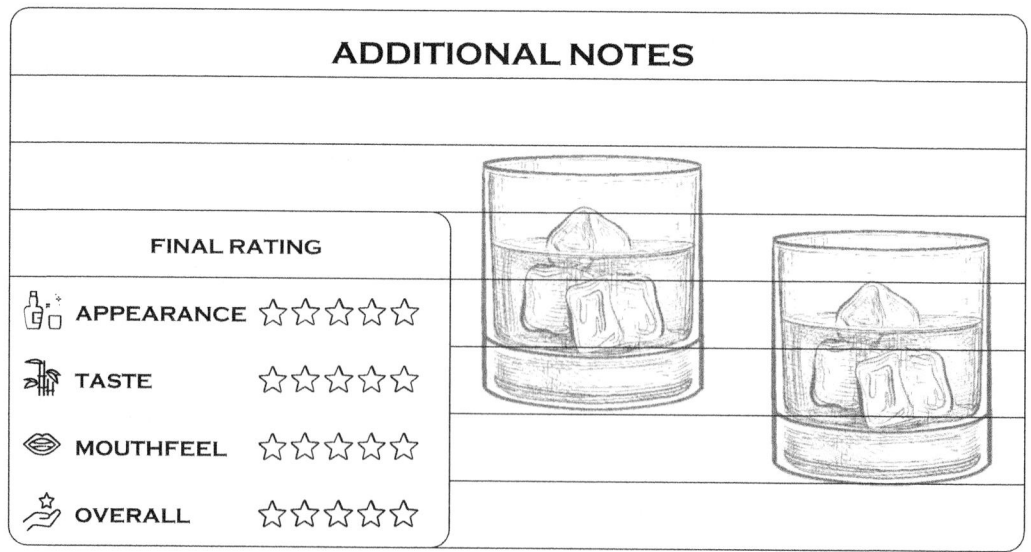

ADDITIONAL NOTES

FINAL RATING

- APPEARANCE ☆☆☆☆☆
- TASTE ☆☆☆☆☆
- MOUTHFEEL ☆☆☆☆☆
- OVERALL ☆☆☆☆☆

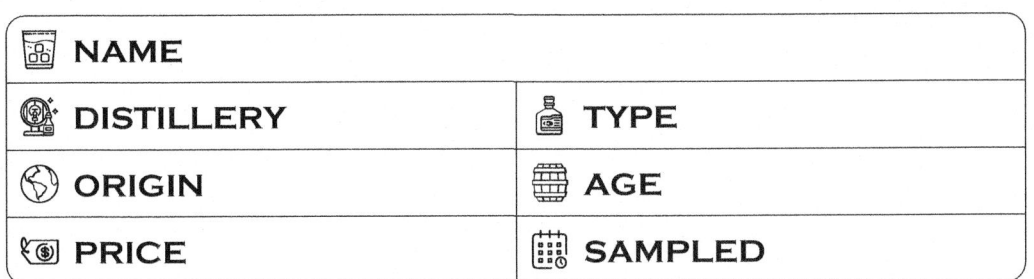
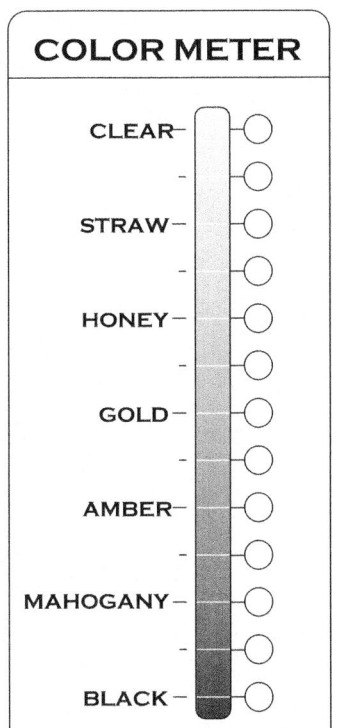
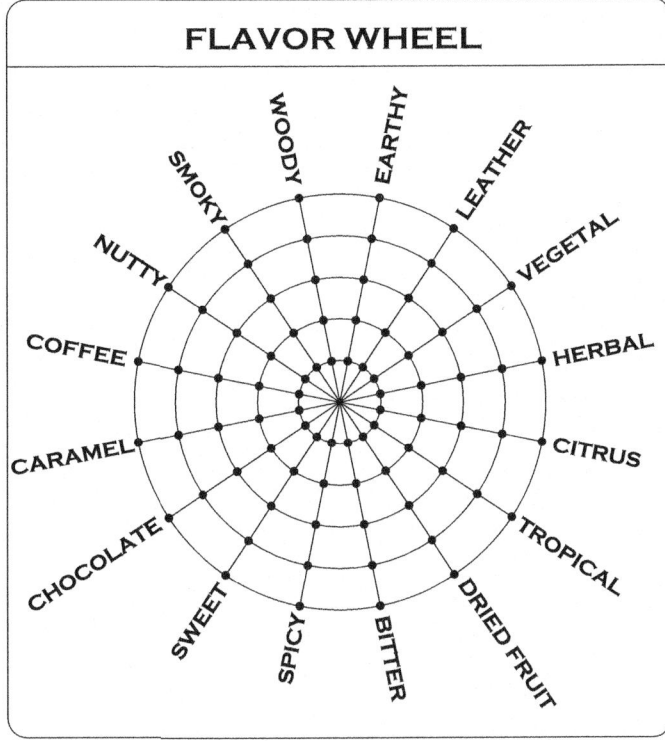
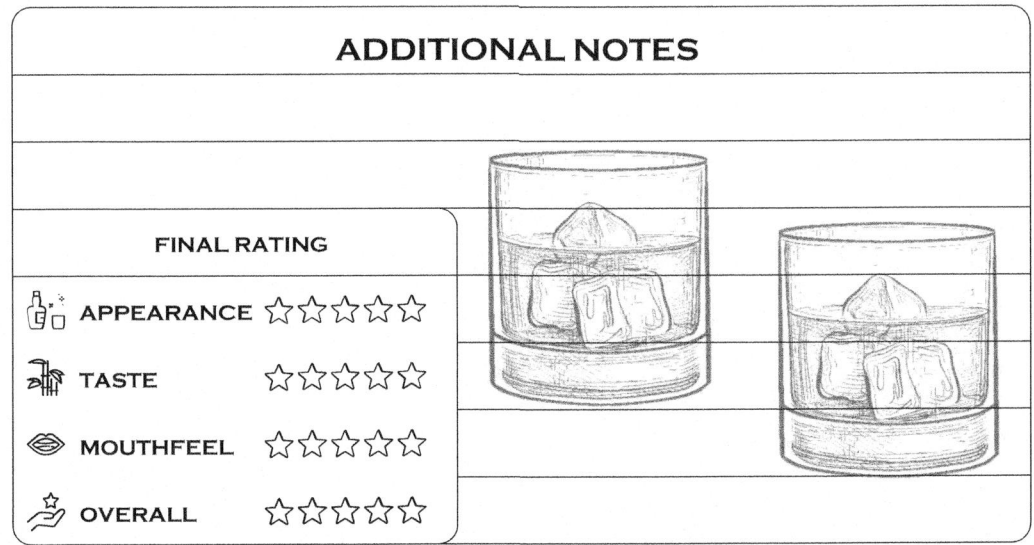

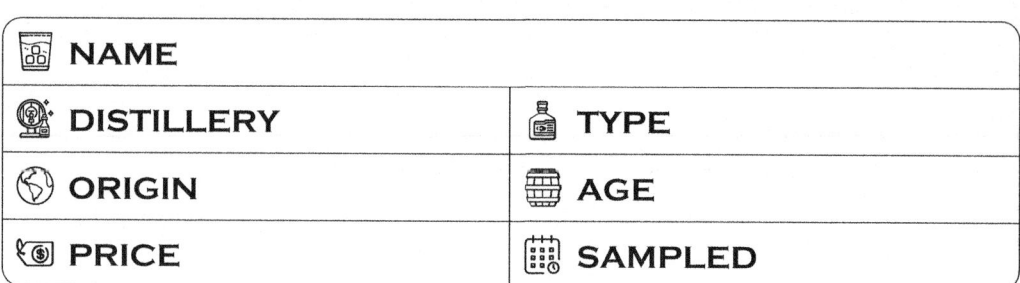

- NAME
- DISTILLERY
- ORIGIN
- PRICE
- TYPE
- AGE
- SAMPLED

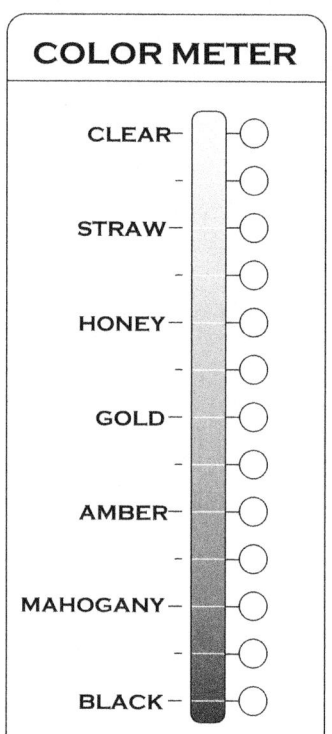

COLOR METER

- CLEAR
- STRAW
- HONEY
- GOLD
- AMBER
- MAHOGANY
- BLACK

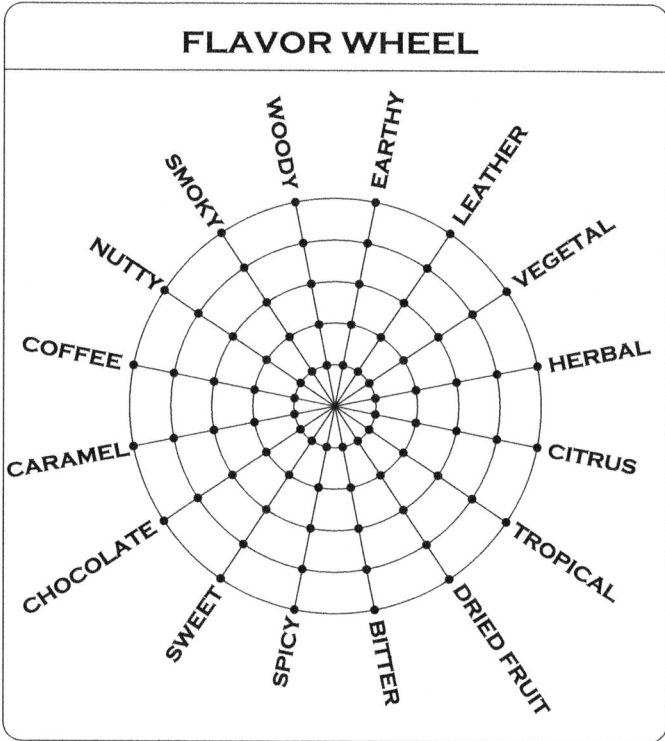

FLAVOR WHEEL

WOODY, EARTHY, LEATHER, VEGETAL, HERBAL, CITRUS, TROPICAL, DRIED FRUIT, BITTER, SPICY, SWEET, CHOCOLATE, CARAMEL, COFFEE, NUTTY, SMOKY

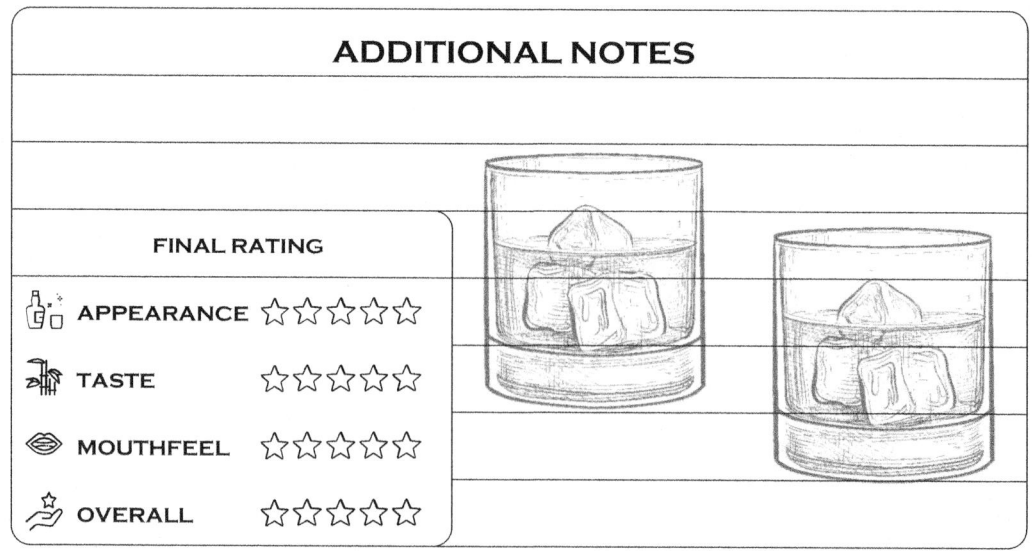

ADDITIONAL NOTES

FINAL RATING

- APPEARANCE ☆☆☆☆☆
- TASTE ☆☆☆☆☆
- MOUTHFEEL ☆☆☆☆☆
- OVERALL ☆☆☆☆☆

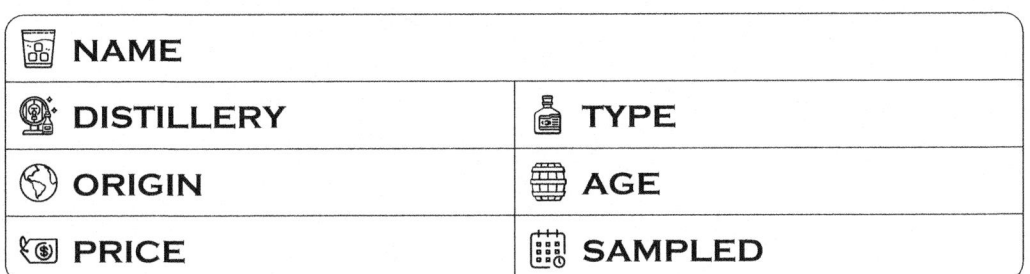

🥃 **NAME**			
🔬 **DISTILLERY**		🍾 **TYPE**	
🌍 **ORIGIN**		🛢 **AGE**	
💲 **PRICE**		📅 **SAMPLED**	

COLOR METER

- CLEAR
- STRAW
- HONEY
- GOLD
- AMBER
- MAHOGANY
- BLACK

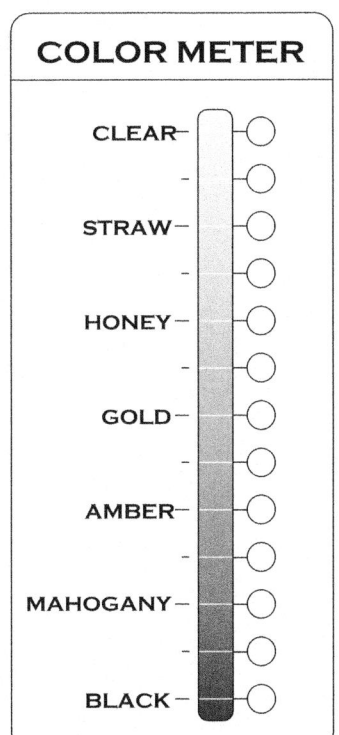

FLAVOR WHEEL

WOODY · EARTHY · LEATHER · VEGETAL · HERBAL · CITRUS · TROPICAL · DRIED FRUIT · BITTER · SPICY · SWEET · CHOCOLATE · CARAMEL · COFFEE · NUTTY · SMOKY

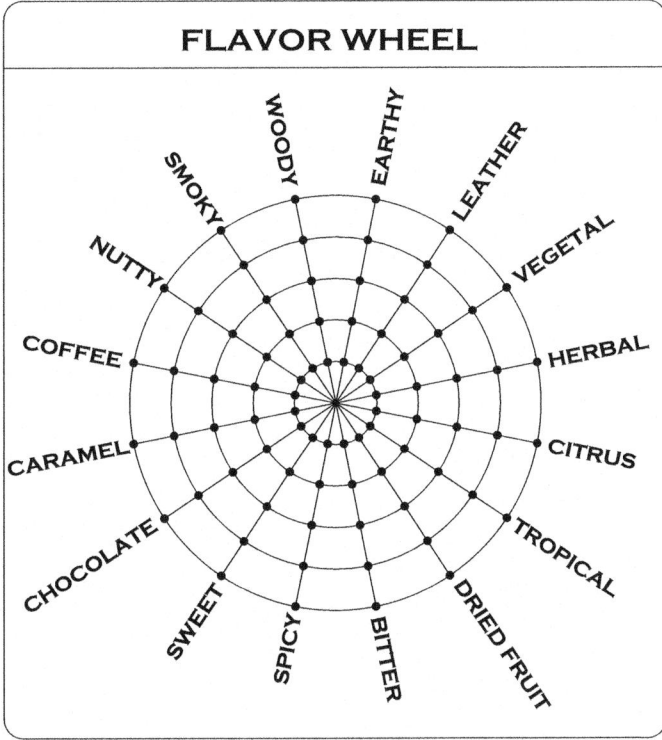

ADDITIONAL NOTES

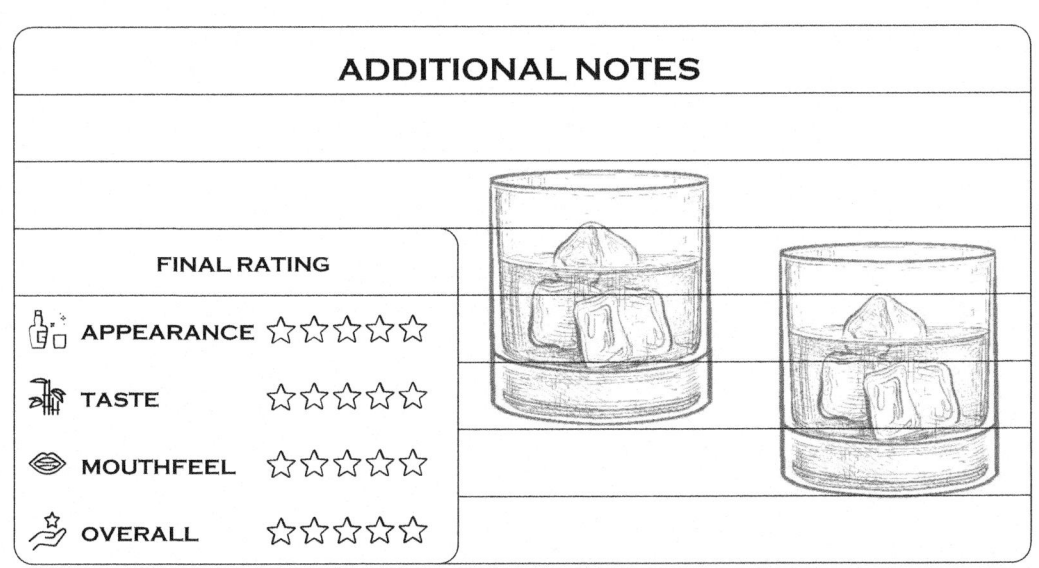

FINAL RATING

- 🍾 APPEARANCE ☆☆☆☆☆
- 👅 TASTE ☆☆☆☆☆
- 👄 MOUTHFEEL ☆☆☆☆☆
- 🤚 OVERALL ☆☆☆☆☆

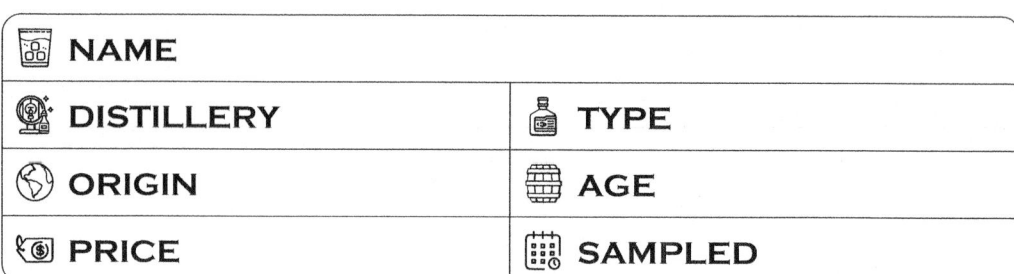

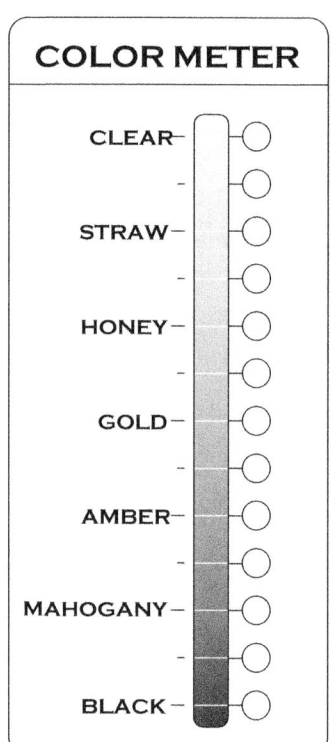

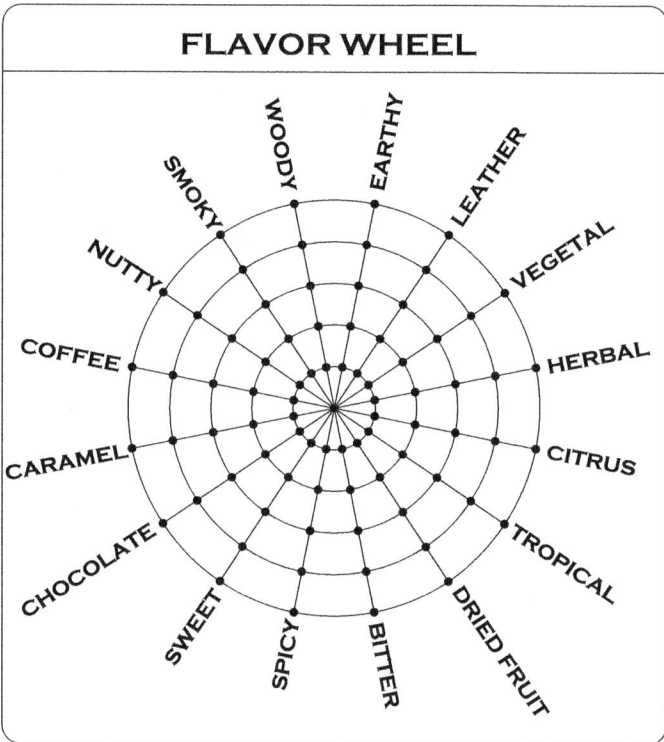

ADDITIONAL NOTES

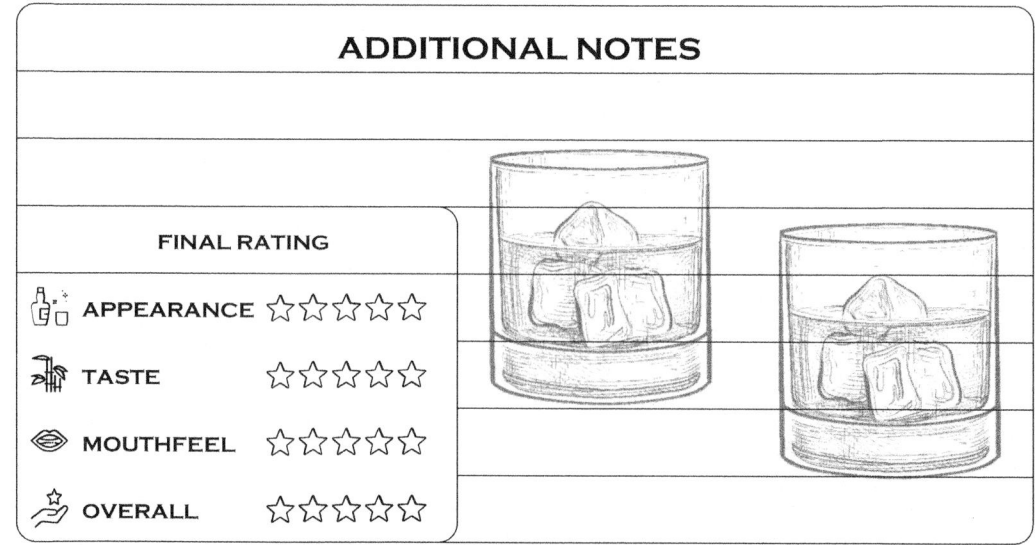

FINAL RATING

- APPEARANCE ☆☆☆☆☆
- TASTE ☆☆☆☆☆
- MOUTHFEEL ☆☆☆☆☆
- OVERALL ☆☆☆☆☆

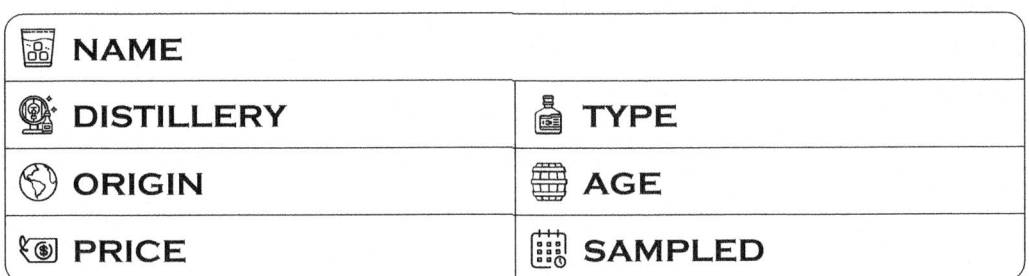

NAME	
DISTILLERY	TYPE
ORIGIN	AGE
PRICE	SAMPLED

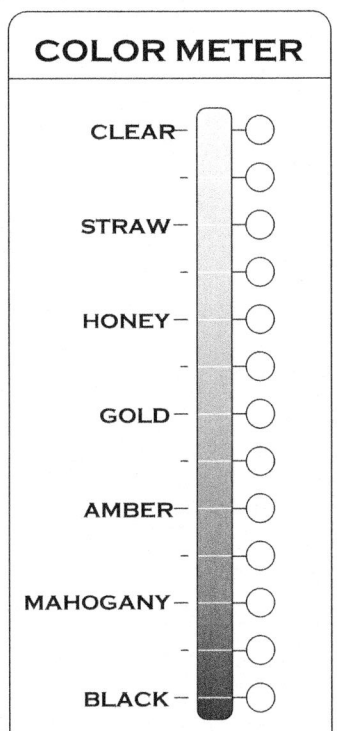

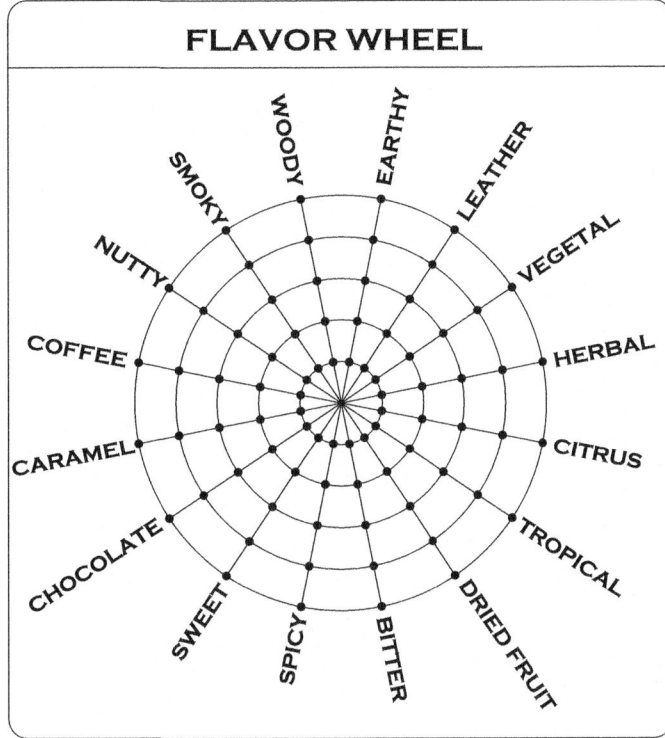

ADDITIONAL NOTES

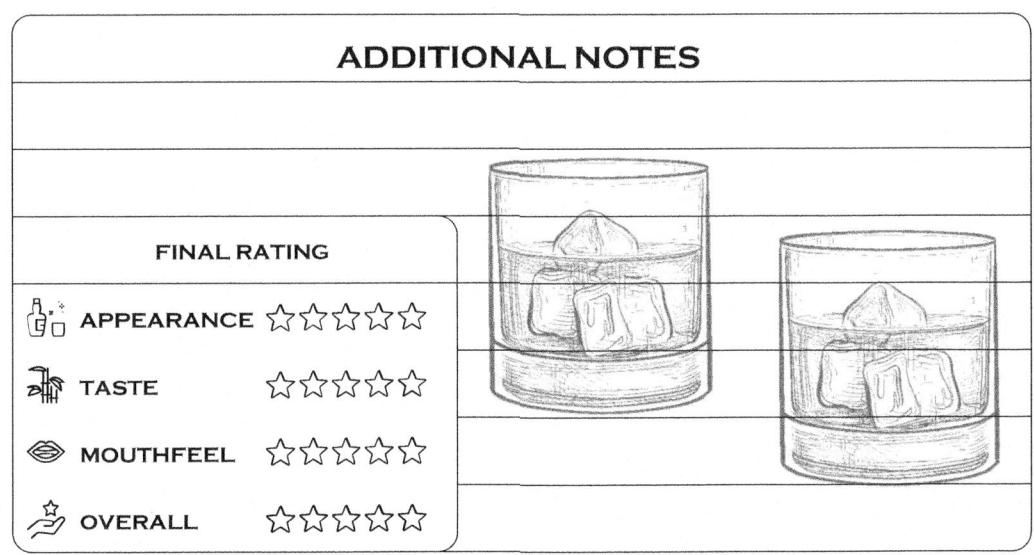

FINAL RATING

- APPEARANCE ☆☆☆☆☆
- TASTE ☆☆☆☆☆
- MOUTHFEEL ☆☆☆☆☆
- OVERALL ☆☆☆☆☆

🥃 **NAME**			
🏭 **DISTILLERY**		🍾 **TYPE**	
🌐 **ORIGIN**		🛢 **AGE**	
💰 **PRICE**		📅 **SAMPLED**	

COLOR METER

- CLEAR
- STRAW
- HONEY
- GOLD
- AMBER
- MAHOGANY
- BLACK

FLAVOR WHEEL

WOODY, EARTHY, LEATHER, VEGETAL, HERBAL, CITRUS, TROPICAL, DRIED FRUIT, BITTER, SPICY, SWEET, CHOCOLATE, CARAMEL, COFFEE, NUTTY, SMOKY

ADDITIONAL NOTES

FINAL RATING

- 🍾 APPEARANCE ☆☆☆☆☆
- 🥃 TASTE ☆☆☆☆☆
- 👄 MOUTHFEEL ☆☆☆☆☆
- 👌 OVERALL ☆☆☆☆☆

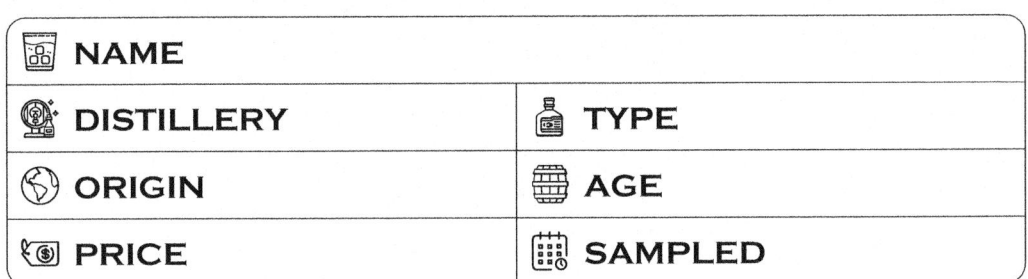

COLOR METER

- CLEAR
- STRAW
- HONEY
- GOLD
- AMBER
- MAHOGANY
- BLACK

FLAVOR WHEEL

SMOKY · WOODY · EARTHY · LEATHER · VEGETAL · HERBAL · CITRUS · TROPICAL · DRIED FRUIT · BITTER · SPICY · SWEET · CHOCOLATE · CARAMEL · COFFEE · NUTTY

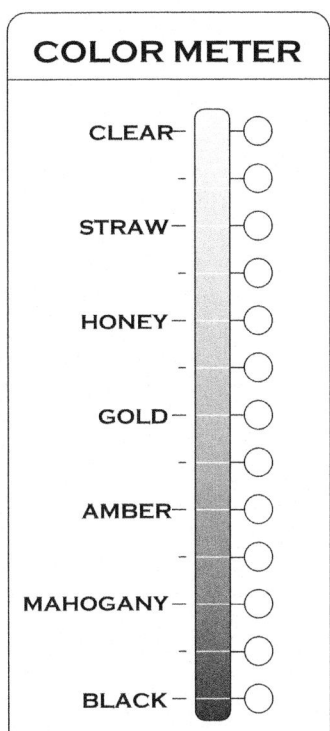
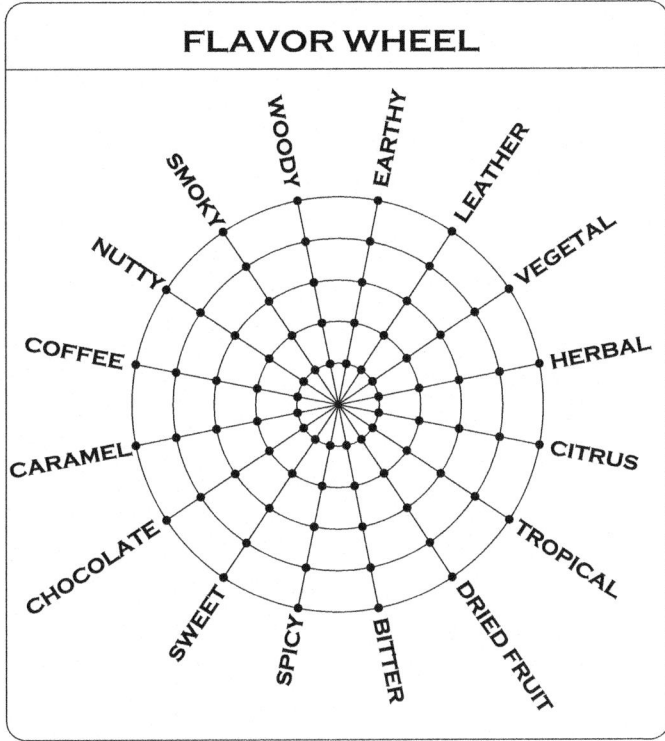

ADDITIONAL NOTES

FINAL RATING

- APPEARANCE ☆☆☆☆☆
- TASTE ☆☆☆☆☆
- MOUTHFEEL ☆☆☆☆☆
- OVERALL ☆☆☆☆☆

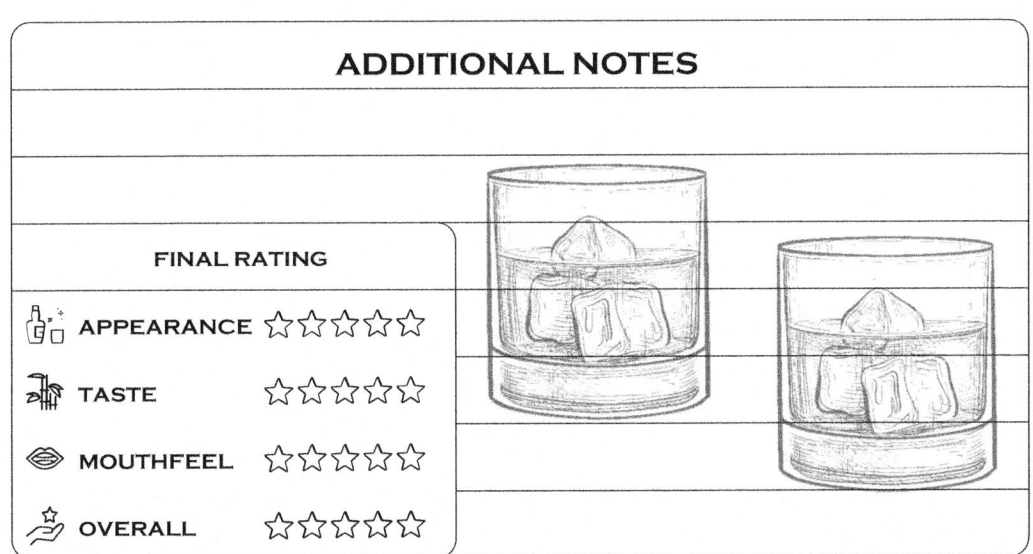

🥃 NAME	
🏭 DISTILLERY	🍾 TYPE
🌍 ORIGIN	🛢 AGE
💰 PRICE	📅 SAMPLED

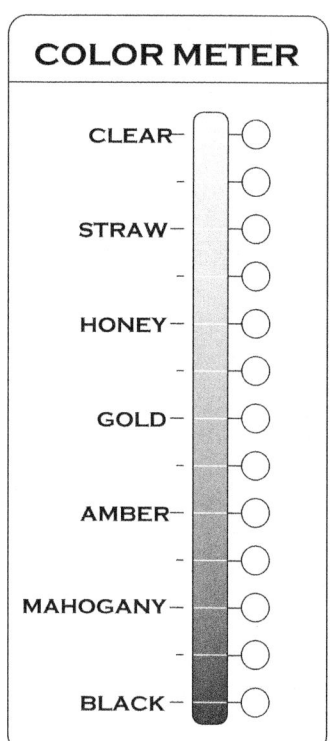

COLOR METER

- CLEAR
- STRAW
- HONEY
- GOLD
- AMBER
- MAHOGANY
- BLACK

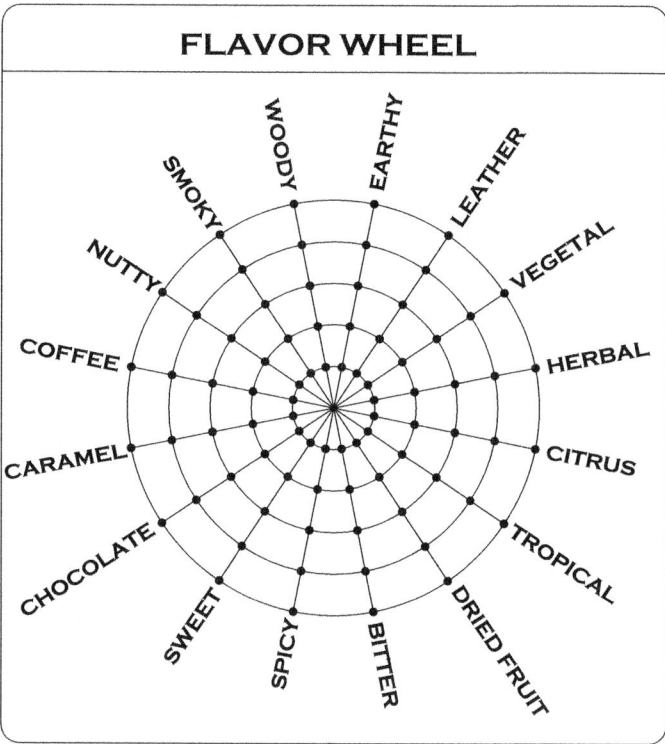

FLAVOR WHEEL

WOODY, EARTHY, LEATHER, VEGETAL, HERBAL, CITRUS, TROPICAL, DRIED FRUIT, BITTER, SPICY, SWEET, CHOCOLATE, CARAMEL, COFFEE, NUTTY, SMOKY

ADDITIONAL NOTES

FINAL RATING

- APPEARANCE ☆☆☆☆☆
- TASTE ☆☆☆☆☆
- MOUTHFEEL ☆☆☆☆☆
- OVERALL ☆☆☆☆☆

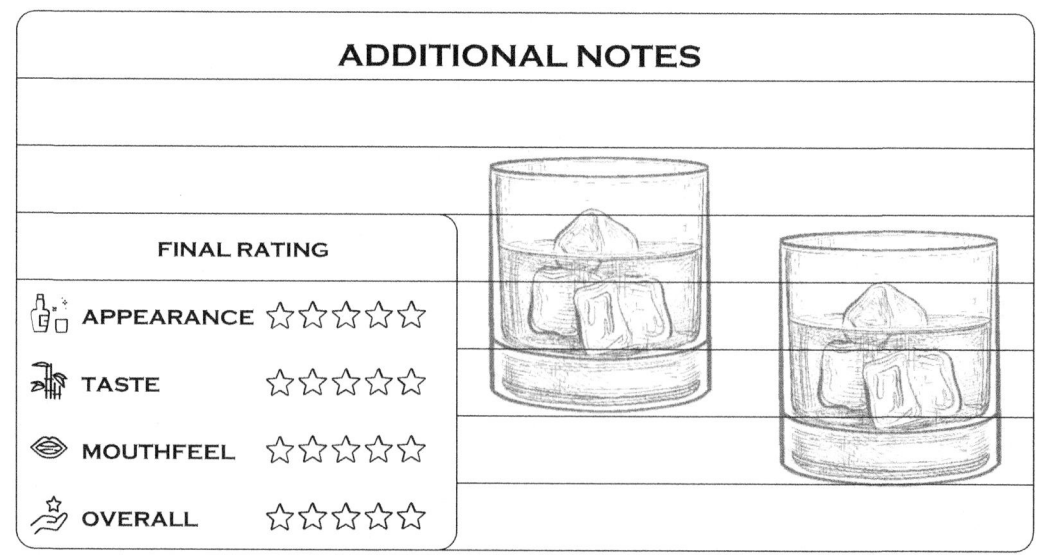

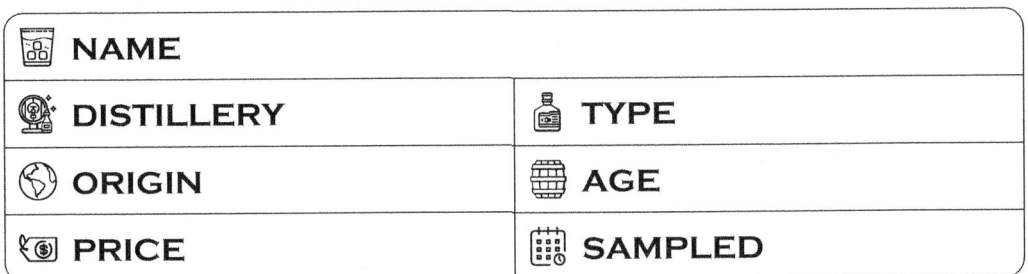

NAME	
DISTILLERY	TYPE
ORIGIN	AGE
PRICE	SAMPLED

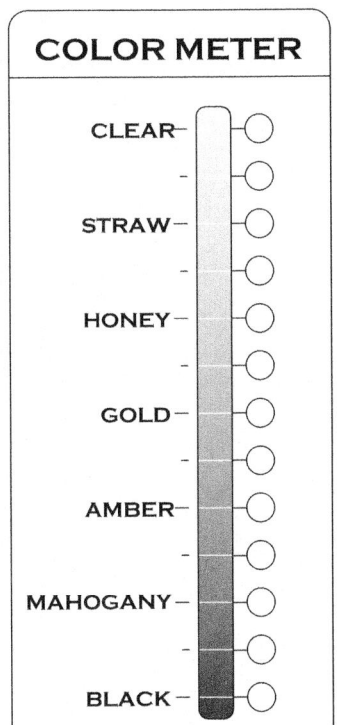

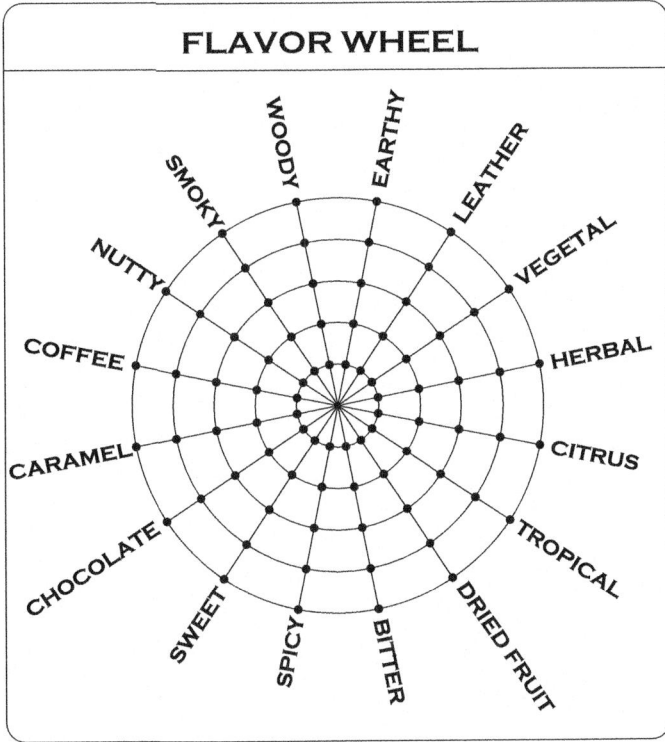

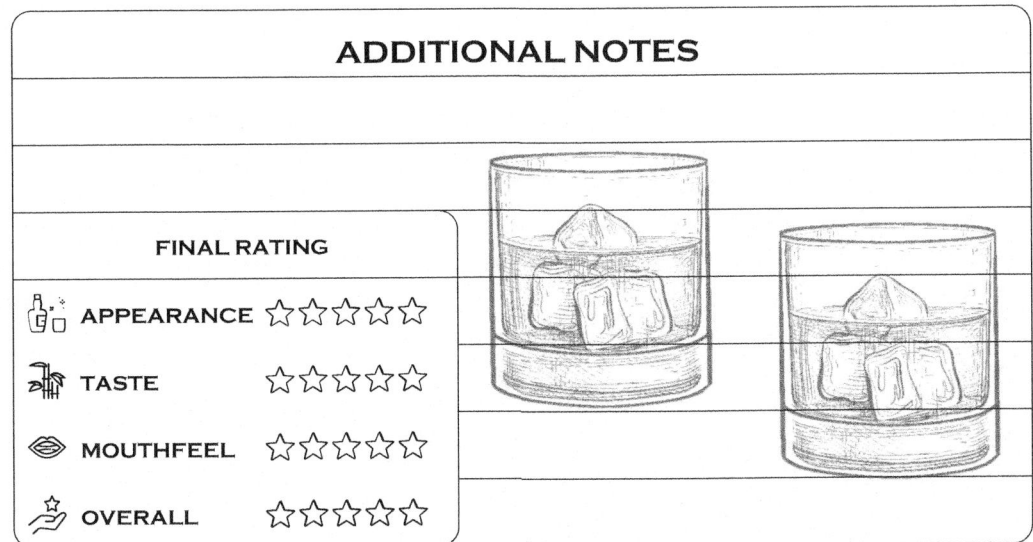

🥃 **NAME**			
🏭 **DISTILLERY**		🍾 **TYPE**	
🌐 **ORIGIN**		🛢 **AGE**	
💰 **PRICE**		📅 **SAMPLED**	

COLOR METER

- CLEAR
- STRAW
- HONEY
- GOLD
- AMBER
- MAHOGANY
- BLACK

FLAVOR WHEEL

SMOKY, WOODY, EARTHY, LEATHER, NUTTY, VEGETAL, COFFEE, HERBAL, CARAMEL, CITRUS, CHOCOLATE, TROPICAL, SWEET, SPICY, BITTER, DRIED FRUIT

ADDITIONAL NOTES

FINAL RATING

- 🍶 APPEARANCE ☆☆☆☆☆
- 🎋 TASTE ☆☆☆☆☆
- 👄 MOUTHFEEL ☆☆☆☆☆
- ✋ OVERALL ☆☆☆☆☆

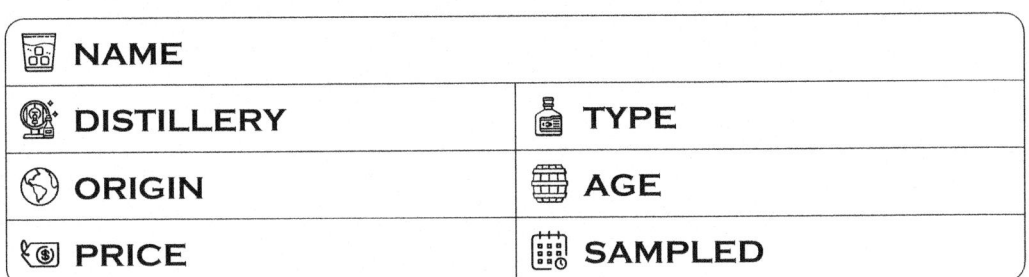

NAME	
DISTILLERY	TYPE
ORIGIN	AGE
PRICE	SAMPLED

COLOR METER

- CLEAR
- STRAW
- HONEY
- GOLD
- AMBER
- MAHOGANY
- BLACK

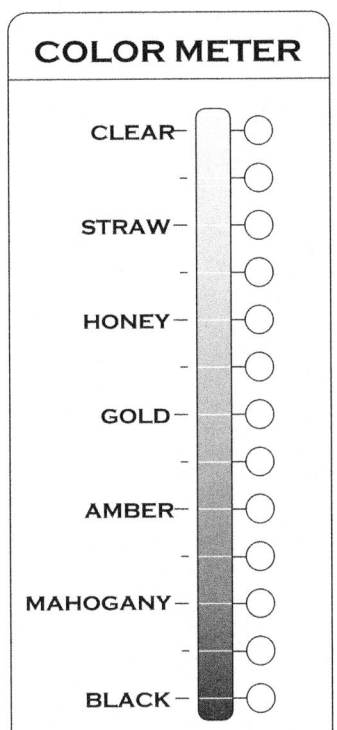

FLAVOR WHEEL

SMOKY, WOODY, EARTHY, LEATHER, VEGETAL, HERBAL, CITRUS, TROPICAL, DRIED FRUIT, BITTER, SPICY, SWEET, CHOCOLATE, CARAMEL, COFFEE, NUTTY

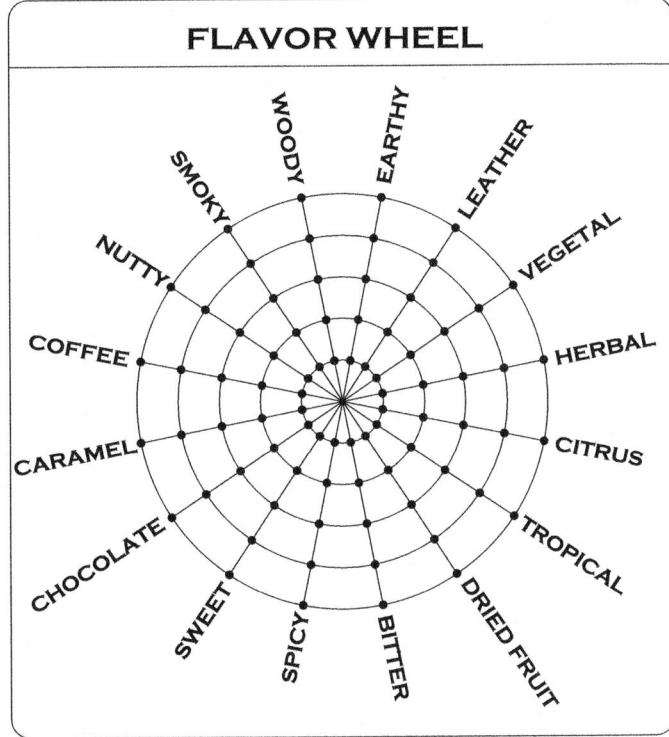

ADDITIONAL NOTES

FINAL RATING

- APPEARANCE ☆☆☆☆☆
- TASTE ☆☆☆☆☆
- MOUTHFEEL ☆☆☆☆☆
- OVERALL ☆☆☆☆☆

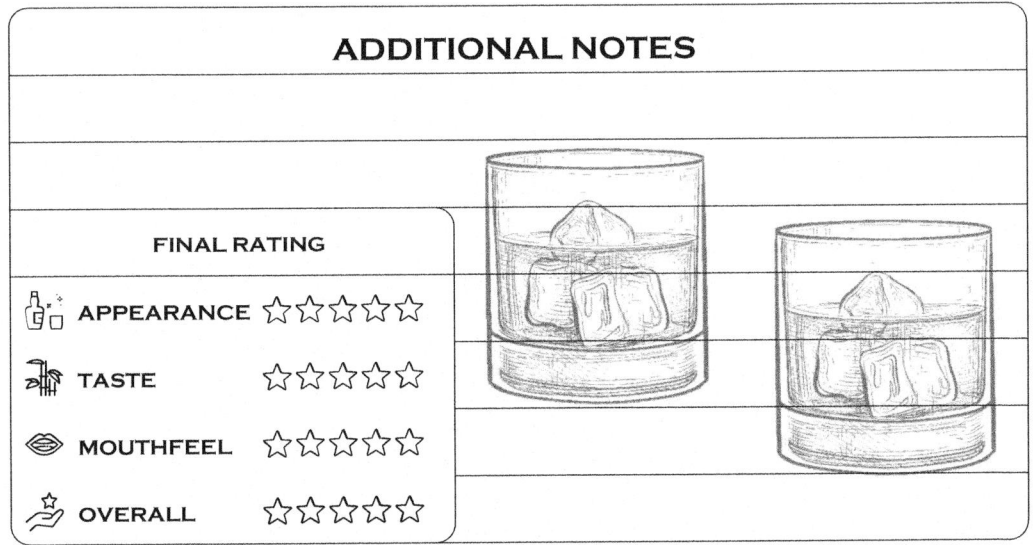

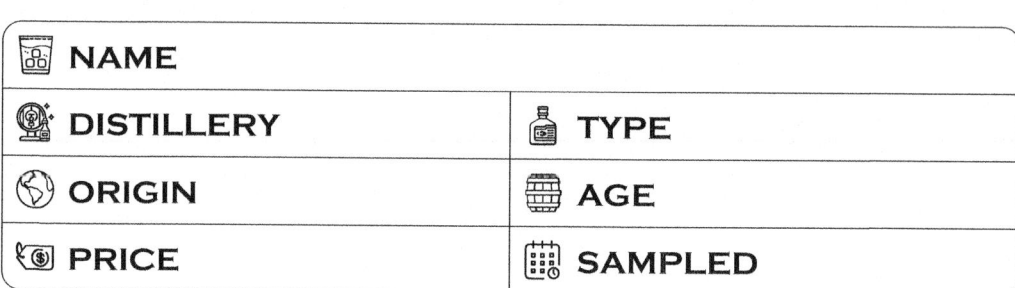

NAME	
DISTILLERY	TYPE
ORIGIN	AGE
PRICE	SAMPLED

COLOR METER

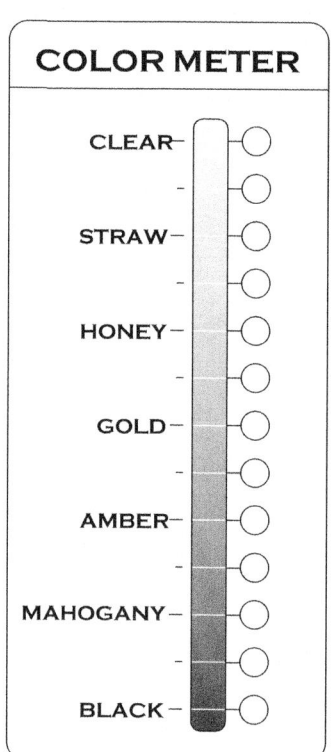

- CLEAR
- STRAW
- HONEY
- GOLD
- AMBER
- MAHOGANY
- BLACK

FLAVOR WHEEL

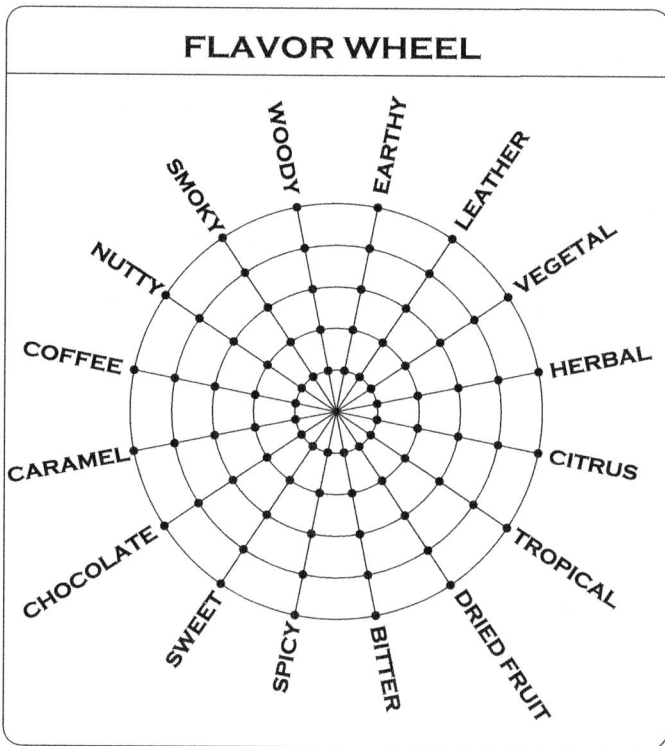

SMOKY, WOODY, EARTHY, LEATHER, NUTTY, VEGETAL, COFFEE, HERBAL, CARAMEL, CITRUS, CHOCOLATE, TROPICAL, SWEET, SPICY, BITTER, DRIED FRUIT

ADDITIONAL NOTES

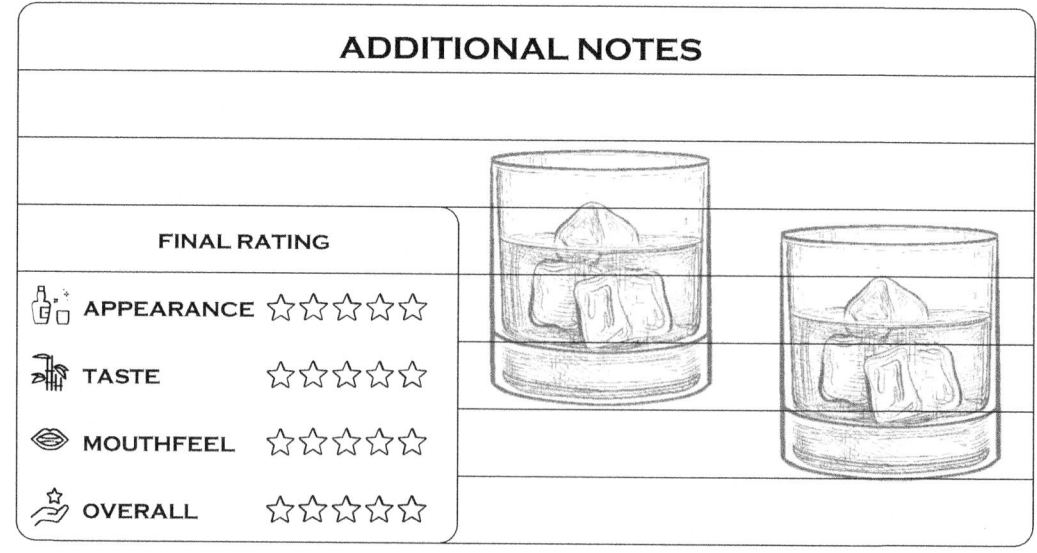

FINAL RATING

- APPEARANCE ☆☆☆☆☆
- TASTE ☆☆☆☆☆
- MOUTHFEEL ☆☆☆☆☆
- OVERALL ☆☆☆☆☆

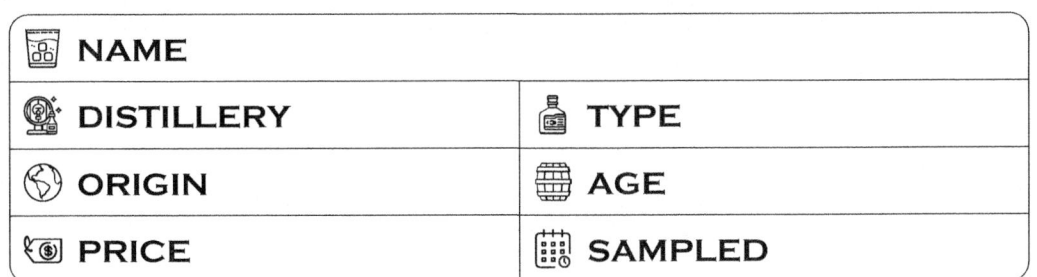

🥃 NAME	
🏭 DISTILLERY	🍾 TYPE
🌍 ORIGIN	🛢 AGE
💰 PRICE	📅 SAMPLED

COLOR METER

- CLEAR
- STRAW
- HONEY
- GOLD
- AMBER
- MAHOGANY
- BLACK

FLAVOR WHEEL

SMOKY, WOODY, EARTHY, LEATHER, VEGETAL, NUTTY, HERBAL, COFFEE, CITRUS, CARAMEL, TROPICAL, CHOCOLATE, DRIED FRUIT, SWEET, SPICY, BITTER

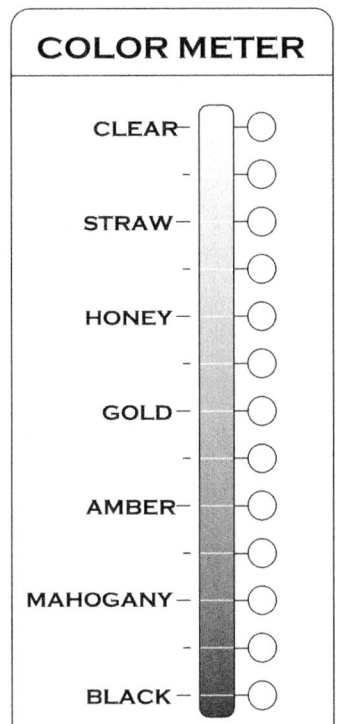
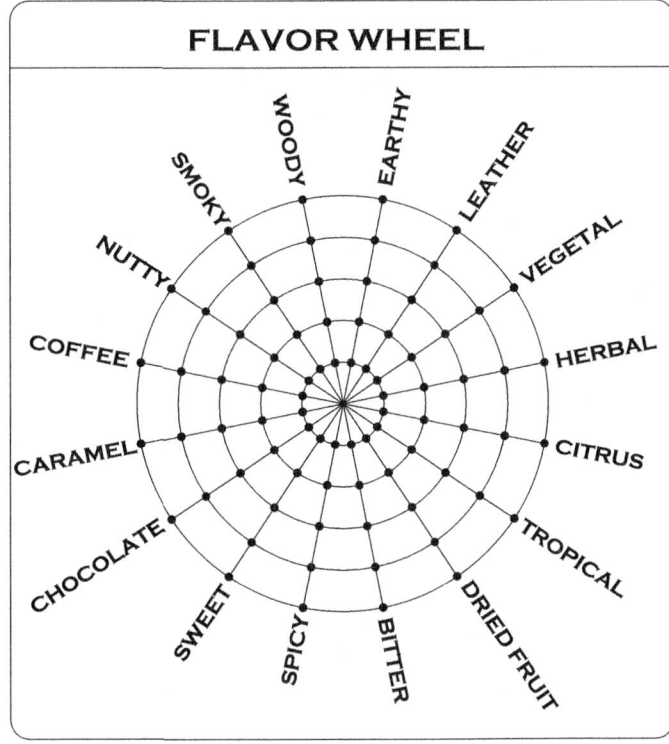

ADDITIONAL NOTES

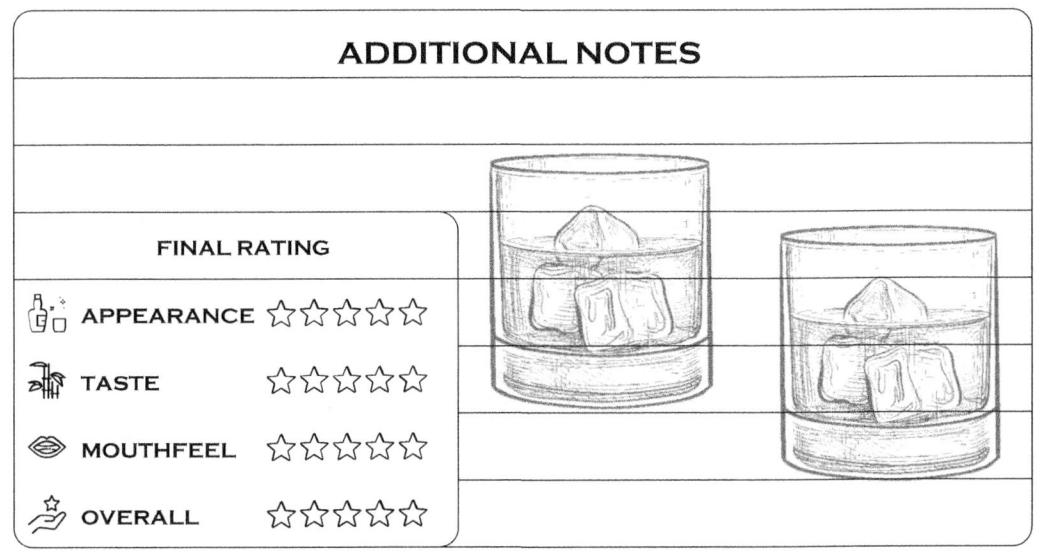

FINAL RATING

- 🥃 APPEARANCE ☆☆☆☆☆
- 🎋 TASTE ☆☆☆☆☆
- 👄 MOUTHFEEL ☆☆☆☆☆
- 🤲 OVERALL ☆☆☆☆☆

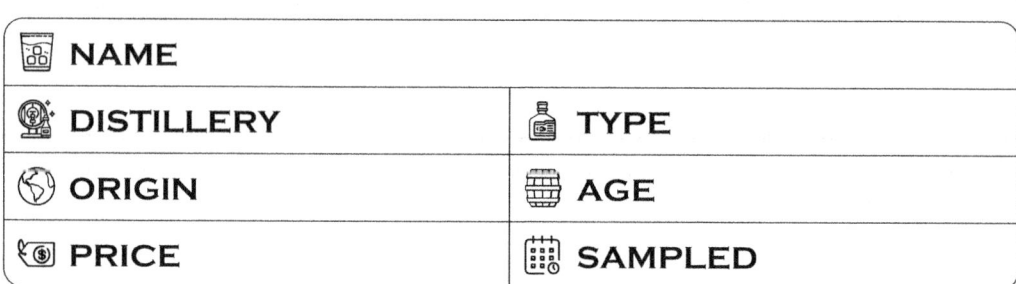

🥃 NAME	
🏭 DISTILLERY	🍾 TYPE
🌍 ORIGIN	🛢 AGE
💰 PRICE	📅 SAMPLED

COLOR METER

- CLEAR
- STRAW
- HONEY
- GOLD
- AMBER
- MAHOGANY
- BLACK

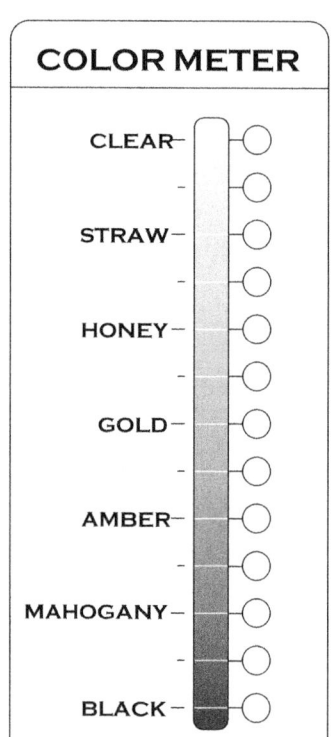

FLAVOR WHEEL

WOODY, EARTHY, LEATHER, VEGETAL, HERBAL, CITRUS, TROPICAL, DRIED FRUIT, BITTER, SPICY, SWEET, CHOCOLATE, CARAMEL, COFFEE, NUTTY, SMOKY

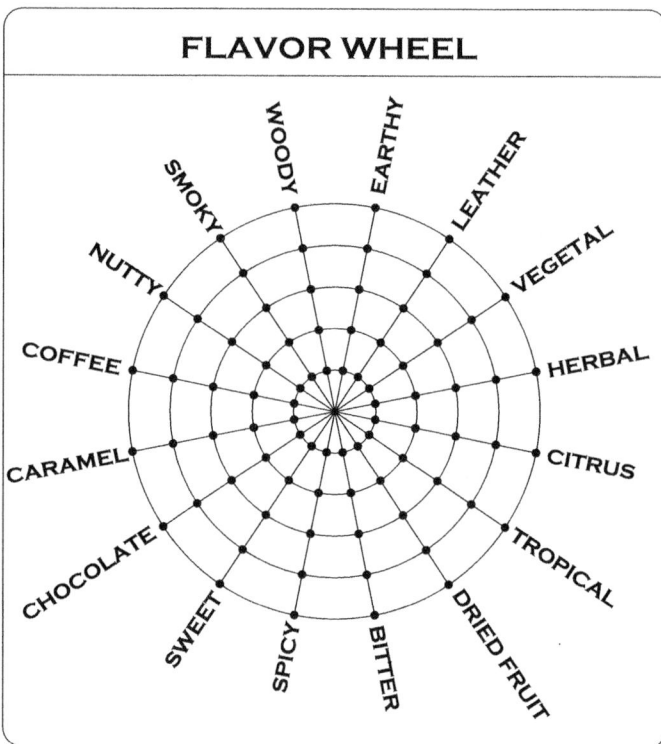

ADDITIONAL NOTES

FINAL RATING

- 🍾 APPEARANCE ☆☆☆☆☆
- 🥃 TASTE ☆☆☆☆☆
- 👄 MOUTHFEEL ☆☆☆☆☆
- ✋ OVERALL ☆☆☆☆☆

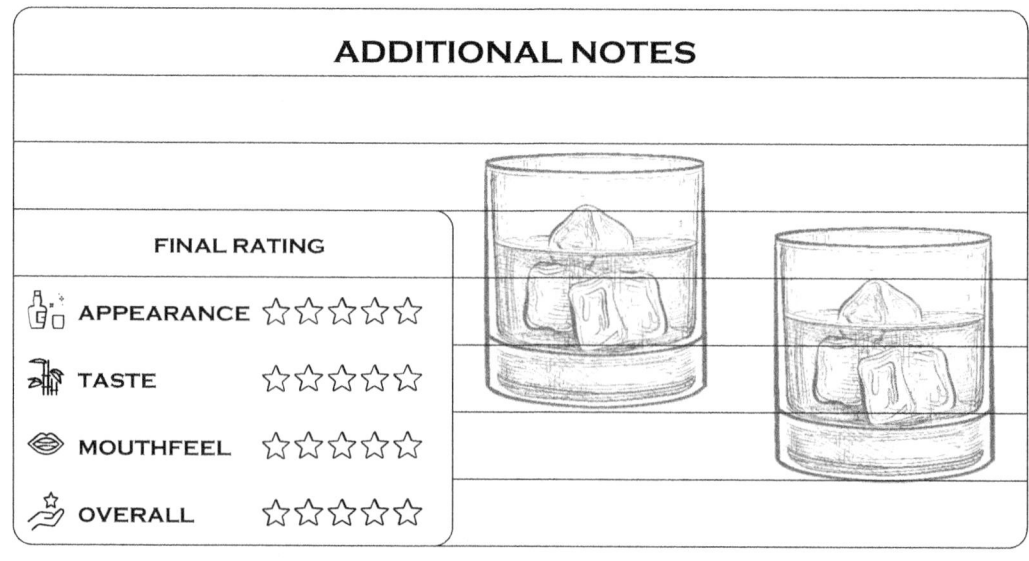

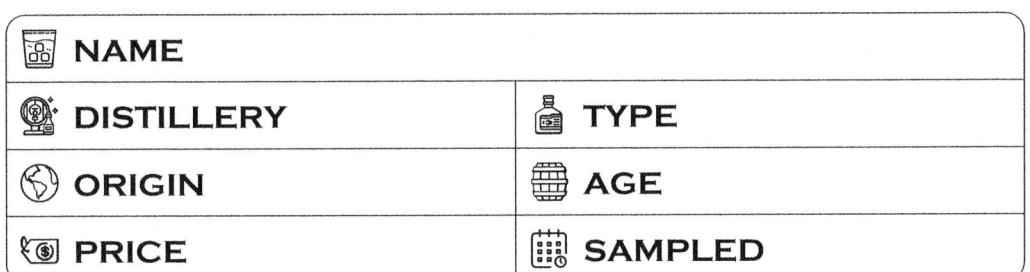

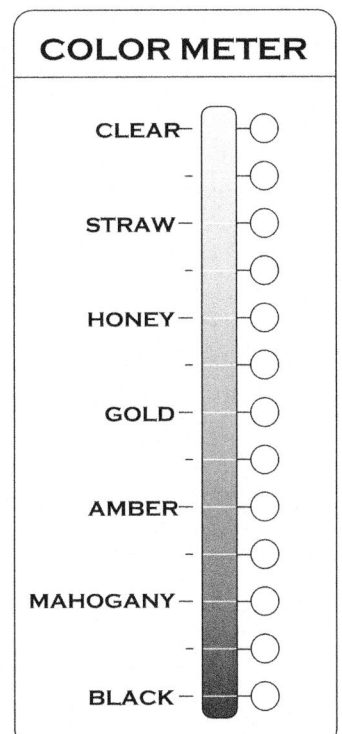

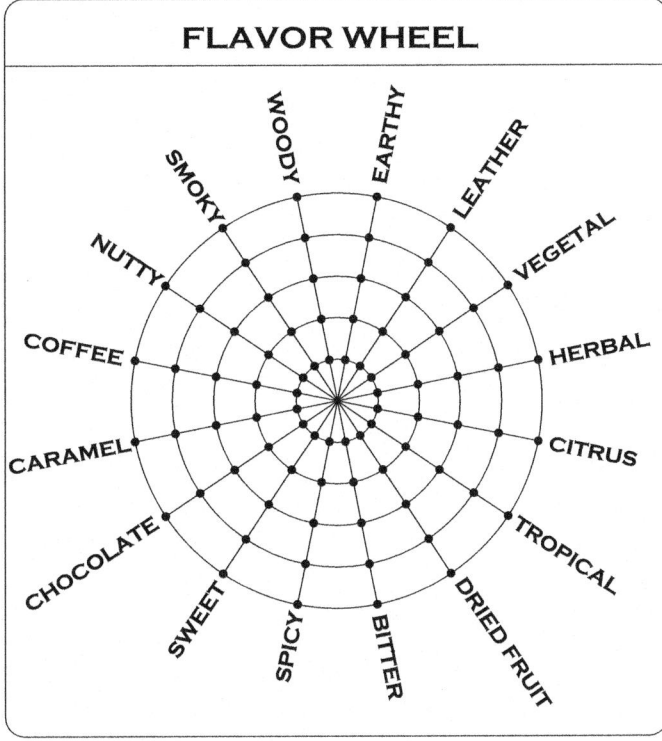

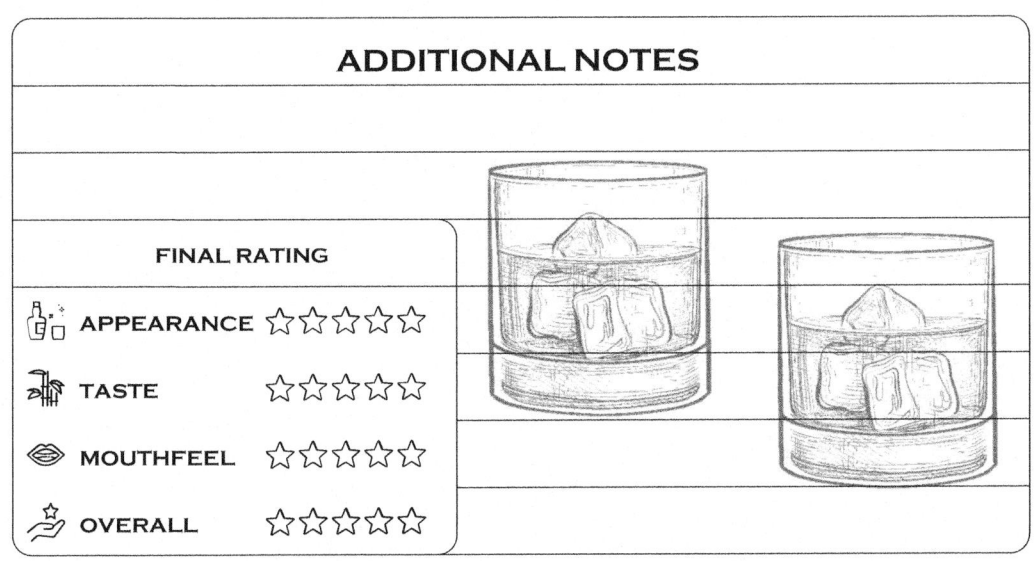

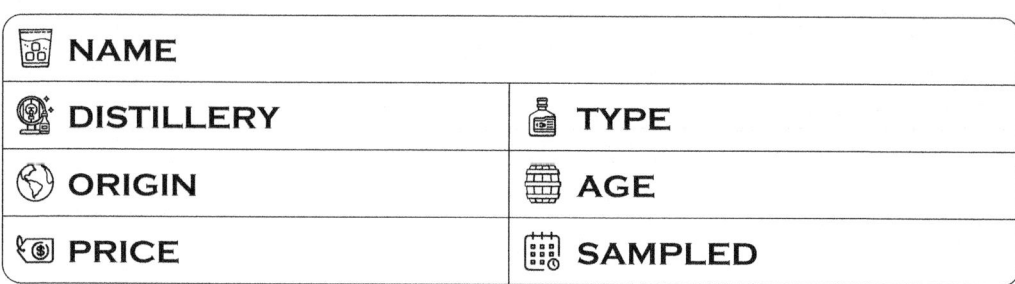

NAME	
DISTILLERY	TYPE
ORIGIN	AGE
PRICE	SAMPLED

COLOR METER

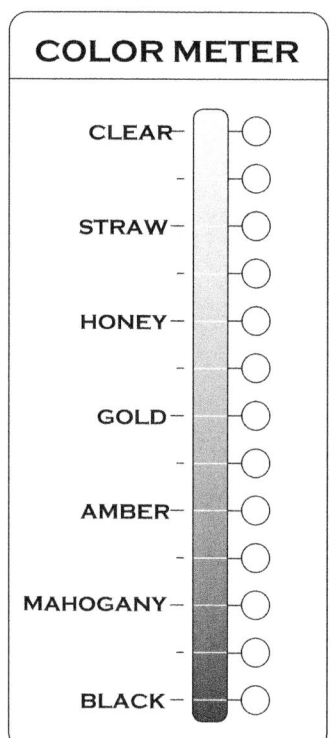

- CLEAR
- STRAW
- HONEY
- GOLD
- AMBER
- MAHOGANY
- BLACK

FLAVOR WHEEL

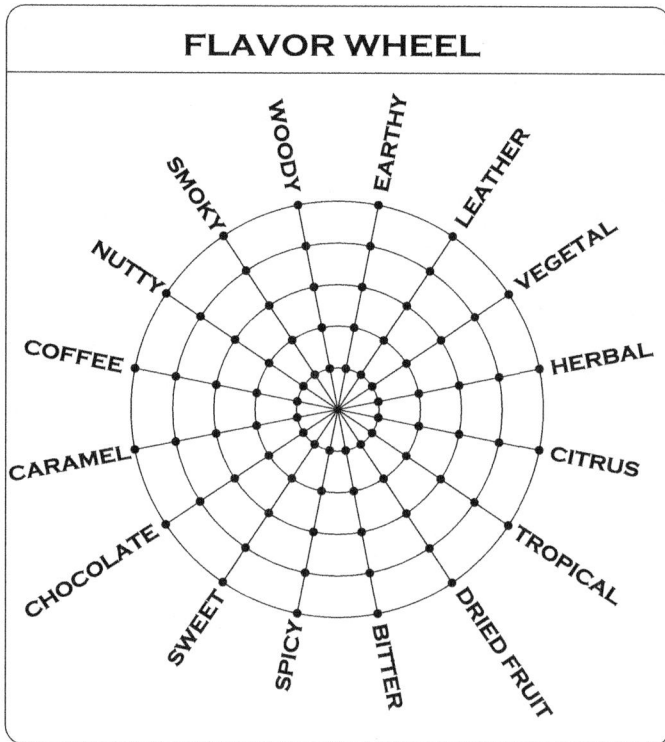

SMOKY · WOODY · EARTHY · LEATHER · VEGETAL · HERBAL · CITRUS · TROPICAL · DRIED FRUIT · BITTER · SPICY · SWEET · CHOCOLATE · CARAMEL · COFFEE · NUTTY

ADDITIONAL NOTES

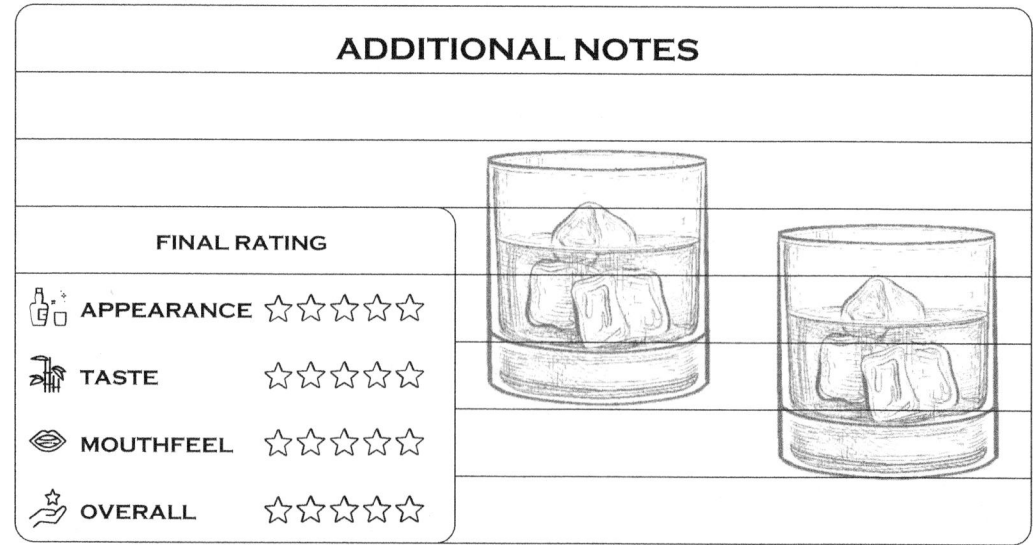

FINAL RATING

- APPEARANCE ☆☆☆☆☆
- TASTE ☆☆☆☆☆
- MOUTHFEEL ☆☆☆☆☆
- OVERALL ☆☆☆☆☆

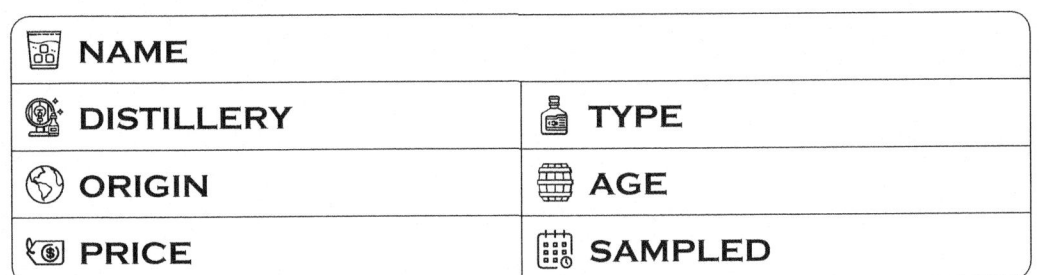

COLOR METER

- CLEAR
- STRAW
- HONEY
- GOLD
- AMBER
- MAHOGANY
- BLACK

FLAVOR WHEEL

WOODY, EARTHY, LEATHER, SMOKY, VEGETAL, NUTTY, HERBAL, COFFEE, CITRUS, CARAMEL, TROPICAL, CHOCOLATE, DRIED FRUIT, SWEET, SPICY, BITTER

ADDITIONAL NOTES

FINAL RATING

- APPEARANCE ☆☆☆☆☆
- TASTE ☆☆☆☆☆
- MOUTHFEEL ☆☆☆☆☆
- OVERALL ☆☆☆☆☆

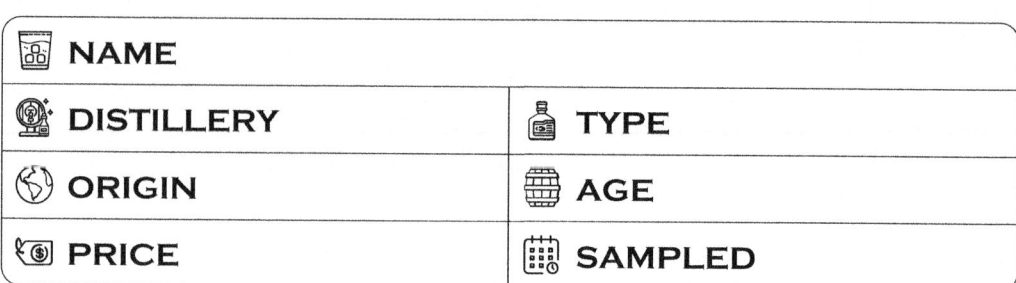

- NAME
- DISTILLERY
- ORIGIN
- PRICE
- TYPE
- AGE
- SAMPLED

COLOR METER

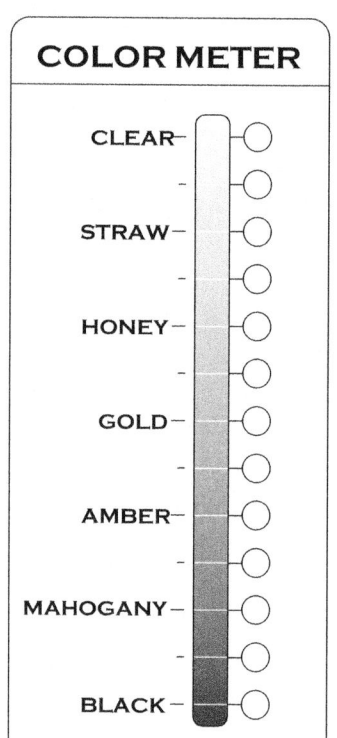

- CLEAR
- STRAW
- HONEY
- GOLD
- AMBER
- MAHOGANY
- BLACK

FLAVOR WHEEL

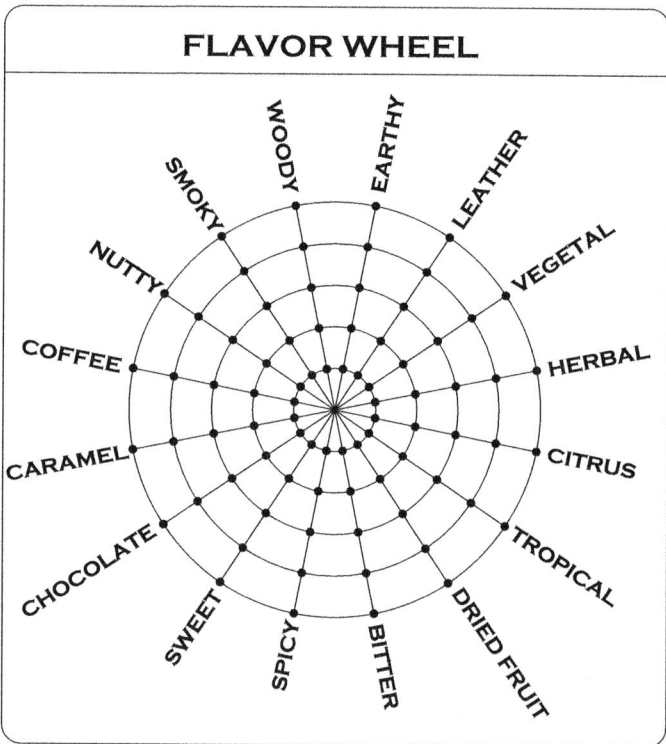

SMOKY, WOODY, EARTHY, LEATHER, NUTTY, VEGETAL, COFFEE, HERBAL, CARAMEL, CITRUS, CHOCOLATE, TROPICAL, SWEET, SPICY, BITTER, DRIED FRUIT

ADDITIONAL NOTES

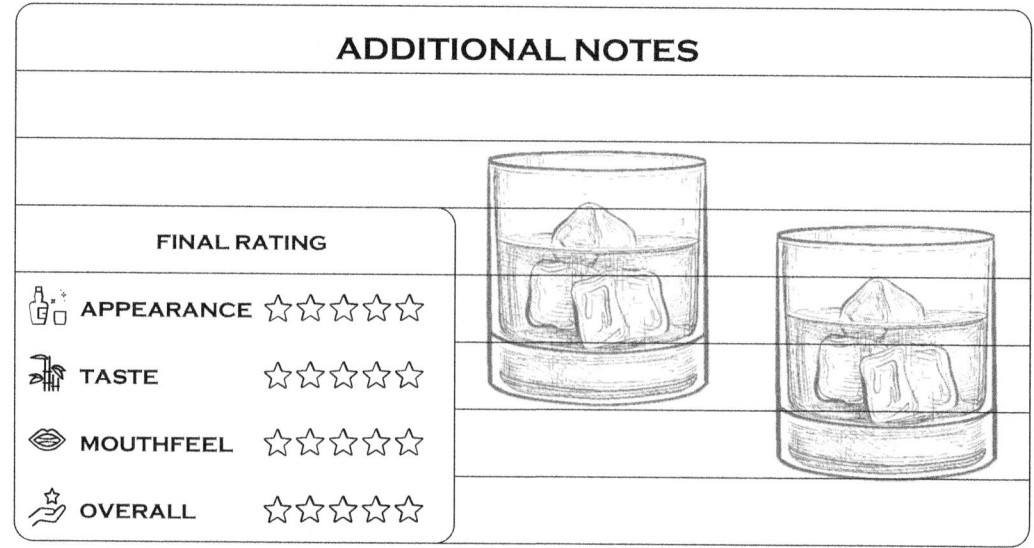

FINAL RATING

- APPEARANCE ☆☆☆☆☆
- TASTE ☆☆☆☆☆
- MOUTHFEEL ☆☆☆☆☆
- OVERALL ☆☆☆☆☆

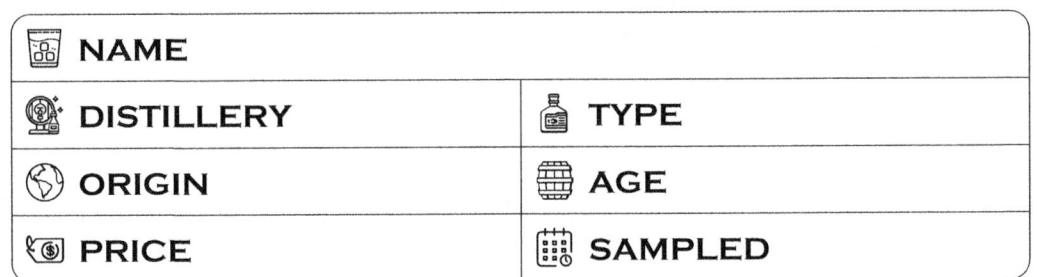

NAME
DISTILLERY
TYPE
ORIGIN
AGE
PRICE
SAMPLED

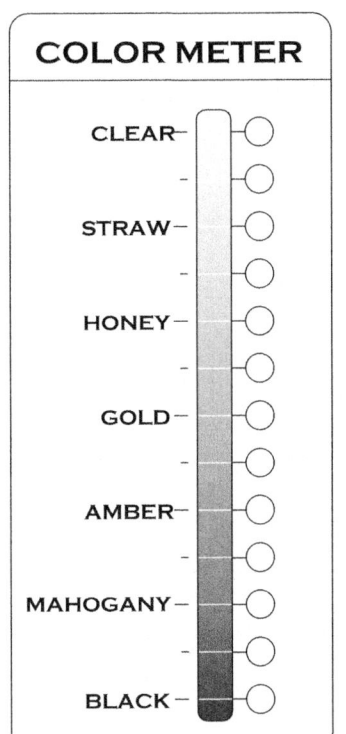

COLOR METER

- CLEAR
- STRAW
- HONEY
- GOLD
- AMBER
- MAHOGANY
- BLACK

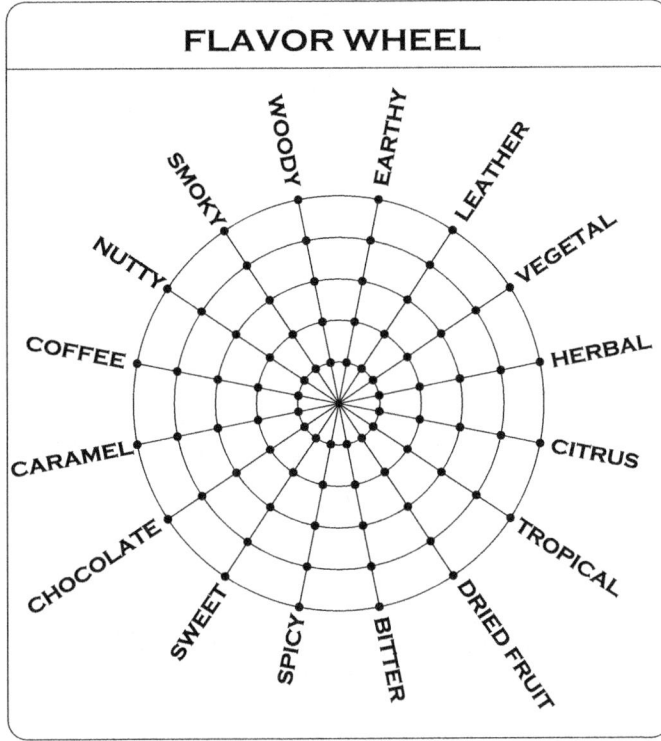

FLAVOR WHEEL

WOODY, EARTHY, LEATHER, VEGETAL, HERBAL, CITRUS, TROPICAL, DRIED FRUIT, BITTER, SPICY, SWEET, CHOCOLATE, CARAMEL, COFFEE, NUTTY, SMOKY

ADDITIONAL NOTES

FINAL RATING

- APPEARANCE ☆☆☆☆☆
- TASTE ☆☆☆☆☆
- MOUTHFEEL ☆☆☆☆☆
- OVERALL ☆☆☆☆☆

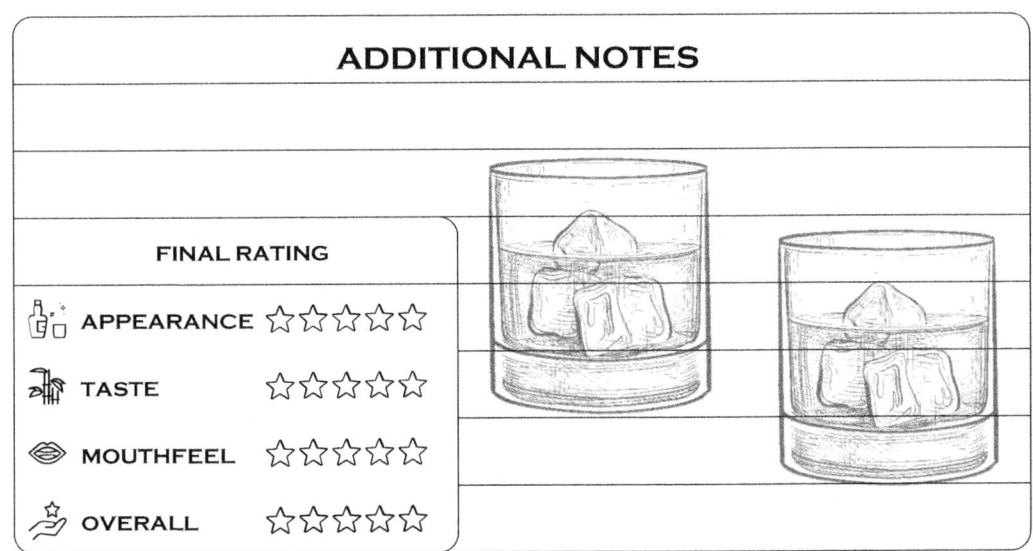

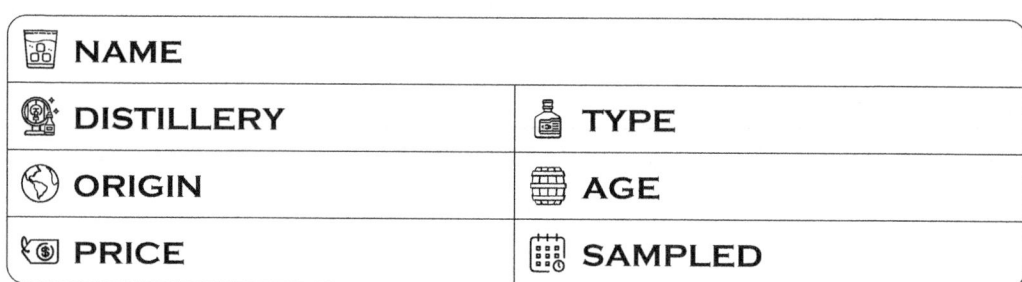

NAME
DISTILLERY
TYPE
ORIGIN
AGE
PRICE
SAMPLED

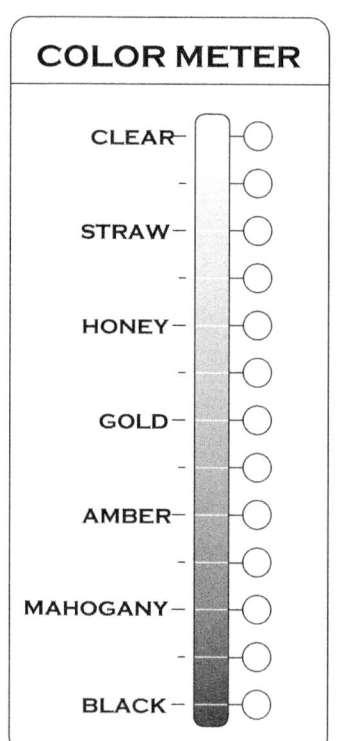

COLOR METER
- CLEAR
- STRAW
- HONEY
- GOLD
- AMBER
- MAHOGANY
- BLACK

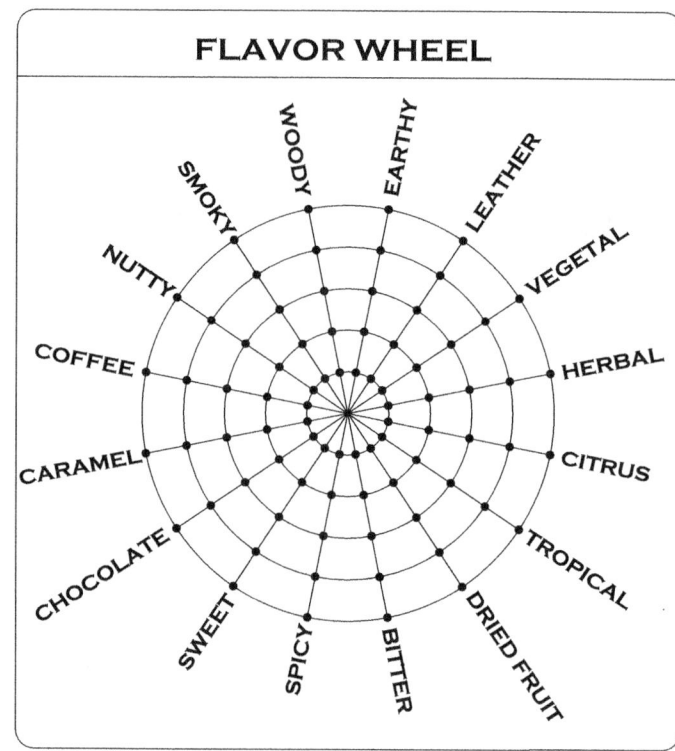

FLAVOR WHEEL
SMOKY, WOODY, EARTHY, LEATHER, NUTTY, VEGETAL, COFFEE, HERBAL, CARAMEL, CITRUS, CHOCOLATE, TROPICAL, SWEET, SPICY, BITTER, DRIED FRUIT

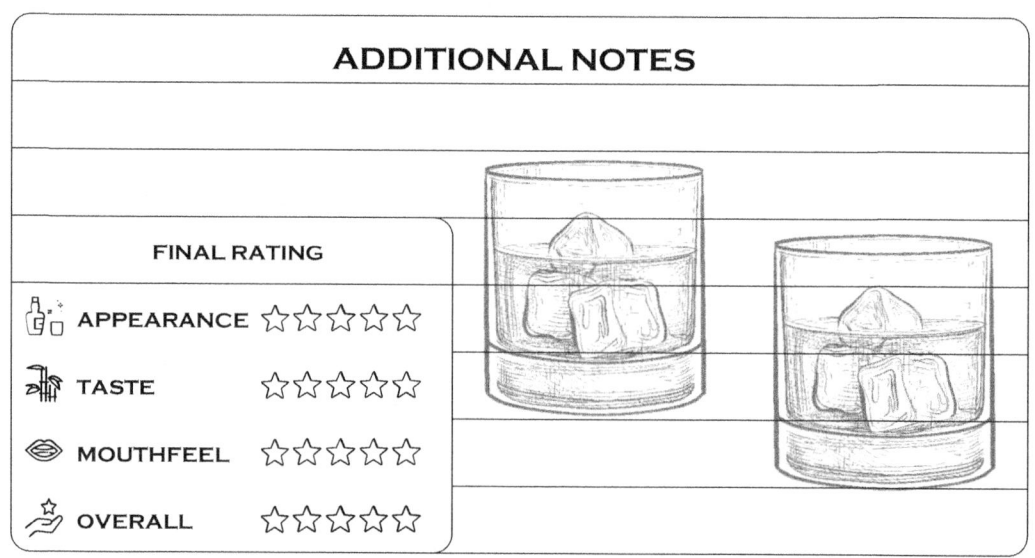

ADDITIONAL NOTES

FINAL RATING
- APPEARANCE ☆☆☆☆☆
- TASTE ☆☆☆☆☆
- MOUTHFEEL ☆☆☆☆☆
- OVERALL ☆☆☆☆☆

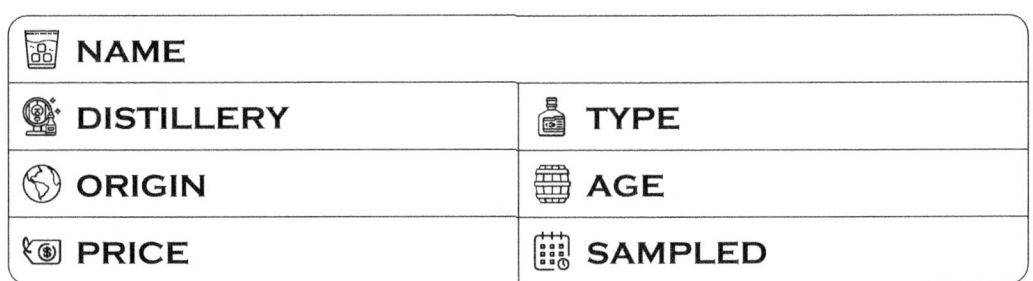

NAME	
DISTILLERY	TYPE
ORIGIN	AGE
PRICE	SAMPLED

COLOR METER

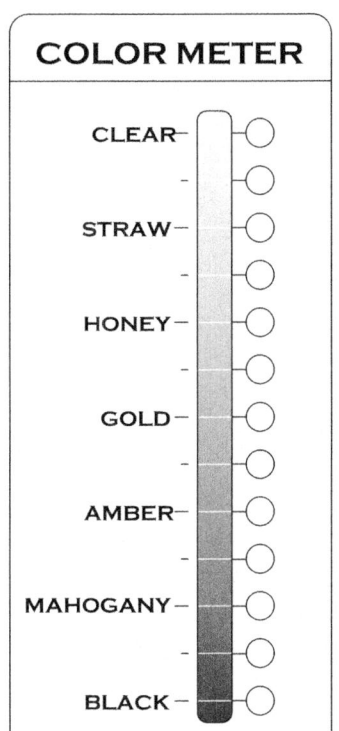

- CLEAR
- STRAW
- HONEY
- GOLD
- AMBER
- MAHOGANY
- BLACK

FLAVOR WHEEL

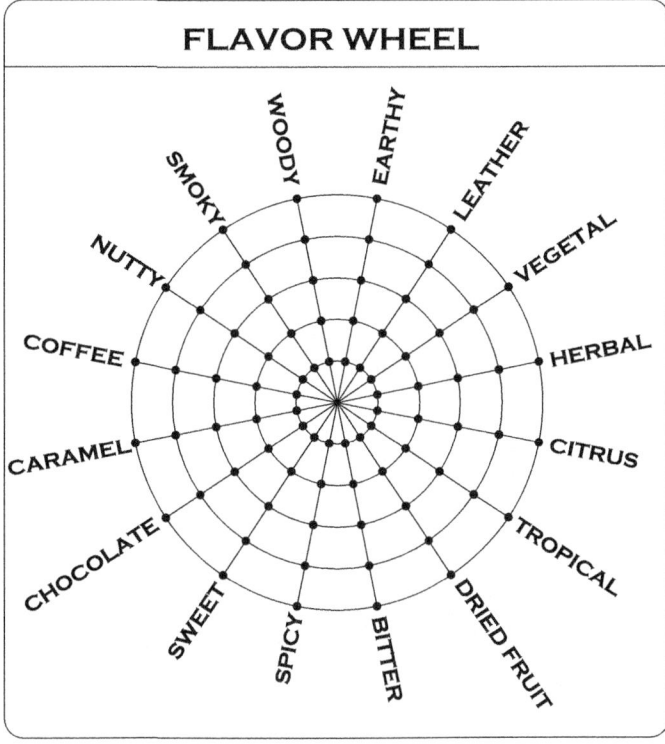

SMOKY, WOODY, EARTHY, LEATHER, NUTTY, VEGETAL, COFFEE, HERBAL, CARAMEL, CITRUS, CHOCOLATE, TROPICAL, SWEET, SPICY, BITTER, DRIED FRUIT

ADDITIONAL NOTES

FINAL RATING

- APPEARANCE ☆☆☆☆☆
- TASTE ☆☆☆☆☆
- MOUTHFEEL ☆☆☆☆☆
- OVERALL ☆☆☆☆☆

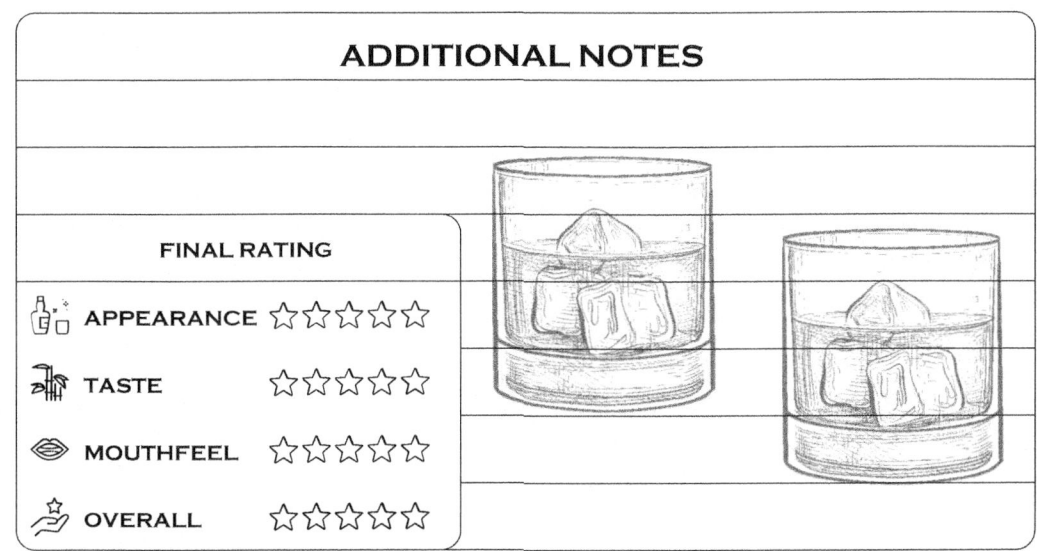

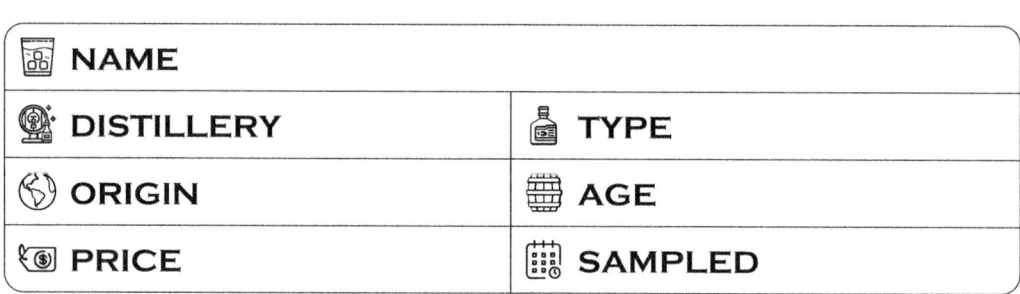

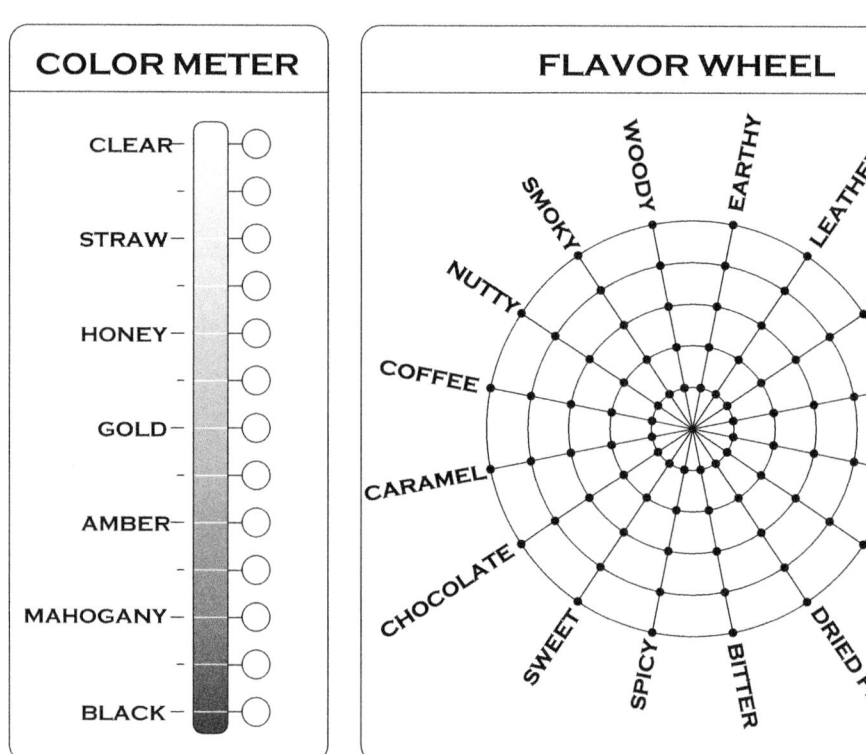

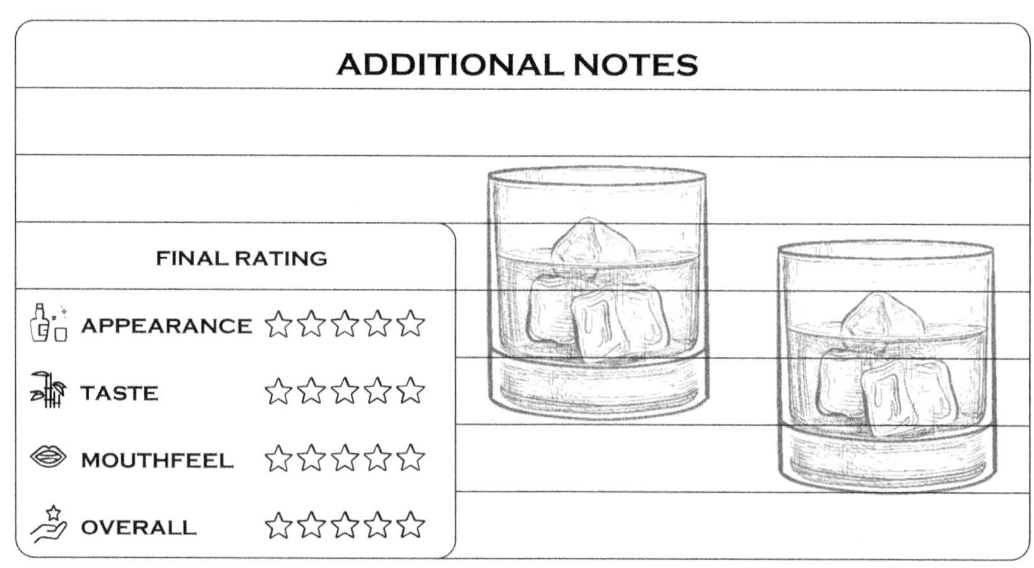

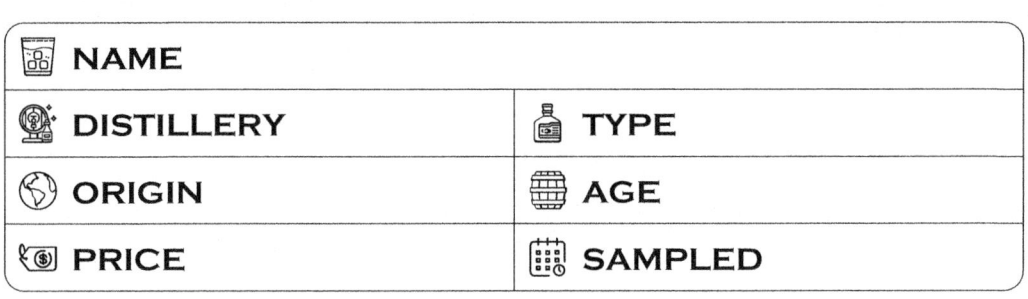

🥃 NAME		
🏭 DISTILLERY	🍾 TYPE	
🌍 ORIGIN	🛢 AGE	
💰 PRICE	📅 SAMPLED	

COLOR METER

- CLEAR
- STRAW
- HONEY
- GOLD
- AMBER
- MAHOGANY
- BLACK

FLAVOR WHEEL

WOODY, EARTHY, LEATHER, VEGETAL, HERBAL, CITRUS, TROPICAL, DRIED FRUIT, BITTER, SPICY, SWEET, CHOCOLATE, CARAMEL, COFFEE, NUTTY, SMOKY

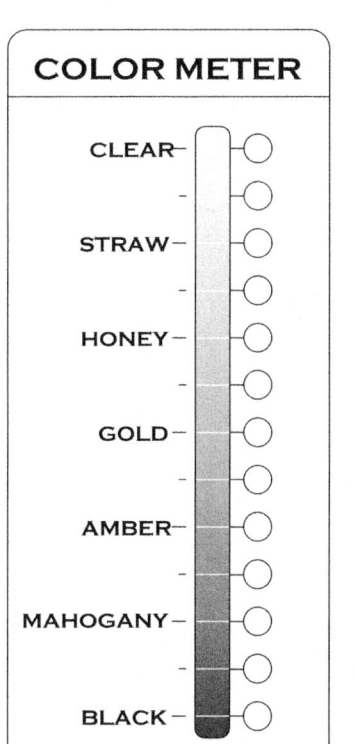
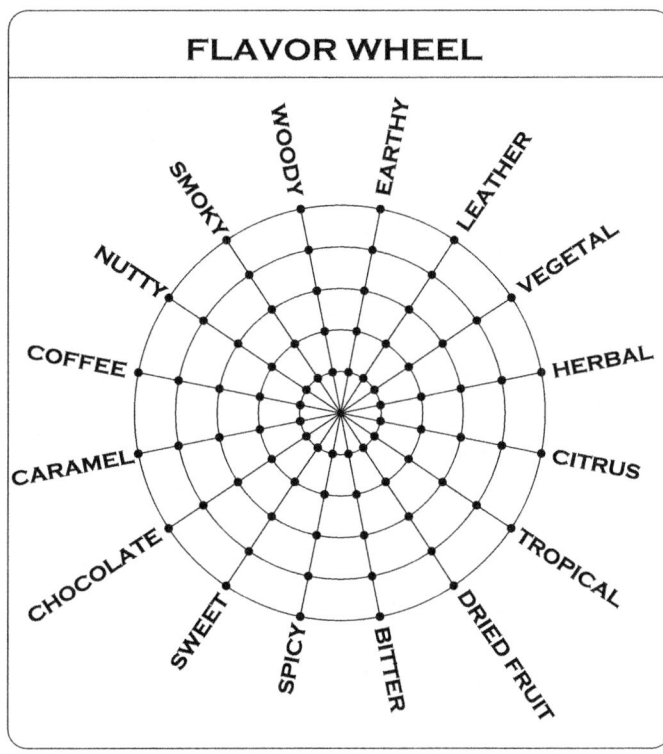

ADDITIONAL NOTES

FINAL RATING

- APPEARANCE ☆☆☆☆☆
- TASTE ☆☆☆☆☆
- MOUTHFEEL ☆☆☆☆☆
- OVERALL ☆☆☆☆☆

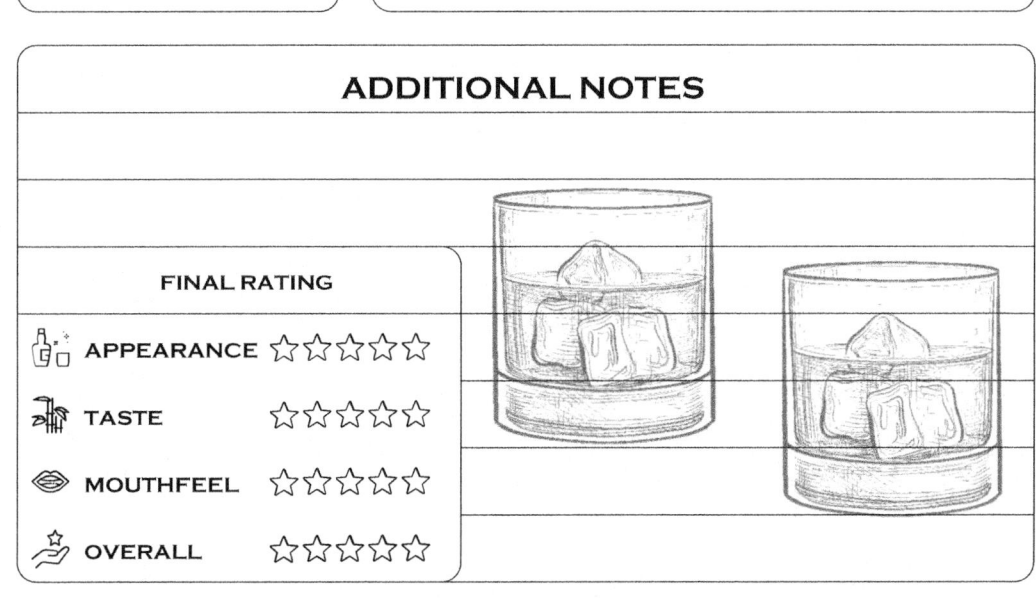

🥃 NAME	
🏭 DISTILLERY	🍾 TYPE
🌐 ORIGIN	🛢 AGE
💰 PRICE	📅 SAMPLED

COLOR METER

- CLEAR
- STRAW
- HONEY
- GOLD
- AMBER
- MAHOGANY
- BLACK

FLAVOR WHEEL

SMOKY, WOODY, EARTHY, LEATHER, NUTTY, VEGETAL, COFFEE, HERBAL, CARAMEL, CITRUS, CHOCOLATE, TROPICAL, SWEET, SPICY, BITTER, DRIED FRUIT

ADDITIONAL NOTES

FINAL RATING

- 🍶 APPEARANCE ☆☆☆☆☆
- 👅 TASTE ☆☆☆☆☆
- 👄 MOUTHFEEL ☆☆☆☆☆
- 👍 OVERALL ☆☆☆☆☆

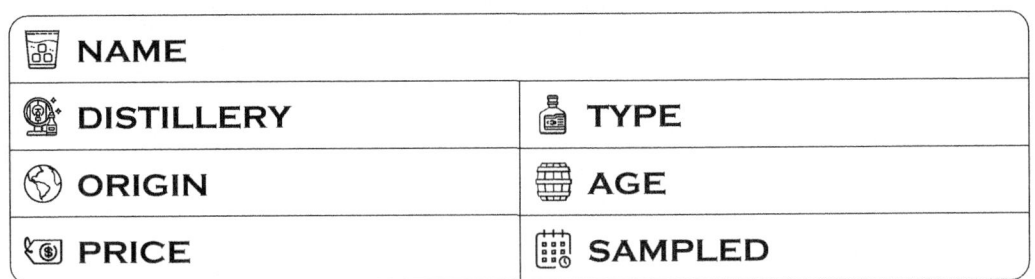

- NAME
- DISTILLERY
- TYPE
- ORIGIN
- AGE
- PRICE
- SAMPLED

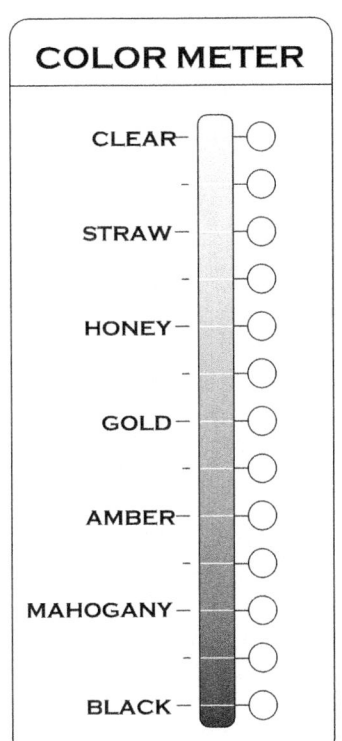

COLOR METER

- CLEAR
- STRAW
- HONEY
- GOLD
- AMBER
- MAHOGANY
- BLACK

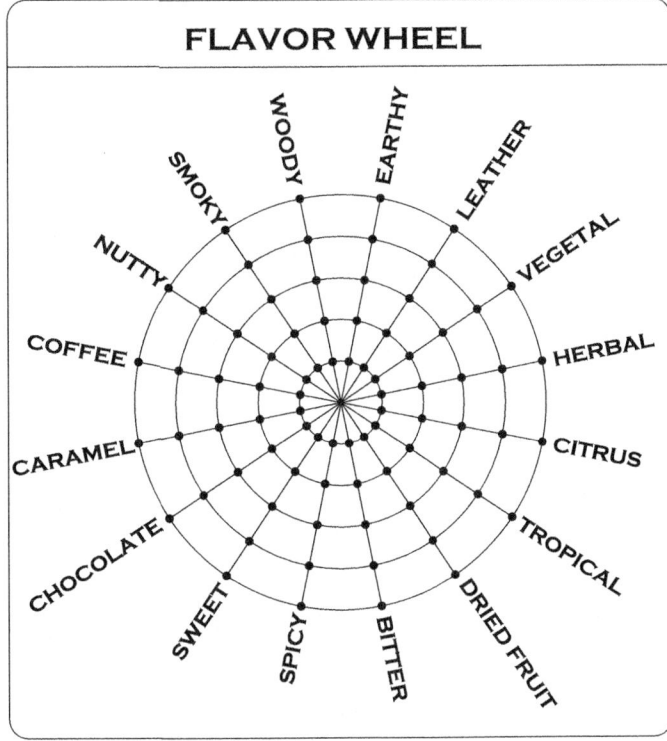

FLAVOR WHEEL

SMOKY, WOODY, EARTHY, LEATHER, VEGETAL, HERBAL, CITRUS, TROPICAL, DRIED FRUIT, BITTER, SPICY, SWEET, CHOCOLATE, CARAMEL, COFFEE, NUTTY

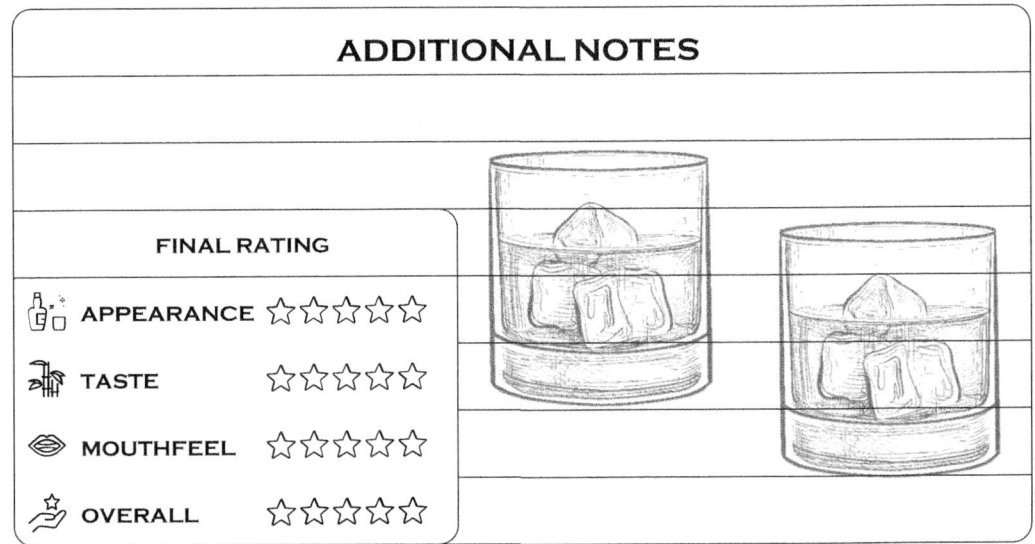

ADDITIONAL NOTES

FINAL RATING

- APPEARANCE ☆☆☆☆☆
- TASTE ☆☆☆☆☆
- MOUTHFEEL ☆☆☆☆☆
- OVERALL ☆☆☆☆☆

NAME

DISTILLERY	TYPE
ORIGIN	AGE
PRICE	SAMPLED

COLOR METER

- CLEAR
- STRAW
- HONEY
- GOLD
- AMBER
- MAHOGANY
- BLACK

FLAVOR WHEEL

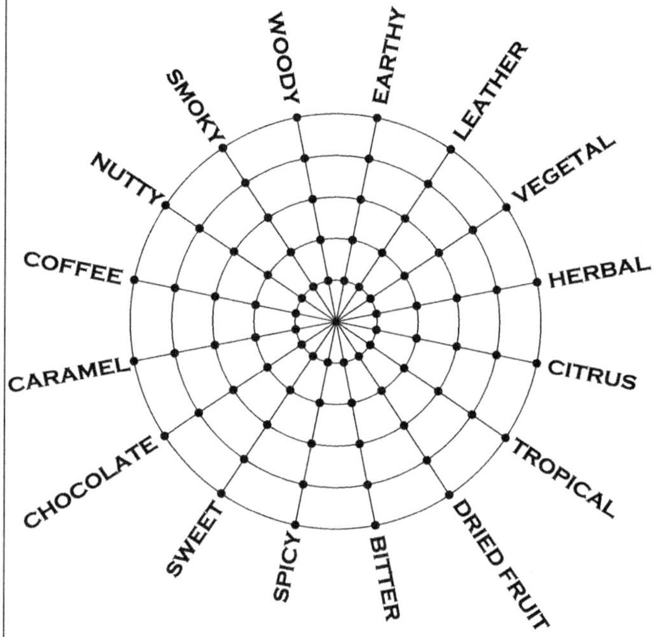

WOODY, EARTHY, LEATHER, VEGETAL, HERBAL, CITRUS, TROPICAL, DRIED FRUIT, BITTER, SPICY, SWEET, CHOCOLATE, CARAMEL, COFFEE, NUTTY, SMOKY

ADDITIONAL NOTES

FINAL RATING

- APPEARANCE ☆☆☆☆☆
- TASTE ☆☆☆☆☆
- MOUTHFEEL ☆☆☆☆☆
- OVERALL ☆☆☆☆☆

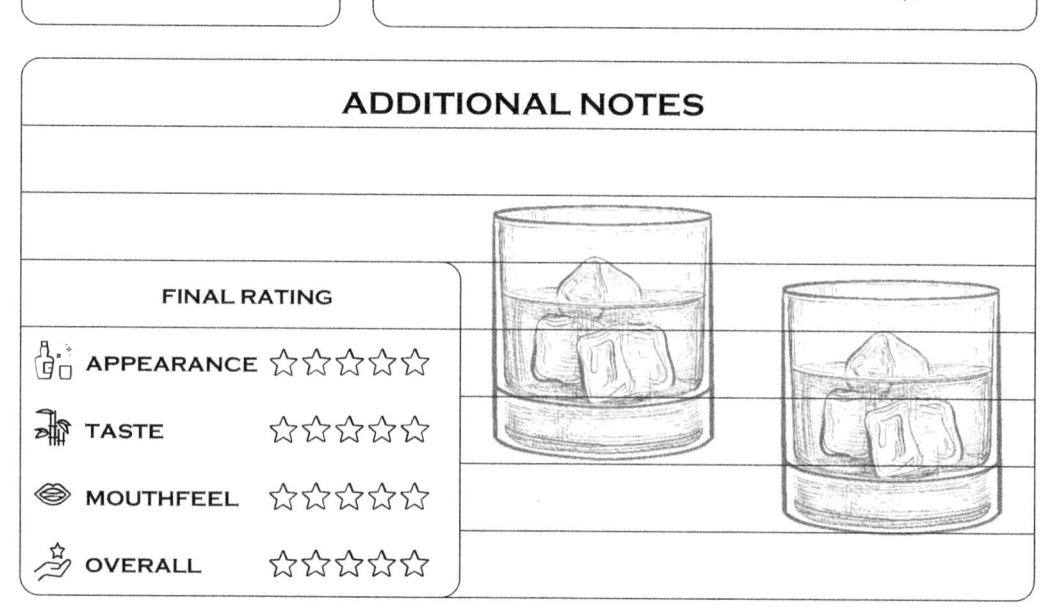

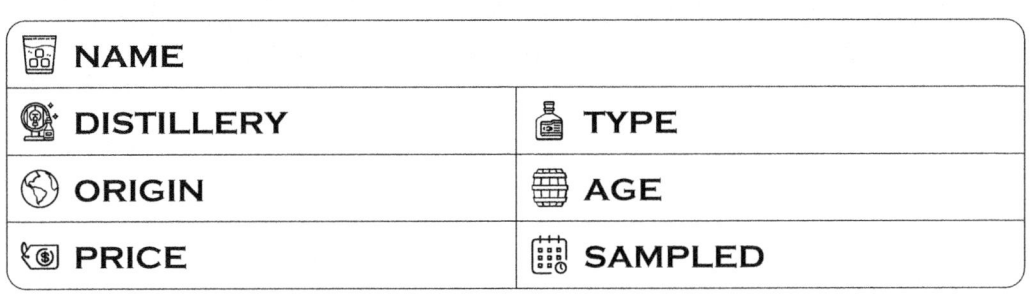

NAME	
DISTILLERY	TYPE
ORIGIN	AGE
PRICE	SAMPLED

COLOR METER

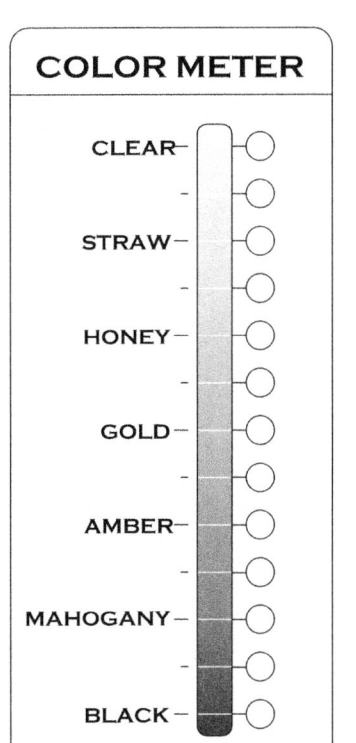

- CLEAR
- STRAW
- HONEY
- GOLD
- AMBER
- MAHOGANY
- BLACK

FLAVOR WHEEL

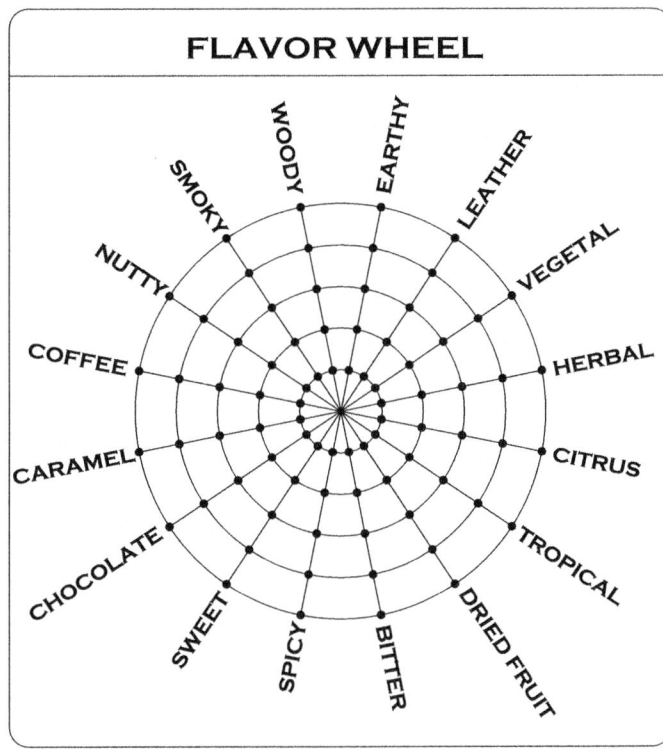

ADDITIONAL NOTES

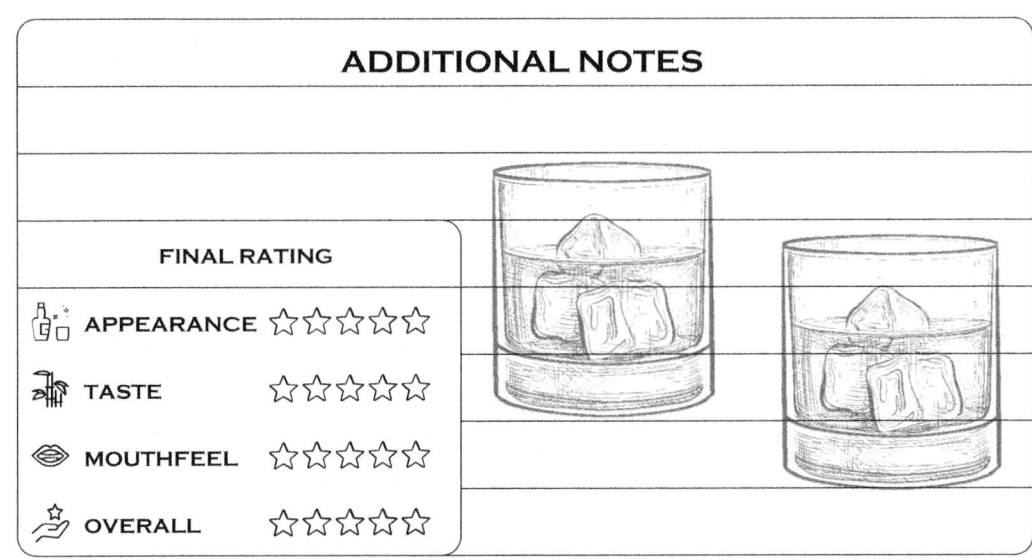

FINAL RATING

- APPEARANCE ☆☆☆☆☆
- TASTE ☆☆☆☆☆
- MOUTHFEEL ☆☆☆☆☆
- OVERALL ☆☆☆☆☆

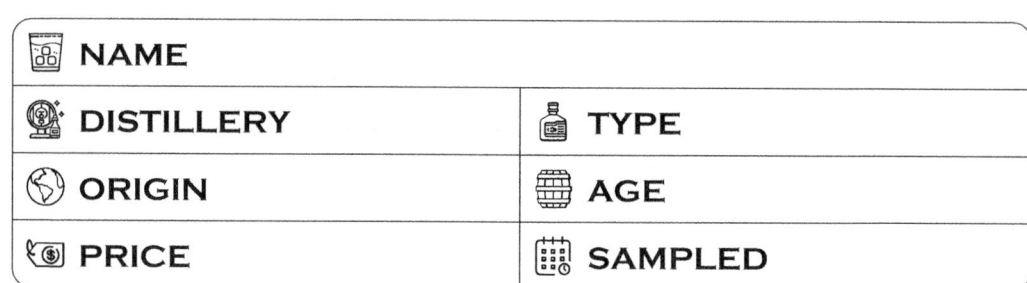

🥃 NAME			
🏭 DISTILLERY		🍾 TYPE	
🌍 ORIGIN		🛢 AGE	
💲 PRICE		📅 SAMPLED	

COLOR METER

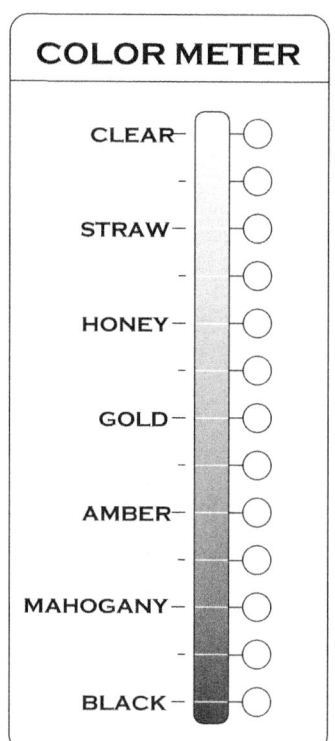

- CLEAR
- STRAW
- HONEY
- GOLD
- AMBER
- MAHOGANY
- BLACK

FLAVOR WHEEL

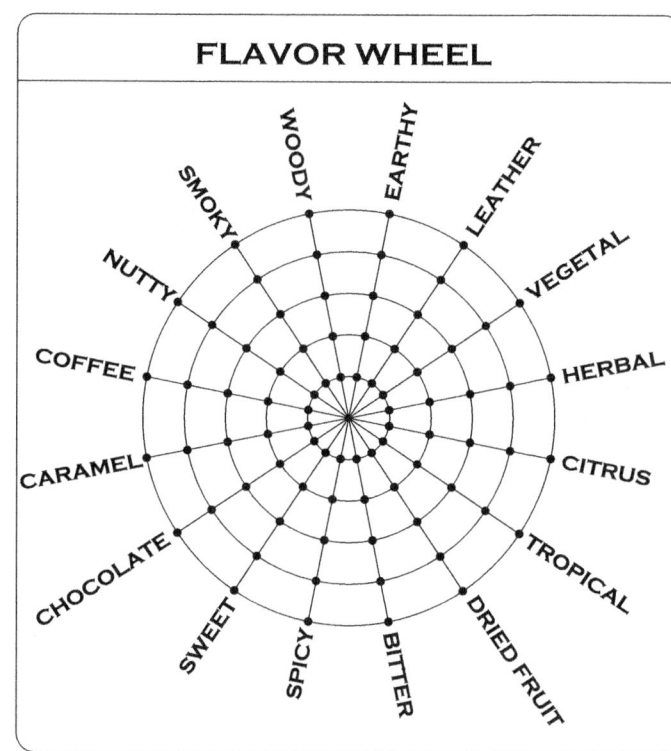

SMOKY · WOODY · EARTHY · LEATHER · NUTTY · VEGETAL · COFFEE · HERBAL · CARAMEL · CITRUS · CHOCOLATE · TROPICAL · SWEET · SPICY · BITTER · DRIED FRUIT

ADDITIONAL NOTES

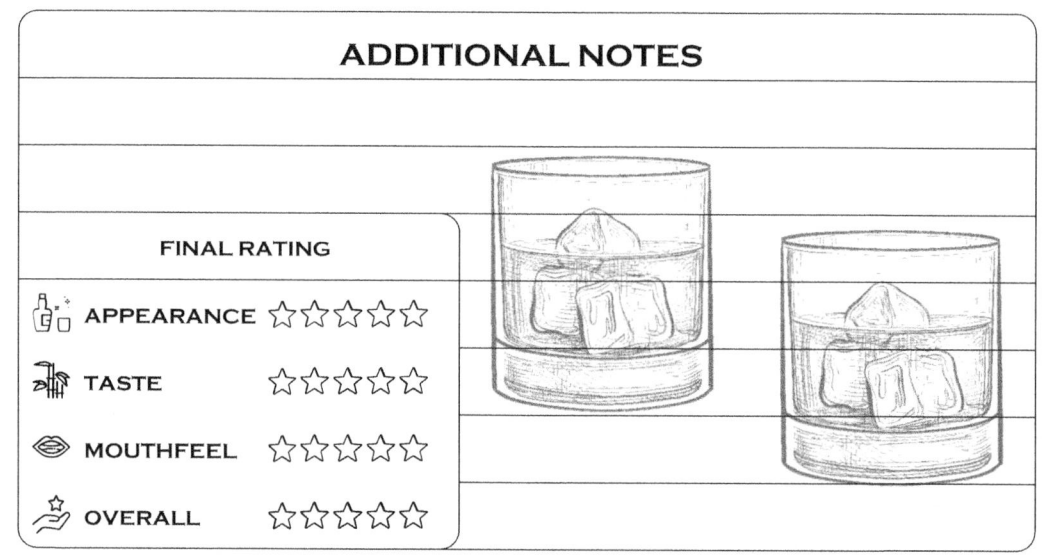

FINAL RATING

- 🍾 APPEARANCE ☆☆☆☆☆
- 👅 TASTE ☆☆☆☆☆
- 👄 MOUTHFEEL ☆☆☆☆☆
- 🌟 OVERALL ☆☆☆☆☆

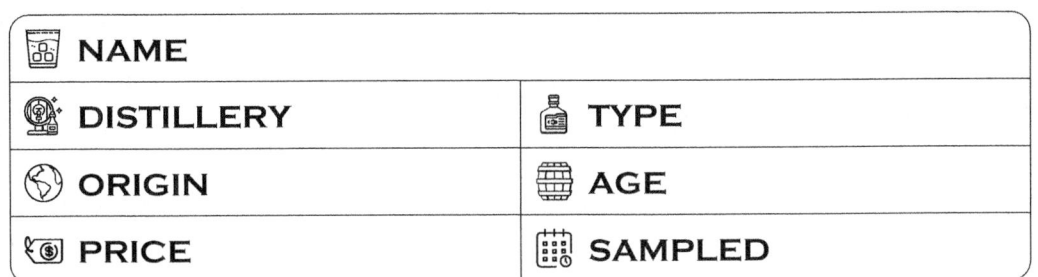

🥃 NAME	
🎛 DISTILLERY	🍾 TYPE
🌐 ORIGIN	🛢 AGE
💰 PRICE	📅 SAMPLED

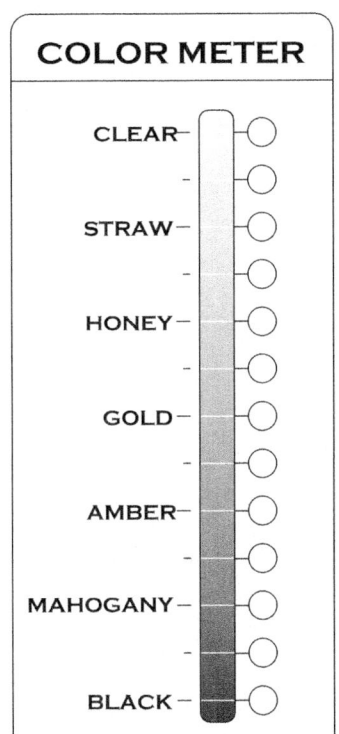

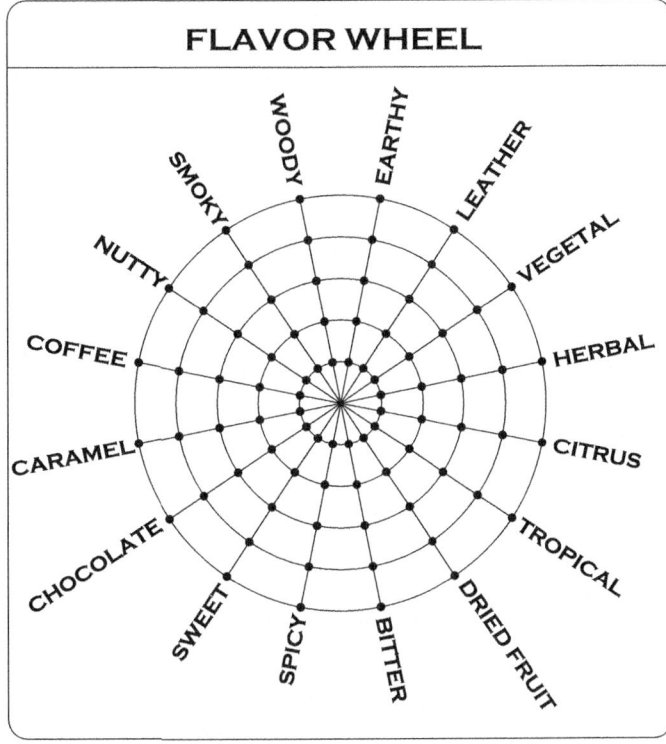

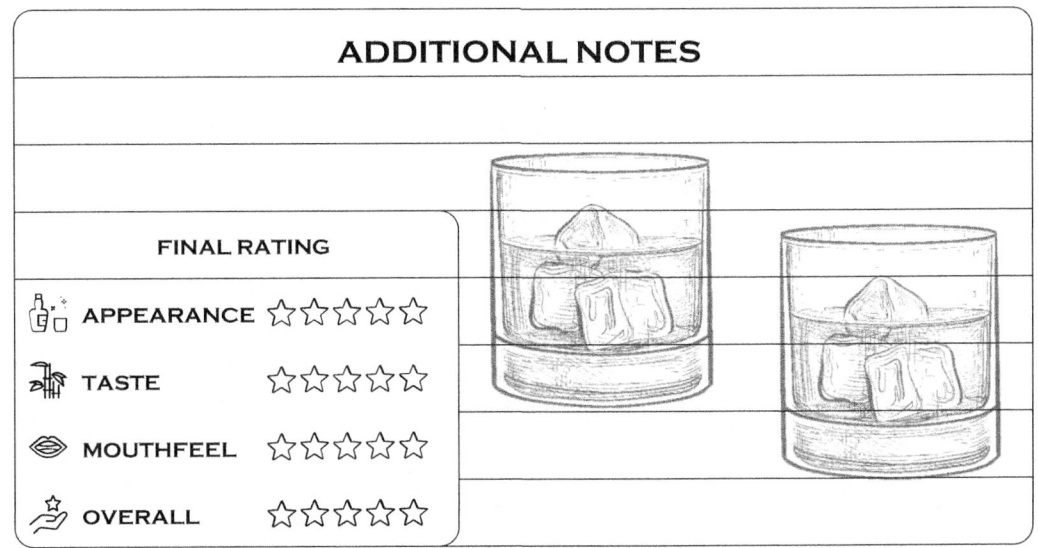

ADDITIONAL NOTES

FINAL RATING

- 🍾 APPEARANCE ☆☆☆☆☆
- 🥃 TASTE ☆☆☆☆☆
- 👄 MOUTHFEEL ☆☆☆☆☆
- 🤲 OVERALL ☆☆☆☆☆

NAME	
DISTILLERY	TYPE
ORIGIN	AGE
PRICE	SAMPLED

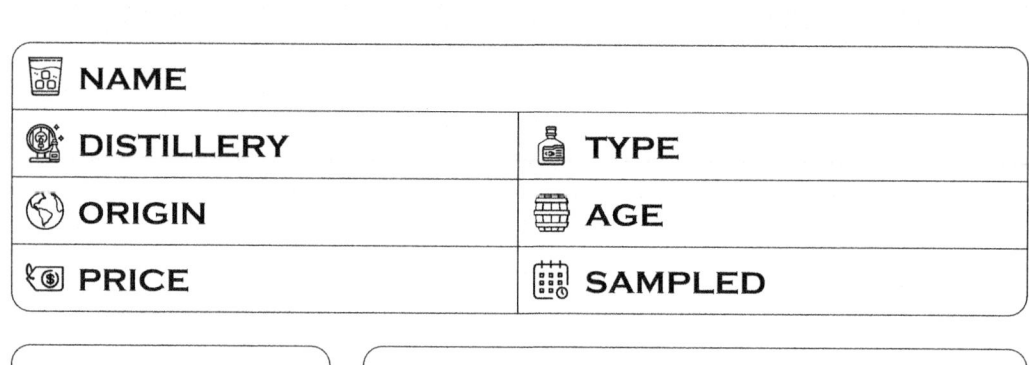

COLOR METER

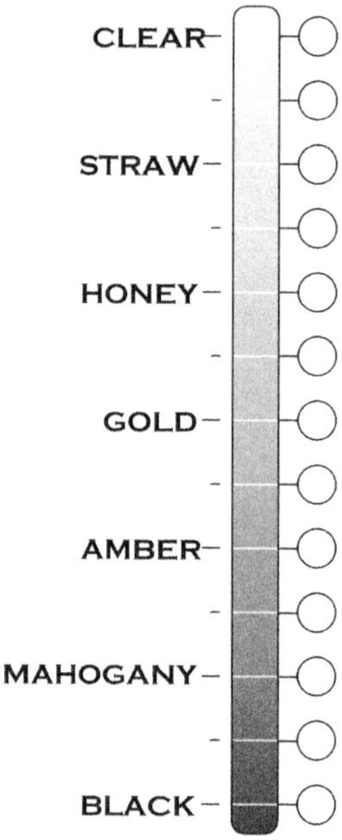

CLEAR
STRAW
HONEY
GOLD
AMBER
MAHOGANY
BLACK

FLAVOR WHEEL

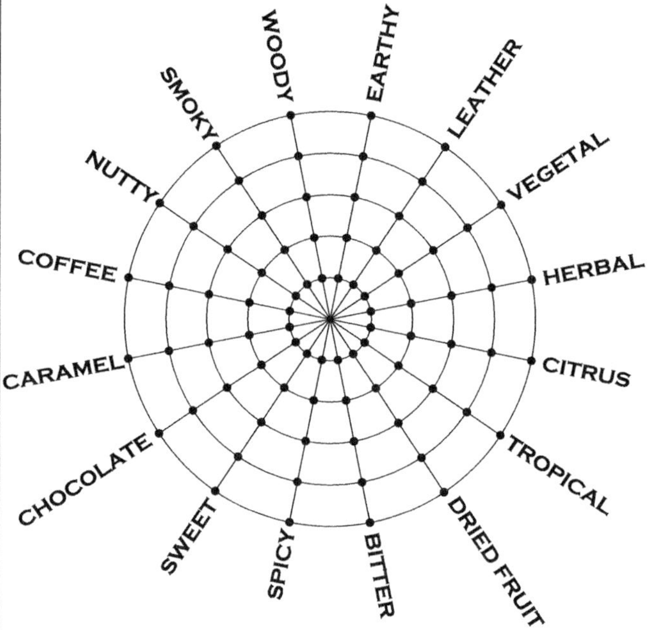

WOODY
EARTHY
LEATHER
VEGETAL
HERBAL
CITRUS
TROPICAL
DRIED FRUIT
BITTER
SPICY
SWEET
CHOCOLATE
CARAMEL
COFFEE
NUTTY
SMOKY

ADDITIONAL NOTES

FINAL RATING

APPEARANCE	☆☆☆☆☆
TASTE	☆☆☆☆☆
MOUTHFEEL	☆☆☆☆☆
OVERALL	☆☆☆☆☆

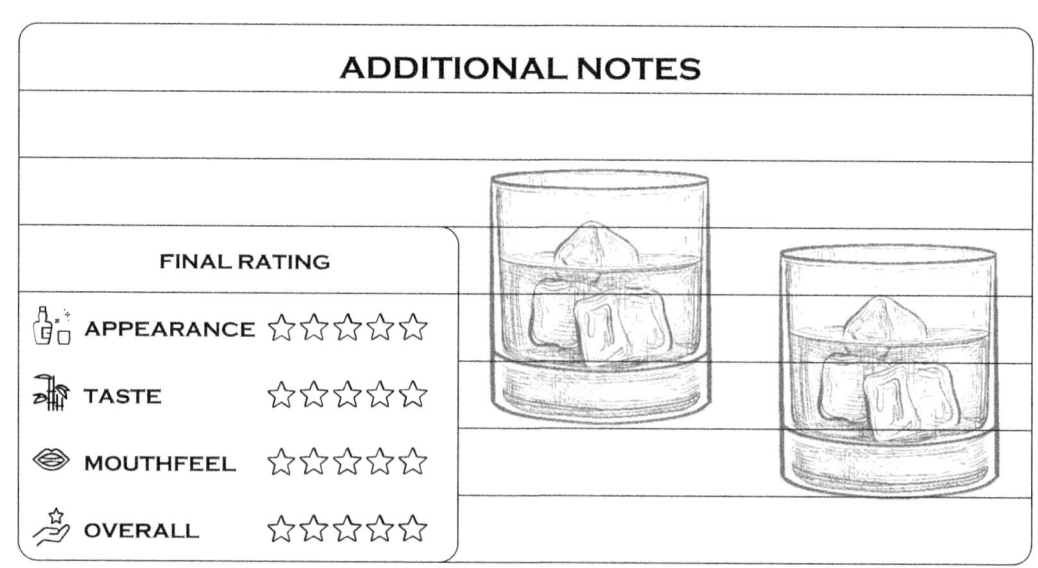

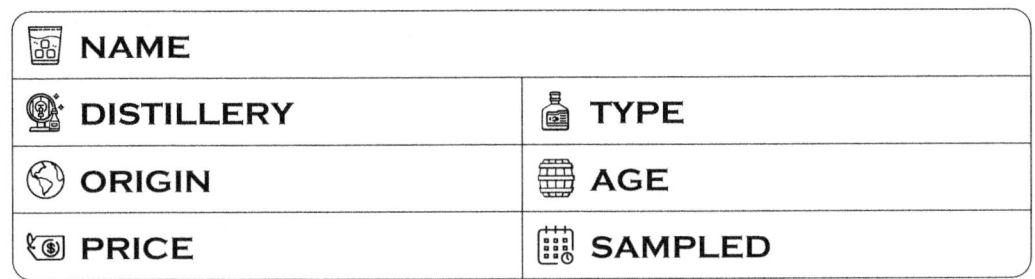

🥃 NAME	
🏭 DISTILLERY	🍾 TYPE
🌍 ORIGIN	🛢 AGE
💰 PRICE	📅 SAMPLED

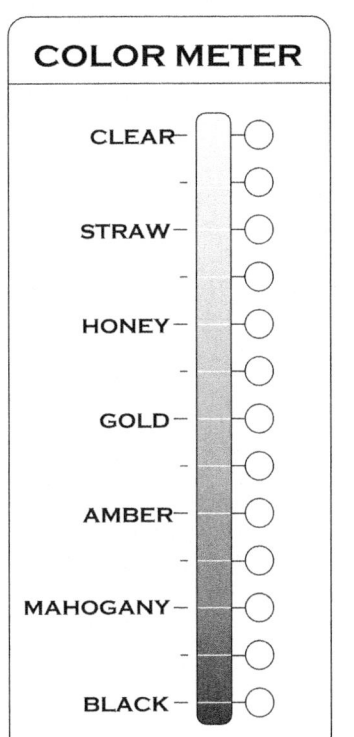

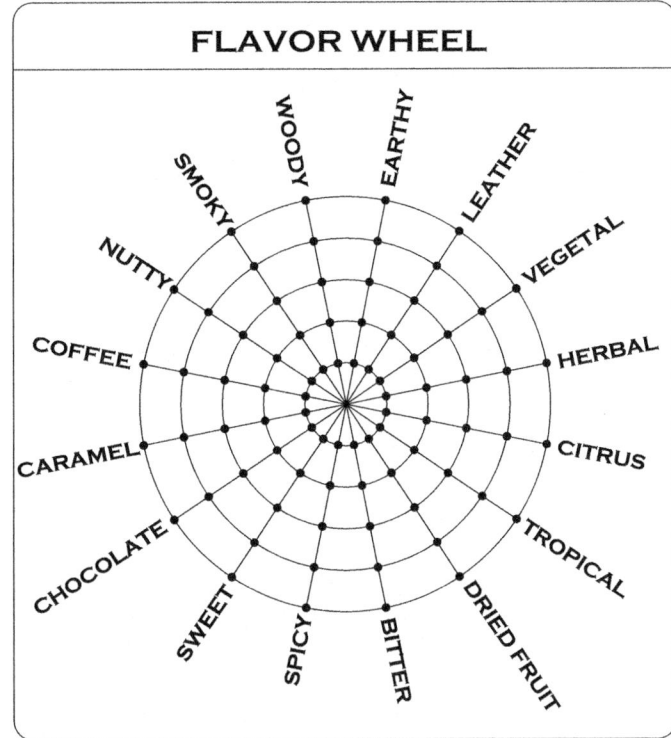

ADDITIONAL NOTES

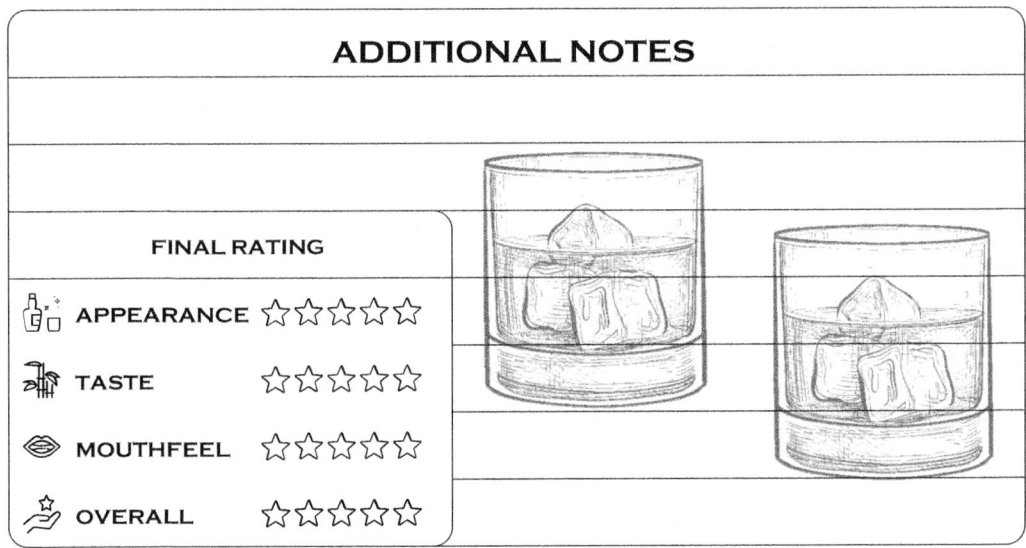

FINAL RATING

- 🍾 APPEARANCE ☆☆☆☆☆
- 👅 TASTE ☆☆☆☆☆
- 👄 MOUTHFEEL ☆☆☆☆☆
- 🤲 OVERALL ☆☆☆☆☆

NAME	
DISTILLERY	TYPE
ORIGIN	AGE
PRICE	SAMPLED

COLOR METER

- CLEAR
- STRAW
- HONEY
- GOLD
- AMBER
- MAHOGANY
- BLACK

FLAVOR WHEEL

WOODY, EARTHY, LEATHER, VEGETAL, HERBAL, CITRUS, TROPICAL, DRIED FRUIT, BITTER, SPICY, SWEET, CHOCOLATE, CARAMEL, COFFEE, NUTTY, SMOKY

ADDITIONAL NOTES

FINAL RATING

- APPEARANCE ☆☆☆☆☆
- TASTE ☆☆☆☆☆
- MOUTHFEEL ☆☆☆☆☆
- OVERALL ☆☆☆☆☆

Printed in Great Britain
by Amazon